Kant's *Critique of Pure Reason*

Edinburgh Philosophical Guides Series

Kant's *Critique of Pure Reason*

An Edinburgh Philosophical Guide

Douglas Burnham with Harvey Young

Edinburgh University Press

© Douglas Burnham with Harvey Young, 2007

Edinburgh University Press Ltd
22 George Square, Edinburgh

Typeset in 11/13pt Monotype Baskerville by
Servis Filmsetting Ltd, Manchester, and
printed and bound by Antony Rowe Ltd, Chippenham, Wilts

A CIP record for this book is available from the British Library

ISBN 978 0 7486 2737 0 (hardback)
ISBN 978 0 7486 2738 7 (paperback)

The right of Douglas Burnham and Harvey Young
to be identified as authors of this work
has been asserted in accordance with
the Copyright, Designs and Patents Act 1988

Contents

Series Editor's Preface

To us, the principle of this series of books is clear and simple: what readers new to philosophical classics need first and foremost is help with *reading* these key texts. That is to say, help with the often antique or artificial style, the twists and turns of arguments on the page, as well as the vocabulary found in many philosophical works. New readers also need help with those first few daunting and disorienting sections of these books, the point of which are not at all obvious. The books in this series take you through each text step-by-step, explaining complex key terms and difficult passages which help to illustrate the way a philosopher thinks in prose.

We have designed each volume in the series to correspond to the way the texts are actually taught at universities around the world, and have included helpful guidance on writing university-level essays or examination answers. Designed to be open alongside the text, our aim is to enable you to *read* philosophical texts with confidence and perception. This will enable you to make your own judgements on the texts, and on the variety of opinions to be found concerning them. We want you to feel able to join the great dialogue of philosophy, rather than remain a well-informed eavesdropper.

Douglas Burnham

Introduction

This book is a short commentary to Kant's *Critique of Pure Reason*. However, it contains several features that you will not find in other commentaries.

First, our primary purpose is not to explain – much less to *evaluate* – Kant's work; rather, we aim to help you read Kant for yourself. We are going to read our way through short key selections from the *Critique of Pure Reason* (as well as sketching in material not covered in depth). In this way, we will build up a picture of Kant's thought by working with Kant's own words. Thus, this book is not really for use on its own. The idea is that you will have Kant's book open in front of you – and next to it, this commentary. We will be moving slowly at first, and then accelerating, as you (the reader) gain in confidence. The passages selected for study are chosen because they meet two criteria: that the passages are among those most commonly assigned by university teachers; and that the passages provide excellent statements of what are commonly regarded as Kant's main ideas and arguments. By applying these two criteria, the aim is to make this book as immediately useful to you as possible.

Second, the number of books and papers on Kant run to the thousands. There are also a good number of 'traditions' of Kant interpretation, which are characterised by making a decisive twist at some pivotal point, usually how one idea is to be understood, weighted or simply dismissed. I shall try to mention a few of these 'pivot points' as they come up, but it is not the job of this book either to take sides on these matters, or even to introduce all the various traditions. (If, as is likely, you are taking a university course, then your professor will have his/her own views; and in any case your library will have many of these thousands of books and papers.) Instead, we are going to try to be naively faithful to the letter of Kant's work. This naivety is, of course, impossible strictly speaking, as we are in the first instance choosing passages according to what is 'commonly' assigned or regarded to be important. This is already interpretation. Further, there are ambiguities and apparent contradictions in Kant's text that mean there can be more than one 'faithful' reading. On the basis of such ambiguities arise many of those traditions of interpretation among which one must make informed choices. Nevertheless, simple explication remains our ideal.

This means that some notions that are less well known in Kant – but which are there in the text – will get an airing. Similarly, some ideas that are assumed to be very important, or are seen as 'pivot points', will receive less attention than is customary – because Kant's text does not emphasise them. These small adjustments add up, and the overall picture of Kant that we provide is thus original and not at every point just a restatement of previous interpretations.

Third, the book contains a study guide at the end, including analyses of sample essays and examination questions, a glossary, and guidelines for writing about Kant. This is part of the function of this book to be as useful as possible to the student of Kant.

There are three English translations that are commonly in use, and another one or two available. So, the best way of navigating through the book is not by page number in the translation, but by the page numbering of the standard German edition. This will be the same for all translations. Conveniently, the translations all give these numbers in the margin or at the bottom of each page. This book uses the translation by Werner Pluhar, published by Hackett, as its standard version, although making the occasional amendment. Conveniently, Hackett also publishes an 'abridgement' of Pluhar, compressing it to roughly one third the length. This abridgement contains most, though not quite all, of the sections we will be working through in this book. Kant's book went through two editions (1781 and 1787). These are often called editions 'A' and 'B'. So, page numbers are indicated by a combination of A or B, and a number. Axii refers to page xii of the first edition preface; A1 refers to the start of the first edition Introduction. Where the second edition has unchanged text, you will see A20=B34 or something similar.

Kant's book has a very complex structure, with numerous subsections and sub-sub-sections. Here are its abbreviated contents laid out using indentation so as to indicate this sub-sectioning more clearly.

It remains for me to thank all of those people who have helped make this book possible. First, Harvey Young, without whom the whole would have been much less well informed and thoughtful. I would also like to thank my wife for all her support and help; my colleagues at Staffordshire University who put up with much grouchiness especially as deadlines loomed, and who are overdue many beers as compensation; all my past students on Kant courses who have taught me so much; and Eleanor, whose Daddy was lost to Kant for too long.

1. Historical Context

The *Critique of Pure Reason* was written and rewritten at the end of the eighteenth century. Immanuel Kant was at this time well into middle age, and a moderately well known professor at the University of Königsberg (now Kaliningrad in Russia, on the Baltic coast due north of Poland). In order to understand Kant's philosophy, we need to know something of the broad intellectual concerns of his era. We are not going to spend too long on this task however; there are many fine books that cover this period (see Bibliography), and our main aim is to tackle Kant's own words.

Let us pose five problems with which Kant and his contemporaries struggled:

First, the eighteenth century was a period of rapid advance in the natural sciences, most obviously physics and related disciplines (such as astronomy). Kant was impressed and even amazed by the pace of advancement. He was not alone in asking the question: what was suddenly being done right by workers in this field? This is, at least in part, a question about epistemology (the study of how knowledge happens). Kant argues that there must have been a fundamental shift in the methodology employed in science; and he sets himself the task of understanding this new method, and exploring its implications. The references in the Second Edition Preface (B-Preface) to the 'secure path of a science' form the beginning of Kant's answer to this question.

Second, Kant wanted to try the 'experiment' of seeing whether this new scientific methodology might be successfully adapted to other topics in philosophy, particularly what he calls 'metaphysics'. We will discuss later the range of notions included in 'metaphysics', but for the moment we will define metaphysics as the attempt to demonstrate truths that cannot be established empirically. 'Cognition through mere concepts', as he writes at Bxiv. Compared to the rapid advance of the natural sciences in the previous 150 years, metaphysics had seen very little consensus but rather a number of vicious controversies. The important empiricist philosophers, such as John Locke and David Hume, seemed poles apart from Kant's own predecessors, such as G. W. von Leibniz. All these philosophers, and many others, were certainly fine minds and creative talents; that was not the problem. Rather, few of these talents could agree about anything. Now, for much of his career, Kant worked in the tradition of Leibniz. By his own report, it was reading Hume that motivated his questioning of all his contemporaries (including Hume himself). So the second 'problem' is whether or not the new model of how science worked would also provide us with a clue as to how metaphysics could work. Again, all this is stated clearly in the Prefaces and Introductions. (Nor is this problem original to Kant; Hume, for example, explicitly sees his own work as borrowing for philosophy the 'experimental method' of the sciences.)

Third, Kant's era followed several centuries of exploration of the world by the European powers. This resulted in a vast quantity of new information about new landscapes, plants and animals – but most importantly about other cultures and modes of human life. So many of these discovered cultures seemed utterly alien. The study of human cultures is anthropology, a science that was barely in its infancy by the time Kant was writing, but the *problem* faced by anthropology was already clear. How deep does this wide variety of humanity – in its modes of thinking, feeling, acting and living together – penetrate? That is, do we only find variety, or is there some hidden essence to human existence, basic laws of thinking and acting that lie behind all that variety? Kant did not agree with many in his day who felt that non-Europeans (or indeed women) were just not fully human and indeed little more than animals. Nor could he agree that it was only European culture that turned 'savages' into human beings. To be sure, Kant too engaged in anthropological description, which emphasised the differences between peoples and sexes in ways that today often seem decidedly prejudiced. However, Kant strove to demonstrate that behind the obvious variety of human life lay fundamental, absolutely universal, structures of thought and experience.

Fourth, what about faith? It seemed to many in Kant's era that since the Medieval period there had been an ever widening split between matters of faith, and everything else. Nations were governed, laws enacted and enforced, economies managed, wars fought – often with very little consideration given to issues of religious faith. Kant was not alone in seeing this split as particularly problematic in the area of knowledge. The great advances in physics, for example, seemed to have happened more or less independently of spiritual questions – indeed, the more independently the better, it would appear. Kant wanted to enquire whether faith could be investigated *scientifically*. Could God and the world *qua* created be an object of physics? If so, with what results? If not, with what implications?

Fifth, the successes of the natural sciences seemed to be built upon a largely deterministic account of nature. That is, the laws of nature as discovered by science seemed to take the form of universal and necessary causal laws. If this view of the natural world is extended into the human world then the old philosophical problem of free will, and with it the problem of the possibility of morality, arises again. How can someone be said to act morally unless they act freely – that is, unless they choose their actions and are not caused to act by something outside or anterior to them. Thus, how could someone act freely if the domain of the natural sciences is truly universal? On the other hand, if metaphysical freedom is possible, then what happens to the universality of the law of causality, and thus science? The importance of the concept of causation in Kant cannot be over-estimated. Not only does it form a cornerstone of science, but only a proper understanding of causation will make possible a proper understanding of human moral freedom.

These five problems set the agenda for the *Critique of Pure Reason*. Kant aimed to arrive at definitive answers to them all.

2. A Guide to the Text

Let us start with the title: *Critique of Pure Reason* (*Kritik der reinen Vernunft*). Sometimes we use the term 'critic' in a negative sense ('he is my most severe critic'); sometimes in a neutral sense ('she is a film critic' – meaning that she makes both positive and negative evaluations of individual films). Kant's use of 'critique' has much in common with the neutral use of 'critic'. But reason is not a thing, like a film, rather a capacity to do some activity. Kant's book is concerned with evaluating what is useful and indeed indispensable about the activities of 'pure reason'. He is also concerned to discover what is futile and even dangerous about it. In this connection, he often speaks in terms of finding the 'limits' of pure reason, which means defining that line beyond which pure reason becomes useless or even dangerous. Similarly, as we shall see, Kant frequently uses a legal metaphor: reason's claims to philosophical knowledge are put to a tribunal.

Prefaces and Introduction

First Edition Preface

You may have noticed that there are two prefaces. Kant wrote a new preface for the second edition of his book. Again, these two are often referred to as A and B; so, below, you can see that the reference is to the A edition, and the page number is in roman numerals to indicate the preface.

The Preface to the first edition begins: 'Human reason has a peculiar fate in one kind of its cognitions: it is troubled by questions that it cannot dismiss, because they are posed to it by the nature of reason itself, but that it also cannot answer, because they surpass reason's every ability' (Avii). In other words, one of the types of activities that reason gets up to finds itself 'troubled by questions' which are in some way natural to it, but which it also cannot answer. In this first sentence we encounter our first translation difficulty. Above we have 'one kind of its cognitions', but some translations read 'knowledge'. The German word is *Erkenntnisse*. Now, if by cognition we mean 'thinking' of some sort, then it is true that all knowledge is rational cognition. But it may not be true that all rational cognition is knowledge. Indeed, this very sentence is speaking of questions that cannot be answered – that is, that could not arrive at knowledge. So, *Erkenntnisse* must be a wider concept than 'knowledge', and that is the reason 'cognitions' is the preferred translation.

Human reason is troubled. What does Kant mean by 'reason'? First of all, above we called it a 'capacity'; Kant uses the term *Vermögen* usually translated as either 'faculty' or 'power'. Reason is a faculty, then. More specifically, we have a broader and narrower usage. First, broadly, reason refers to any thinking that operates according to basic logical principles, whether it is about geese or God. This is what we are refer-ring to in everyday situations by expressions such as 'figuring something out', 'problem-solving', etc. Kant summarises all these employments of reason as discovery of the 'conditions' of things. By 'conditions' Kant means that which explains something; thus, he means answers to questions such as 'what?', 'why?' or 'how?'. This broader use of reason is not dispensable, Kant believes; it is required as part of our everyday engage-ment with our world. In the second usage of the term 'reason' – and this is the 'one kind' of cognition in the quotation above – reason refers to a type of thinking that attempts to discover knowledge simply through reasoning and 'pure' concepts; 'pure' here meaning not empirical (however, see pp. 24–5). Such pure reason seeks to reach conclusions purely, rather than through any empirical investigation of the world. This type of cognition is what is meant by 'pure reason'. Kant believes that this kind of thinking is typical of philosophers such as Plato or Descartes. The history of philosophy indeed sometimes calls such philosophers 'rationalists'. We will find Kant discussing this type of cog-nition in more detail soon. (It is worth pointing out, even this early, that although this pure use of reason troubles reason, it is by no means a dis-aster; even this pure use has its proper and indispensible use.)

So, it is reason in the second sense that is troubled by questions. If such reason is typical of Plato and Descartes, among others, then their philosophies must also be 'troubled'. Kant, it seems, is launching an attack on such philosophy. Moreover, he is not objecting to this or that idea in Plato, or this or that argument in Descartes. Rather, he is objecting to nothing less than the *use to which reason is put* in Plato or Descartes. Now, Hume famously makes a similar attack: that which is arrived at entirely through reasoning and yet also claims to be knowledge of reality, he argues, must be 'committed to the flames, for it can contain nothing but sophistry and nonsense'.

But Kant is not making a simple attack of this type. There is something quite inevitable about reason being troubled, because the questions arise out of the 'nature' of reason in general; that means, even from reason in the first sense. And, as we noted above, reason in this wider sense is an essential part of normal human thought. Reason can no more avoid these questions than a mammal can avoid being warm-blooded. So, Plato and Descartes are not to be blamed for raising and being troubled by such questions. Rather, they are to be blamed for failing to also realise that such questions 'surpass reason's every ability'. In short, they did not realise that all questions of the type that they raise could never be answered. In other words, Plato and Descartes did not perform a critique of pure reason (Axii). Likewise, Kant implicitly claims, Hume also missed this opportunity. Hume's sceptical rejection of the role of reason in knowledge is *just as thoughtless* as any rationalist's affirmation.

The second, longer paragraph of the first Preface clarifies this. Reason (in the first and broadest sense now) has 'principles' that it employs to discover conditions, and our experience bears out the usefulness of these principles. Reason in the broadest sense, then, is natural, necessary and playing an important role. On the other hand, *the same function* of reason also inevitably 'ascends . . . to ever more remote conditions' (Avii–viii). Reason in the first and second senses, then, is one and the same faculty, employed with different objects. This is a hugely important claim, and one Kant will be defending throughout the 'Transcendental Dialectic' explored in the chapters below. If reason in the first, broader, sense leads one 'naturally' to reason in the narrow sense, then the questions that trouble reason, and the philosophies that arise to answer such questions, are not a mistake that this or that person happened to make, but are everywhere and always a temptation against which we must guard.

By 'remote' and 'ascend' he means to move towards thoughts that are essentially different from immediate experiences. Importantly, 'ascend' does not mean merely to become more abstract (there is nothing intrinsically wrong with abstraction for Kant). Rather, to ascend to remote conditions means to search for *total* or *complete* conditions. That is why, here, Kant makes so much of the incompleteness of tasks and answers. Our experiences of the world, and even our most advanced knowledge of it, are both characterised by being *partial*. I hear an event, but not all of what happened before or after; I see an object, but not its complete web of relationships to all other objects. In the course of our experience we can never encounter the totality of experiences. (Kant will return to just this point much later in his 'solution' to the 'Antinomies of Pure Reason'.)

Similarly, if I form an abstract concept (say, a concept of a mammal) then this concept says more than an experience of a particular animal – it refers to all mammals – but importantly also it says less – it doesn't specify species, size, age, location and so forth. Even a universal concept (like those in the very principles of science Kant is writing about here) – one that applies to everything everywhere – would be abstract because it would be only a partial account. Kant's usual example is the concept of causation. This concept is abstract (importantly, this does not necessarily mean it was abstracted *from* something) because it cannot specify what caused what, when or how. For Kant, then, both my concepts and my immediate experiences of the world are abstract in this sense: they exist only insofar as they are separated from the totality of their conditions, and do not include compete definition or explanation.

However, only this totality would count as the complete condition of something; only that totality could satisfy reason's natural urge to discover conditions. Indeed, on previous accounts of the physical sciences (for example, in Descartes and Leibniz), only the possibility of such a totality guarantees the possibility of science. Otherwise, the discoveries of science would seem to be imperilled by doubt. Thus reason feels the need, as Kant describes it, 'to resort to principles that go beyond all possible use in experience'. The totality of conditions would itself be unconditioned; there would be nothing outside it that would serve to explain or define it. We have names for such total entities – God, the soul, the cosmos. If we accept Kant's definition of both experiences and concepts as partial, then both the principles of pure reason, and the entities that it posits as complete conditions, can have no legitimate meaning. Reason – the faculty by which we come to experience and know the world – would have arrived at something that cannot be an object of experience or knowledge. So, somewhere along the line we went wrong. This is Kant's point. Eventually, in the pursuit of its normal and natural activity, reason in the first sense leaves behind experience altogether, and becomes reason in the second sense. That is, its search for conditions takes place purely and without reference to the experiential. Reason plunges into 'darkness and contradictions' (Aviii) or, in other words, into what Kant often calls 'metaphysics', intending this in a *negative* meaning. If 'critique' is Kant's name for the type of reasoning that sorts out the limits of reason, then such metaphysics in a negative sense we can call 'uncritical metaphysics'. Kant's point is that the perfectly ordinary and valuable functioning of reason leads directly and necessarily to 'darkness', and thus *needs* critique.

The following few paragraphs develop the theme of philosophy losing its way by way of an elaborate metaphor of philosophy as the queen of the sciences. The result of 'civil war' among philosophical factions has been ultimately an 'indifferentism' – a situation in which no one has the strength to care where truth lies. Critique is Kant's remedy for such long-standing and destructive forces in the history of philosophy. Significantly, Kant is sweeping up the *whole history of philosophy* in this single notion of 'troubled reason'. This whole previous history will be in one gesture unified and also subjected to critique, insofar as its basic organising principles are discovered within reason.

Let us turn to the first short paragraph on Axii. The 'critique' is not a critique of philosophers, their books or their philosophical systems. Kant is not very interested in what so-and-so happened to think. Particular philosophers are just examples of universal reason at work. (See also B-Introduction, B23: Kant argues that, for the purposes of critique, specific attempts at 'dogmatic' metaphysics 'can and must be regarded as if they had never occurred'.) Nor is he interested here in empirical or experiential uses of our reason: history, botany, physics or psychology, for example. Particular discoveries in these areas are outside the scope of the critique of *pure* reason. Rather, he is interested in what the structure of human reason requires anyone to think, in its pursuit of cognition independently of (pure of) all experience. Kant is after what is essential to reason, not in any particular use to which reason might be put (excepting only the fact that critical philosophy itself is just such a particular use). Only in this way could the limits of reason in general be drawn. The critique will therefore 'decide on the possibility or impossibility of metaphysics in general, and determine its sources, its extent, and its limits – all in accordance with principles' (Axii).

Thus, the purposes of Kant's critique: first, to try to identify the line that separates reason in the first and second senses; and second to evaluate what is essential about the function of reason on one, and what is 'troubling' about reason on the other, side of this line. Let us go back now to the footnote at Axi. It begins by arguing against those who claim Kant's age is shallow. For reasons he shall introduce later, Kant believes the sciences are in fact on a properly conceived methodological foundation, and their progress anything but shallow. To make other disciplines (even, Kant says, religion and governmental legislation) equally grounded would require this same activity of 'critique'. Therefore, Kant's philosophical revolution is intended to be wide-ranging indeed, and 'our age is properly the age of critique' (Axin).

Second Edition Preface

In the First Preface, for the most part, Kant writes *as if* he is a sceptic. Reason is troubled, questions cannot be answered, darkness follows all those who try, and so forth. In the second preface, he turns about-face, writing much more positively: to be sure, metaphysical questions have not previously yielded reliable answers, but that is because the wrong questions have been asked, or at least that these questions have not been addressed properly, using a genuine understanding of how metaphysical cognition happens. The two Prefaces commence with different tones and approaches, but in fact say the same thing. They are, in effect, both talking about the limit of reason. The First Preface warns against exceeding that limit; the Second praises those who have remained within it.

The major theme in the first paragraph is the idea of a 'secure path of a science' (Bvii). The outward signs of something on this secure path are that it mostly moves forwards rather than constantly restarting (this is often called 'progress'), and that it is conducted according to procedures widely known and agreed, on objects widely known and agreed (it is universal). How, we might have asked in our reading of the First Preface above, is reason supposed to sit in critical tribunal *concerning itself*? Is this not like asking the accused in a criminal court to judge himself? Part of Kant's answer to this is to investigate the extent to which the products of reason conform to the notion of a 'secure science'. Kant more specifically wants to ask to what extent metaphysics is, or could ever be, a science, and why. The implication is that metaphysics as practised in Kant's day is far from being scientific (it is, as we put it above, 'uncritical'), but that there may be some hope that a more modest and critical metaphysics can be made scientific.

Kant gives three examples of sciences: logic, mathematics, physics. Logic, Kant thinks, was established once and for all by Aristotle; its basic principles have remained unchanged ever since. The success of logic, significantly, is ascribed to its 'limitations'; that is to its complete removal from any concern with the object about which we think (Bix). What Kant here calls simply 'logic' is later referred to as 'pure general logic' (A54=B78). There, such pure general logic is distinguished both from applied logic – the function of logic under empirical or psychological conditions – and from transcendental logic, which will be Kant's concern from then on. Here in the Preface we must note that because it does not produce any cognition *of objects*, logic is in fact a 'vestibule' of science, and thus not a very helpful model of science in general.

Next, Kant provides an imaginative history of mathematics, and describes the turning point when it became a 'science'. Geometry, Kant claims, is neither an empirical science that investigates the properties of objects in space (Kant's example here is an isosceles triangle), or a purely conceptual endeavour that aims to prove something about the properties of objects from their mere concept. He argues that the former could never yield the *necessary* quality of geometric demonstrations. (This is by no means a new claim, and is a sub-species of the argument often used against empiricist accounts of either natural science or indeed philosophy.) The latter, however, is futile: no analysis of the *concept* of a triangle will yield information about the angles within it. Instead, the geometric demonstration proceeds by the 'construction' of the triangle, and its interior angles, on the basis of the concept of it. That is, the concept governs a spatial activity.

Importantly, this spatial activity is not then just another empirical object (because then we would be back to the objection to mathematics as empirical); rather, the construction of the figure in space somehow has the necessity and rigour of proof. We will discover how later, in the 'Transcendental Aesthetic'.

Let us turn to the paragraph about natural science starting at Bxii. Kant refers to a 'revolution' (Bxii) or a light that 'dawned' concerning how empirical science was understood. His specific examples are chemistry and physics and, within the latter, the inclined-plane experiments of Galileo. Galileo demonstrated some of the basic principles of gravitational acceleration by timing the descent of polished metal balls down flat, smooth planes inclined at various angles. Once the principles were demonstrated, Galileo was able to extrapolate geometrically to the case of bodies in free fall, a case for which the technical means to test directly were lacking at the time.

What was realised when natural science finally embarked on the road of science, Kant argues, was that 'reason only has insight into that which it produces after a plan of its own' (Bxiii). What is required, then, is not the mere accumulation of 'accidental observations', but the pure framework of a scientific method within which alone observations could yield knowledge. This method is to 'adopt as its guide . . . that which reason has itself put into nature' (Bxiv). Kant seems to have in mind the idea that experiments such as Galileo's must be: 1. subject to the rigorous control of variables, which in turn makes possible: 2. an idealisation of nature such that its laws first become discoverable. The experiment is a highly constructed event, indeed it is 'artificial'. The laws of nature only become discoverable under the condition of nature being subjected to this controlled procedure. In other words, the starting point of empirical science, and also the only basis for carrying it out, are *not empirical*. (Neither, however, is it entirely rational, and based simply on the analysis of concepts without, for example, experimentations.) Rather, it is a scientific method for the interrogation of nature, built on rational principles. In order to become known, nature must agree with these principles.

Let us think about one widely discussed principle: the principle of sufficient reason. This has a long history in philosophy and is often associated with both Aristotle and Aquinas, but in Kant's mind would be above all the German Enlightenment tradition beginning with

Leibniz. Leibniz writes that by this principle 'we hold that no fact could ever be true or existent, no statement correct, unless there were a sufficient reason why it was thus and not otherwise – even though those reasons will not usually be knowable by us' (*Monadology*, section 32). In brief, things don't just *happen*. Now, as Leibniz recognises, in ordinary acts of reasoning we do not necessarily know or even feel the need to inquire into these reasons. If I notice the kettle is boiling, I may not feel the need to inquire into the reasons, beyond noticing that it is plugged in and switched on. In ordinary acts of reasoning, there is a natural termination of questioning, based upon the context and upon our habitual behaviours. A child who keeps asking the question 'Why?' has not learned this natural termination of reason-giving and treats the repeated question as an abstract game of reasoning. In ordinary acts of reasoning, the principle of sufficient reason is not employed throughout.

In a similar way, one might argue that natural science does not require complete chains of explanation. Science too relies upon local contexts and customary procedures; the answers it seeks are not absolute but bound to the demands of the scientific context. In Hume, this observation itself becomes a principle. Both everyday reasoning and scientific reasoning concerning an idea are based upon context (that is, relations to other ideas) and customs. Hume accordingly rejects as nonsense a notion such as the principle of sufficient reason, claiming that not only has it no legitimate grounds, but is likewise unnecessary. Indeed, for the later Wittgenstein, it is not just that our ordinary and even scientific reason *happens to* have a natural termination, but a context is the condition of any reason-giving. Therefore, it does not make sense – it is not a legitimate question – to inquire after the reason for contexts and customs (Wittgenstein 1958).

Why, then, might Kant feel the need to re-emphasise the legitimacy and importance of such rational principles? First, it is entirely possible to inquire into the reasons for some context of question asking and answering. These new inquiries, to be sure, will also have their contexts and natural terminations, but they are possible. Second, it often happens in both ordinary and scientific contexts that the natural end to questions needs to be overcome. If the results of a scientific procedure are not what is expected, then it is part of the protocol of scientific rationality to inquire into the conditions of the procedure:

Were the samples pure? Were the instruments properly calibrated? and so forth. The explanations for deviations can even lead to new discoveries. This has happened repeatedly in the history of astronomy, for example, where small discrepancies in the data compared to the current model led to revisions, perhaps wholesale, in the model. That is, there seems to be a genuine and fruitful demand *within the nature of reason itself* for inquiry beyond or outside the scope of given contexts and customs. Relatedly, something absolutely without explanation – a miracle – would not only be quite outside science but would signify the end of scientific explanation as such. Science (even a science conceived entirely empirically) perhaps does not prove that there are no miracles, but rather its rationality must assume it. (Compare Hume on miracles in the *Enquiry*.) Third, the question-asking of a discipline of science, although it may be contextualised locally to that discipline, is rarely understood as bounded by space and time. The chemistry of nitrogen here on Earth is the same as on the moons of Jupiter; the mechanics of the human skeleton are the same all across the world, and back thousands of years in time. This presumptive universality of scientific rationality, and its importance for scientific inquiry are, for Kant, marks of the action of rational principles within science. Fourth, specifically against the Humean account of rationality based upon habits or customs, Kant argues repeatedly that the identification of order or patterns in our experience requires an underlying conceptual order that is not merely empirical. Thus, here in the B-Preface, we find Kant talking about nature revealing, empirically, 'that which reason has itself put into nature' (Bxiv). Again, the reasons for the intelligibility of experience are not to be found in experience. This last argument is one that Kant makes in many and forceful ways throughout the first half of the *Critique of Pure Reason*.

All of these arguments are implicit when Kant speaks of science. (And others, too; see the Introduction, and the discussion of the communicability and systematicity of science in the Doctrine of Method.) While to be sure, in every instance the rationality of scientific inquiry is informed by contexts and customs, it is not *closed off* by these from more fundamental inquiry. The revolutionary change of which Kant is speaking is itself the broadest and clearest example. The rational structure of pre-modern scientific inquiry involved conceiving of science as merely a passive observer of things and accumulator of data. This was its context and custom. This context and custom is overthrown in the move to the modern situation of compelling 'nature to answer reason's own questions' (Bxiii).

To be sure, the confidence in the principle of sufficient reason can go too far. Leibniz and others, in the pursuit of the chain of reasons, recognised that the reasons for the intelligibility of experience are not to be found in experience. However, these philosophers were thus led to speculate *as if it were experiencable* on that which is *not itself a possible experience*, for example, the uncaused cause that is God. A philosopher such as Hume will reject the viability of such speculation, and centuries-long disagreements ensue. For Kant, agreement (on basic issues, objects and on strategies for resolving differences) is one sign of a science. These unresolved and unresolvable debates make it clear that metaphysics is not (yet, at least) a science. As we saw above in discussing the A-Preface, the problem will turn out to be that one should not claim the legitimacy of a rational principle without also investigating the limits of that legitimacy (thus, the concept of 'critique'). Kant will explicate how the principle of sufficient reason should be understood, and will indeed offer proof of its validity *within the limits proper to it*, at A200–1=B246.

The next two paragraphs (Bxiv–xv), accordingly insist that metaphysics is certainly not on the scientific road. Recall the sceptical tone of the First Preface – 'Human reason is troubled by questions it cannot answer' (Avii) – where Kant described pure reason plunging towards darkness in its pursuit of metaphysical questions. Uncritical metaphysics appears to be a domain of unending conflict with no hope of resolution. Here Kant seems to be saying that there is metaphysics in this negative sense, historically, but it is certainly no science. However, he also implies that there may also be a 'scientific' or a 'critical' metaphysics. Could metaphysics ever be on the scientific road? Kant then wishes to try the experiment of understanding metaphysics through imitating (Bxvi) the model of mathematics and natural science. In other words, just like in mathematics and natural science, perhaps it is the activity of reason that first constitutes the proper objects of metaphysics. Kant writes, famously: 'Thus far it has been assumed that all our cognition must conform to objects. . . . Let us . . . try to find out by experiment whether we shall not make better progress in the problems of metaphysics if we assume that objects must conform to our cognition' (Bxvi). The assumption of all previous metaphysics has been that true knowledge means that cognition (what we think) is made to conform to objects (what really is, 'out there'); that we aim to form an accurate image of things. But suppose we invert that, suppose that *to be cognisable* an object must first of all conform to our cognitive abilities? Kant then compares this proposed inversion of our common sense approach to the revolution in astronomy in Copernicus. Rather than building an understanding of the solar system on the basis of the sun orbiting the motionless earth, Copernicus put forward the bold hypothesis that it is the sun that is still, and the earth in circular motion.

Kant immediately tries out his new idea on the notion of 'intuition' (*Anschauung*). We will shortly talk a great deal about intuition, but for the moment we will say that intuition in general means our sensory relation to things. I intuit a bird when I see or hear it; I intuit my own state of mind in feeling happy or hungry. If, Kant argues, intuition comprised a mere image of an object – in for example the way Locke describes the formation of ideas – then how could I ever even know if the image were accurate? I cannot verify an image by forming another image; that would be a fruitless circle. Because I start by assuming that the image is *outside*, or only contingently related to, the object of the image, there is in principle no way of verifying the image. Moreover, on this supposition, I could not speak about objects metaphysically (that is, a priori or independently of any particular experience of them), for my pure thinking would be still more groundless and disengaged from the world. It is this groundlessness that Hume emphasised in his criticism of metaphysics.

If, however, the basic metaphysical structure of objects had to conform to the nature of my intuiting, then everything is different. My intuitions are not outside the world, formed as detached images; rather, intuitions are the world presented to me. Or, expressed using the phrases Kant employs here, objects are always objects 'of the senses', or objects 'of experience'. It becomes difficult, perhaps impossible, to conceive of a mind without a world, or a world without a mind. Now, a priori cognition of objects becomes possible. That is, if objects are always objects in intuition, I can come to know something a priori about objects by studying the nature of my intuition (of any object) in itself. In other words, metaphysical truths can be established by carefully studying the necessary structure of intuiting. The nature of my ability to intuit (which ability Kant calls 'sensibility') forms the topic of the first main section of Kant's book: the 'Transcendental Aesthetic'.

Just like Copernicus, Kant is proposing an inversion in how we ordinarily understand the relation between our minds and the objects presented to us. Recall that for Copernicus' new cosmology, we are not on a still earth surrounded by things that move circularly; on the contrary, *we* are the ones who move, and our motion results in the appearances of the sun and stars rising. In Kant's terms, this means that the knowing subject is active – not a passive 'viewer' of a moving, changing and active world – and understanding knowledge means understanding the constituting role of this activity. Moreover, the previous Ptolemaic cosmology distinguished between the perfect, eternal and circular motion of sun, planets and stars, on the one hand, and motion or change on Earth, on the other. The stars moved circularly, but did not change; things on Earth were subject to change, but did not move circularly. For Copernicus the Earth is not separated in its essence from the sun, stars and planets. Rather, change and motion were understood universally, as being the same everywhere. The Copernican revolution to which Kant is referring is partly the reversal of the picture of what moves, but is also the elimination of the ontological separation of the Earth from the celestial spheres. So analogously, in Kant, the activity, structures and principles of the knowing mind should not be understood as originally or essentially separated from that which appears to it. Much of the rest of his book will be concerned with pursuing the meaning and implications of this insight.

It is worth pointing out at this stage three additional points. First, Kant has more than one word translated as 'object', perhaps with a translator's note indicating the original. We will not go into this problem just yet but will return to it in our discussion of the A edition of the 'Transcendental Deduction'. Suffice it to say that this distinction allows him to articulate the subtleties entailed by the collapse of the separation between object and cognition in his new Copernican revolution. Second, on an earlier philosophical usage of 'object' (still found in Descartes, for example in *Meditation* III) 'object' did not mean 'the thing outside me'. Rather, it meant 'the property of my ideas insofar as they refer to things'. So, insofar as Kant is stressing the lack of separation between objects and their presentation, Kant's new Copernican revolution is restoring this lost philosophical usage. Third, the notion that all objects for us are objects 'of experience' raises the theoretical question of what objects are not 'for us'. That is, does the set of experiential objects exhaust the set of all things that can be said to exist? Kant's name for such hypothetical objects that are not objects of experience is 'thing in itself'. The thing in itself is a problematic and controversial notion in Kant's work, and we will have to return to it often. For the moment it is enough to notice the question, and perhaps also to wonder whether the notion of the thing in itself might have something to do with Kant's answer to the fifth of the issues we mentioned under 'Historical Context' above: namely, the problem of the possibility of human freedom and its relationship to science.

Back in the Second Preface, Kant makes the same basic move in regard to concepts as he did with respect to intuitions. If my concepts simply originate in objects as things outside and separate from me, then both the rigorous empirical verification of these concepts, and a priori knowledge of objects through concepts, are impossible. If my concepts are not empirical, but innate, a similar problem arises: how can it be established that these innate concepts have any validity, that they actually apply to real objects? Their innateness is in itself certainly no proof. If, on the other hand, the experience of objects must conform to my concepts, then a variety of metaphysics looks possible. It would involve the study of pure concepts and, above all, the study of how these concepts are put to work in the presentation of objects. This would be cognition of objects a priori, 'before they are given to us' (Bxvi). Such a study might be expected to yield metaphysical truths based upon the necessary function of pure concepts. This study is the topic of the second and much longer section of the book, the 'Transcendental Logic'.

Recall above we said that 'critique' does not mean to attack, rather to evaluate neutrally. Kant is going to show that reason can and does lead to certain illusions; but it is reason itself (in the form of critical philosophy) that will be doing this 'showing'. The critique of pure reason evaluates such reason and shows that pure reason is both productive of positive metaphysical knowledge, *and also* troubled by questions that are metaphysical in a negative sense. The task of critique is to identify the criteria by which the two forms of pure reason can be differentiated. In other words, to show both the possibility *and the limits on the validity* of this positive or critical metaphysics.

Clearly Kant believes that these odd inversions are more than hypotheses, but can be proved true descriptions of how cognition happens. In the Prefaces he offers nothing more than glimpses of the proofs he intends to offer later. We will get to these proofs in due course. The rest of the Second Preface pursues some of the implications of Kant's challenging hypothesis and in particular returns to consider the sceptical themes of the First Preface. We will now turn to the Introduction. (Kant's new 'Copernican revolution' is a major point of discussion for commentators because it seems to lay out so boldly what is at stake in Kant's philosophy. However, we will postpone a survey of some of these discussions until the 'Transcendental Aesthetic', because it will help to have a few more Kantian notions under our belts.)

B-Introduction, Section 1

Here, we will look at passages from the B-Introduction, because this second edition proceeds at a more manageable pace than the first. We are going to spend a good deal of time on the Introduction, because it contains so many important new concepts.

The opening two paragraphs of the B-Introduction recast once again the Copernican revolution idea we saw in the Prefaces. 'There can be no doubt', Kant says, 'that all our cognition begins with experience' (B1). For, what else is there to think about, and what motivation to think at all, except experiences of the world? Objects outside of us 'bring about' presentations (*Vorstellungen*) in part directly, and in part presentations are brought about by mental activities that process the 'raw material' of our impressions into something coherent and knowable. What happens first, 'in terms of time', is that there is an experience of things; all other thinking happens afterwards. All this, Kant says, is pretty obvious. So far, this sounds like empiricism of a straightforward Lockean variety. The world impacts upon our senses producing simple ideas, as Locke calls them; then the mind combines and compares, producing complex and even abstract ideas.

But then Kant throws a spanner into the works. In the second paragraph, he argues that although it is true that all cognition starts *with* experience, this does not entail that all cognition arises *from* experience. In fact, all our experiences are composite, with only part arising directly or indirectly in the Lockean fashion, together with something supplied by 'our own cognitive power'. Empiricists, Kant adds mischievously, are not to be downcast about not recognising this fact; it takes 'long practice' to separate out the elements of experience (B1–2).

The rest of this first section of the B-Introduction introduces two new ideas, in the form of two distinctions. The purpose of these distinctions, and of several others to follow, is to help us to define and separate out the elements of experience. Kant is aiming to describe especially those cognitions that arise from the activity of the mind. The first new idea is 'a priori' as opposed to 'a posteriori' (B2). These are Latin expressions meaning, respectively, 'prior' and 'after' something; they had been used in philosophy for a long time but Kant will give them a new twist. An a priori cognition is one that arises independently of any experience. Kant's amusing, concrete example of someone removing the foundations of their home is meant to stress this 'any'. The person in the example should have known better, we say. They shouldn't have had to wait to see what would happen to their house, but should have known from other, previous experiences. So, knowledge about houses and foundations is a priori *relative* to this or that present experience, but is not a priori with respect to *all* experiences. Notice, importantly, that 'prior' does not necessarily mean prior in time to; rather, it means *independently* of. This is why in the first paragraph Kant did not have to talk about cognition prior in time to experience.

The second new idea is, 'pure' as distinguished from 'not pure' (B3). Kant has already introduced the idea that our cognitions are normally a mixture of experiential input and the contribution from the mental powers. This notion of a mixture, however, suggests the possibility that if we could isolate the contribution of the mind, then it would be 'pure' (pure means unmixed with something of a different origin). Insofar as it is Kant's aim to investigate just this contribution of the mind, then what he will be looking for initially are pure cognitions, or what he also calls 'a priori principles of cognition'. Kant claims here that 'every change has a cause' is an a priori proposition. However, he also claims that it is not pure, insofar as 'change' has, in part, an origin in temporal intuition. Notice that, in passing, Kant has asserted something very important. Change is an experiential concept – it comes from my experience of things. But given this empirical concept of change, I am *nevertheless able to say something a priori about it*. This claim is so startling and far-reaching in its consequences that even Kant sometimes forgets it, and writes as if 'pure' and 'a priori' just meant the same thing.

B-Introduction, Section 2

A priori and pure are descriptions of the kind of cognition Kant is seeking; but as concepts they are not very helpful in actually identifying when such cognition has been found. In the second section of the 'B-Deduction', Kant introduces further characteristics of a priori cognition that will allow us to 'safely distinguish a pure cognition from empirical ones' (B3). He commences with two very old philosophical arguments about the contingency of experiences. Experience shows us how things *happen to be* but does not show us that they *could not* be otherwise. A pure, a priori proposition would, on the contrary, be *necessary*. It would be a proposition that could not but be true. In addition, experience may reveal to us patterns of things, but cannot demonstrate them to be *everywhere and always the same*, that is, *universal*. A pure, a priori proposition would be universal, without any exception here, there or anywhere. To be sure, Kant adds, some empirical propositions are held to be universal (his example is 'all bodies have weight'). However, this is an instance of a proposition, which has proved true *so far*, being 'upgraded' to a proposition that is assumed always to be so (B4). A true universal proposition is one that needs no such 'upgrading'. These two 'characteristics' are sure signs of an a priori cognition.

In the next paragraph, Kant comes up with some examples. From the sciences, he includes all mathematical propositions; from the 'most ordinary' use of the understanding, his example is the one we've already seen 'all change must have a cause' (B4–5). It is important to notice that Kant is not just speaking about science here. His analyses in the Prefaces of the history of logic, mathematics and science – and the notion also in the Prefaces that metaphysics should be put on the 'secure path of a science' – all suggest that he might be only speaking of how scientific cognition is possible. But, this second section of the B-Introduction makes it clear that Kant is concerned with *all* cognition. Even the most ordinary or common uses of our minds are in some way informed by a priori cognition. Our critical understanding of how cognitions are possible can, Kant hopes, be made scientific. But, the cognitions the possibility of which is thus understood can in themselves be quite ordinary. This statement will prove of immense importance just a few sentences later.

Kant adds that the proposition 'all change must have a cause' should be entirely obvious. If one, like Hume, challenged either the necessity or universality of the connection of cause and effect, then the whole concept of cause would 'get lost entirely' (B5). (In fact, this is also just what Hume says. But Hume is happy with the conclusion that, strictly speaking, the concept of causation is 'lost'.) Hume's sceptical empiricism was hugely significant for Kant, and we will see throughout the book a running skirmish between these two philosophers, especially on the subject of causation. However, claiming that the proposition is obvious, and therefore proves that there are a priori principles, is not much of an argument.

Kant writes: 'But we do not need such examples in order to prove that pure a priori principles actually exist in our cognition. We could, alternatively, establish that these principles are indispensable for the possibility of experience as such, and hence establish their existence a priori' (B5). With this move, Kant's novelty as a philosopher really emerges. It is one thing to be able to establish a few examples of pure a priori principles. Kant states in fact that this is 'easy'. But it would not achieve a great deal, since these examples themselves might be isolated and relatively unimportant. It would not, for instance, prove that such principles are involved in *all* cognition, even the most 'ordinary'. (Please see what Kant has to say about examples at Axviii.) Kant is, not for the first time, going to turn this problem on its head: he will instead 'establish' that experience would not be possible were it not for the a priori principles of our cognition. A priori cognition, that is, is a *condition of the possibility* of experience. Thus, the mere fact that we all of us have experiences would prove the presence and operation of these principles. That is why it is so significant that Kant is speaking of all types of experience and cognition, and not just the specifically scientific. Even the most trivial encounters of mind and world – my counting change in a shop, say, feeling a bit nauseous, or feeding the cat – prove the existence and activity of the a priori structure of the mind.

The second section finishes with Kant arguing that an a priori origin can be established not only for some 'judgements' (we shall assume here that he is referring to the 'cognitions' or 'principles' discussed above), but also some concepts. The apparently merely empirical concept of a 'body' contains, after we dissect the concept removing everything inessential (everything, that is, that could be either true or false in experience), the notion of 'space'. Thus space is *necessary a priori* for the concept of body. 'Body' is a mixed or impure concept, in the same sense as 'all change must have a cause' is a mixed or impure cognition. So, a similar example would have to be the concept 'change'. This or that can change, and the change can be of any number of different types – but *all* change necessarily entails *time*. Just as the concept body has space as an a priori element, so the concept of change has time. The fact that both some concepts and judgements/principles exhibit signs of a priori cognition shows that there is a deep relation between concepts and judgements. Kant will be exploring this relation in the fourth section of the B-Introduction.

B-Introduction, Section 3
The third section of the B-Introduction returns us to the problem of pure reason, which was discussed in both Prefaces. There are types of cognition, Kant says, that are not only independent of experience though apply to it, through making it possible, but *leave experience behind*. That is, using the language we employed in discussing the Prefaces, types of cognition that cross the line between legitimate and illegitimate uses of reason. Kant adds a bit more detail here; for example, he lists the key types of question that, in the words of the first lines of the A-Preface, 'trouble' human reason. There are, for reasons we will discover later, three basic troubling questions: concerning God, freedom and immortality. The so-called 'science' that attempts to address such questions is called 'metaphysics'. The rest of the third section elaborates on the reasons why reason crossing this line is understandable, if illegitimate, and why these questions are unanswerable.

What is the connection between the discussion of necessary and universal, a priori cognitions, on the one hand, and this discussion of the illegitimate employment of reason? Kant will argue that, insofar as the a priori principles of cognition make experience possible, they also define the *limits of* experience. Therefore, they define the limit that reason crosses when it passes from a legitimate to a illegitimate employment. The conditions of the possibility of experience also define the limits of the use of reason. Therefore, a critique of pure reason will have to first explore the conditions of experience – and this is exactly what Kant does.

B-Introduction, Section 4

In the fourth section of the B-Introduction commences one of Kant's most famous analyses. First of all, we need to notice that Kant has moved from speaking of 'cognitions' to 'principles' and now 'judgements'. This is most confusing, and it might have been better had he begun with 'judgement'. Roughly, Kant tends to say 'cognitions' when he is referring to judgements that do, or claim to, present experiential objects. He writes 'principles' when he is referring to that select category of pure, a priori judgements that form universal, necessary conditions of possibility of cognition. (This definition is true of the principles of the understanding. More broadly, a principle is that which governs the activity of a faculty; thus reason too will have its principles.) And he uses 'judgement', especially in the singular, when referring to particular mental acts of any cognitive kind. Here, for simplicity, he is focusing on judgements that are normally expressed by a proposition that connects a subject phrase with a predicate phrase. For example, 'The sky [subject term] is blue [predicate phrase]', or 'My hair has gone grey.'

In this section, Kant is adding to the earlier distinction between a priori and a posteriori judgements a new distinction between analytic and synthetic judgements. A judgement is analytic if it simply 'elucidates' the already existing content of the subject concept. To use a very common example: 'A bachelor is an unmarried man.' The predicate phrase ('is a married man') is an expression of part of the meaning of the concept phrase ('A bachelor'). Nothing is added; rather, what was already (though covertly) contained in the concept is spelled out.

A judgement is synthetic, on the other hand, if the predicate is not already part of the subject concept. To be sure, it is *connected* to that concept, but its connection with the subject needs to be established by reference to some other source. Establishing this connection is what is indicated by the adjective 'synthetic' or the noun 'synthesis'. So, for example, 'That car is blue' requires that I refer beyond the concepts 'car' and 'blue' to the car in question (by looking at it), in order to establish whether it is in fact blue. I have to, Kant says, go 'outside' the concept; accordingly, such judgements are 'expansive' since they add to the information already available within the subject concept by 'synthesising' it with something else.

The result of combining these two pairs is four types of judgement:

	analytic	synthetic
a priori	An identical or tautological judgement, such as 'A is A'.	'All changes have a cause.'
a posteriori	'All primates are warm-blooded'. (See discussion below.)	'All bodies have weight', or 'That car is blue.'

Table 1. Types of judgement

An eighteenth-century empiricist might have objected that 'a posteriori' and 'synthetic' mean the same thing. Since my only source of information about the world is data collected from it, which is then combined, sorted or compared, then synthetic cognition is simply identical to empirical cognition. Obviously, it is one of Kant's major claims, as yet unproven, that there is a genuine difference here, and thus that synthetic a priori judgements are a unique, newly discovered, and all-important class. Kant begins his second paragraph by writing *'Experiential judgements, as such, are one and all synthetic'* (B11), something a contemporary empiricist would appreciate. But the further suggestion is that the reverse is not the case: not all synthetic judgements are experiential.

The class of 'analytic a posteriori' is a curious one which Kant does not discuss here but raised earlier. 'All primates are warm-blooded' is of course an empirical discovery, and is in fact synthetic. But it has become 'upgraded' to a universal statement, just like 'all bodies have weight' at B4. For some purposes – in certain cognitive contexts such as taxonomy – the upgraded judgement serves as part of a definition of 'primate'. Therefore, for these purposes it functions as analytic.

(This 'upgrading' is also similar to Kant's example of removing the foundations of the house at B2.) There are no statements that can be classed as analytic a posteriori in all cognitive contexts.

Many twentieth-century philosophers rejected the distinction between analytic and synthetic judgements. This is part of a general rejection of any account of language that understands it *either* as grounded in ostensive definition (establishing the names of things by pointing them out) *or* as comprising truth claims that are adequate reflections of states of affairs in the world. This attack on naive notions of meaning or sense is found in the work of Wittgenstein and Quine, for example. Quine argued that any attempt to prove supposedly analytic statements based upon definitions of terms was inevitably circular, relying on unstated assumptions. Wittgenstein emphasised that the constraints on the sense of words, and thus on the meaning of propositions, depends upon considerations that earlier philosophers would have seen as outside language altogether: for example, pragmatic considerations or social contexts. (See Wittgenstein 1958, Quine 1961, and for a general discussion, Miller 1998, Dancy 1984.)

Analyses like these are then used (by Bennett, for example) to interpret Kant's work as built on an initial mistake. The distinction between analytic and synthetic judgements is founded on normal use or custom, and not on a priori constraints. (That is, just like we noted that analytic a posteriori is not a real class, but only appears to be in certain cognitive contexts.) Bennett argues that Kant's distinction is thus a piece of empirical psychology, rather than transcendental philosophy. Beck defends Kant on this point, arguing that concepts can be seen as governed a priori within a pragmatic project of continuously improving one's definitions. Beck's account, however, has to begin from an essentially realist understanding of language and concepts; it could therefore be accused of not having taken on board the arguments of Quine and Wittgenstein to the effect that language is not a tracking of real essences. How might we interpret Kant so that there is both an a priori determination of sense and a historical, pragmatic or indeed free determination of use? This is and remains a problem; see also our discussion of commentators at the end of the 'Second Analogy of Experience'.

The significance of synthetic a priori judgements is huge. As synthetic, they would be expansive and would enlarge our knowledge of things. As a priori, however, they would also be independent of experience, and therefore independent of the limitations of experiential knowledge, such as contingency or doubtful universality. Synthetic a priori propositions – together with the knowledge of how such propositions are possible at all – constitute what Kant means by 'metaphysics' in the *positive* sense, what we have called 'critical metaphysics'. (Kant begins to make these immense implications clear at B19.)

In this second paragraph, we should look at Kant's account of how synthetic a posteriori judgements can take place. Kant's example is again 'all bodies have weight (or heaviness)'. (This is not a good example, because although synthetic a posteriori Kant had spoken of it being 'upgraded' in some contexts so as to appear analytic.) First, I look to my experience of things I call 'bodies' and the characteristics I already know bodies possess. Then, Kant writes: '[B]y looking back to the experience from which I have abstracted this concept of body, I also find heaviness to be always connected with the above characteristics; and so I add it, as a predicate, to that concept synthetically' (B12). This seems a conventional description of basic inductive reasoning. The object that answers to 'body' and the quality that answers to 'weight' have always been found together, in 'the same experience' of the body. There is, of course, a certain contingency to this synthetic combination: the two (object and quality) did in fact occur in the same experience, but perhaps did not have to (that is, according to some natural law). Thus, inductive reasoning always involves an element of probability. However, before moving on, Kant then further analyses what happens by saying that 'body' and 'heaviness' 'belong to each other, though only contingently, as parts of a whole; that whole is experience, which is itself a synthetic combination of intuitions' (B12). What does this mean? Again, it is the traditional account of induction. However, Kant is also asking what makes it possible that two characteristics can occur together, and for us to even raise the possibility that they *belong* together. Kant argues (in later passages alluded to here) that experience is a synthetic whole; it is unified both by the fact that it is *my experience* (I 'have' it), and by the fact that it is my experience *of a single world*. Only because of this wholeness does it make sense to ask whether two elements of my experience might be related. For example (and supposing this to be possible, which Kant argues it is not), if the part of my experience of the body were of *one* world, but the part about weight were of *another* world, then it would be silly to expect the two to 'belong to each other' and to be in any real relation, such that empirical observation in one would be valid also in the other. Only because we treat our experiences as of one world can we learn about that world by correlating the characteristics of the things we experience. Or, expressed differently, only because experience is 'one' can it be the third thing that makes possible the synthesis of subject and predicate concepts in a synthetic a posteriori judgement. This line of thinking becomes extremely important later, in the 'Transcendental Deduction' for example.

It is also worth noting that in his *Prolegomena*, an attempt to represent the philosophy of the first *Critique* in a slightly more popular form, Kant makes a famous distinction between judgements of perception and judgements of experience (Akademie IV, 297ff.). The former are subjective, the latter objective. However, in the *Prolegomena* passage, Kant explicitly says that judgements of perception do not depend upon any pure concept of the understanding (i.e. category), and this has led to considerable debate in the literature. Apparently similar accounts of subjective judgement can be found in the *Critique*, including here in the Introduction, and talking of 'empirical consciousness' at B133 in the 'Transcendental Deduction'. In these passages it is clear that either: 1. judgements of perception are an insignificant class to be linked with either empiricists or animals (see Leibniz, *Monadology*, section 28, and Hume on animal intelligence in the *Enquiries*); or 2. judgements of perception are apparent only, and in fact are implicitly dependent upon a horizon of *experience*. Here, Kant's move to the 'whole of experience' suggests the second interpretation. This is also true of the passages in the 'Deduction', where we will explore the whole issue further.

Let us return to the specific problem of synthetic a priori judgements. For such judgements, we can obviously no longer talk about consulting our particular experiences and observing which characteristics occur consistently in the 'same experience'. A priori judgements are supposed to be independent of particular experiences. Nevertheless, Kant says, I need to 'go beyond' the subject concept in order to make a synthetic connection with the predicate concept. If the connection could be made on the basis of the concept alone, then the proposition would be analytic. In the case of our running example, I need to go beyond the concept 'change' to some other thing X, in order to grasp the validity of its connection to the predicate 'have a cause'. But go beyond *to what?* That is the key question; much of Kant's epistemology follows from his answers to this question.

Well, we know it cannot be experience. However, the some other thing X cannot be another concept, either. Kant's reasoning goes something like this. The other concept would either be empirical, in which case the resulting connection would not be a priori. Or, the other concept would be a priori, in which case the connection would certainly be a priori but wouldn't be *expansive* – that is, would not provide new knowledge about the world. Such a connection between two a priori concepts would only be superficially synthetic. Consider, analogously, a simple logical syllogism, such as 'All men are mortal; Socrates is a man; therefore Socrates is mortal.' The last proposition is entailed by the first two, and this is often interpreted to mean that it is 'contained' in the first two. Thus, the last proposition does not provide *new* knowledge, but merely draws out or 'explicates' what is already known. So, similarly, were the X to which we refer in forming a synthetic a priori judgement just another concept, the judgement would not be genuinely synthetic. (Kant makes a similar argument in section six, at B23–4.)

So, again, the question: go beyond *to what?* Teasingly, perhaps, Kant is not going to provide an answer to this question for some time. Instead, he will first pursue the significance of the question itself, and also the method for answering it.

Here, we are going to skip section five because Kant is only adding detail to the problem of science introduced in the Prefaces, and restating his conception of science in the language of the synthetic/analytic distinction and the notion of synthetic a priori cognition.

B-Introduction, Section 6

In the first paragraph, the question of 'go beyond *to what?*' is recast more generally as 'How are synthetic judgements possible a priori?' (B19). This question, Kant claims, is the 'proper problem of pure reason'. It is, first of all, the question of how specific sciences (mathematics, physics, etc.) are possible. And, Kant adds, these must be possible because they are actual (B20–1); science exists so the question of *how* it exists must have an answer. The general question is also, as we have seen, the problem of how *any experience of the world* (whether fully scientific in nature or not) is possible. Again, such experience is actual for us all. Notice that we are framing Kant's arguments in this way: experience of type X (which might be an ordinary experience, or a science such as geometry) is actual; therefore it must be possible; therefore, any principle Y which is a universal and necessary condition of its possibility must be synthetic a priori and objectively valid. Kant does in fact frame his 'transcendental arguments' in this way, sometimes. But, when later we encounter such arguments in detail, it will be worth asking if this is the most authentic way of understanding how they are supposed to work, or if it over-simplifies.

The general question of synthetic a priori judgements also concerns how metaphysics is possible both in its uncritical and critical or scientific senses. Now, Kant argues that uncritical metaphysics, at least, is actual. In this section he refers back to metaphysics as a natural and unavoidable disposition of reason (see first paragraph of A-Preface), and thus terms it *'metaphysica naturalis'* (B21). '[T]hus all human beings, once their reason has expanded to speculation, actually have always had in them, and always will have in them, some metaphysics.' Understanding this 'natural metaphysics' would mean both understanding the natural 'urge' to ask troubling metaphysical questions, as well as understanding the limits of reason itself. Uncritical metaphysics is not something that critique could eliminate (because natural), but which it could at least understand and show to be different from critical metaphysics.

Metaphysics in a positive sense – necessary and universal knowledge not confined to one science or the other, together with the knowledge of how the former is possible – has not yet been attempted. So, its possibility cannot be demonstrated from its actuality. Indeed, it may turn out to be impossible. But in that case at least we will have gained insight into that impossibility of metaphysics – for example, insight into the limits of reason. So, it is impossible to work towards a positive metaphysics from its actuality. Instead, we must follow that path of science Kant has been describing, and (to borrow the metaphor he employs at the end of the section, B24) grow an entirely new plant, and nurture it to fruitfulness.

B-Introduction, Section 7

The first paragraph of this section introduces several important new ideas. It begins with the idea of critique as a special science, which has as its object not the objects of reason (that is, the things about which we reason) but reason itself. Now, such a special science, if it were complete and had identified 'the sum of those principles by which all pure a priori cognitions can be acquired' (B24–5) could be called an 'organon', a 'doctrine' or even a 'system' (B24–5). Kant claims his task is much less ambitious. He wishes to provide instead a 'propaedeutic' (a preliminary or orienting set of studies), which he calls 'critique'. In regard to metaphysical speculation, the purpose of this critique would be primarily negative, showing the limits of reason and puncturing the pretensions of dogmatic philosophy.

This first paragraph switches direction with the sentence 'I call *transcendental* all cognition that deals not so much with objects as rather with our way of cognising objects in general insofar as that way of cognising is to be possible a priori' (B25). We already know that Kant's purpose is not to compile a system of the a priori concepts of reason. Instead, he wishes to focus on *transcendental knowledge*: a priori knowledge about how ordinary forms of knowledge are possible. Thus he writes a few lines later: 'What here constitutes the object is not the nature of things, which is inexhaustible, but the understanding that makes judgements about the nature of things, and even this understanding, again, only in regard to its a priori cognition' (B26). This notion of the 'transcendental' is clearly important. It defines not only: the new manner in which Kant's work will proceed (he will be finding a way to uncover the transcendental conditions of cognition); and its new philosophical discovery (that there are such transcendental conditions); but also its limits (these are the conditions of cognitions about objects, and thus neither directly cognition of objects themselves, nor about anything other than the conditions of cognition). We will return, on several future occasions, to this key notion of 'transcendental'.

Now it becomes clear why the critique is only a 'propaedeutic': it is essential, Kant argues, to establish how knowledge is possible before any inventory of it can be made. Critique thus provides a 'touchstone of the value, or lack of value, of all a priori cognition' – where 'value' means truth value in the realm of critical metaphysics. Without critique, 'unqualified historians and judges [of metaphysics] pass judgement on other people's baseless assertions by means of their own, which are just as baseless' (B27).

Let us skip to the last paragraph. Kant is, again, discussing what structure his book must have in order to perform the above task of critique. There must be, he says, both a doctrine of elements (that is, the elements or parts that constitute the possibility of a priori cognition) and a doctrine of method (how the investigation must proceed). (We'll overlook the slip here: Kant has just finished saying that he is not going to provide a 'doctrine'. Here, it is a 'doctrine' of transcendental elements, rather than of those cognitions made possible thereby.) Now, Kant claims, 'Human cognition has two stems, namely *sensibility* and *understanding* . . . Through sensibility objects are *given* to us; through understanding they are *thought*' (B29). This is an all-important distinction for Kant, with huge implications, as we shall see later. For the moment, Kant is simply asking whether each of these 'stems' might individually contain conditions of a priori cognition. If so, each stem must be subjected to critique. Accordingly, Kant will begin the doctrine of elements with a transcendental analysis of our ability to sense, or for objects to be given to us (e.g. by sight). This faculty in general Kant calls 'sensibility'. In this first section (the Transcendental Aesthetic), he will ask if sensibility contains 'a priori presentations constituting the condition under which objects are given to us' (B29–30). The faculty of thinking about objects with concepts is the understanding; Kant analyses this faculty immediately after tackling sensibility (in the first division of the 'Transcendental Logic').

Transcendental Aesthetic

Section 1

(Notice that Kant starts to number sections in his book section 1, section 2 and so forth, and then stops again after the 'Transcendental Deduction'.)

So, the book proper opens with a consideration of 'sensibility': our ability to sense objects or for objects to be given to us in sense. The question is whether there is an a priori aspect to sensibility and, above all, whether this aspect must be part of the transcendental condition of cognition in general.

The first paragraphs lay out some important terms. Cognition refers to or 'presents' objects, Kant says, in many different ways, but it is 'intuition' (*Anschauung*) by which it refers to them *directly*, or *without mediation* (A19=B33). An intuition is a direct presentation (*Vorstellung*) of an object. Or, in other words, an intuition is the object as given. This happens only insofar as the mind is 'affected in a certain manner' – for example, being affected by something visual through the eyes. In general, our ability or capacity to be affected in this manner Kant calls 'sensibility' (*Sinnlichkeit*) (A19=B33).

Kant is distinguishing this 'direct' manner of presentation from any indirect manner. By the latter, he means conceptual presentation. My concept of a wall, say, is indirect in the sense that it does not immediately refer to any particular wall, but rather refers to all walls or to walls in general. In order to get from the reference to all walls (or walls in general) to *this* wall, the concept needs to be mediated by the process of recognising wall-like characteristics in an intuition of *this* wall (A19=B33). Only through the mediation of intuition can concepts reach particular, real things. This is an important part of what Kant means in calling human concepts and their usage 'discursive'. We'll need to return to how Kant understands conceptuality later.

In the short second paragraph, Kant writes that the effect of an object on our sensibility is called 'sensation' (*Empfindung*). (Notice that although in English sensibility and sensation have a common etymology, this is not so in German. These are two distinct notions.) And, 'intuition that refers to the object through sensation is called *empirical* intuition' (A20=B34). The object, before it is determined to be this or that (a wall or a walrus), is called 'appearance' (*Erscheinung*). There are two potential misunderstandings that lurk here. Both in German and in English we might be led to confuse 'appearance' with 'illusion'. This is most definitely not what Kant has in mind. Rather, 'appearance' means just what it says: something gives or shows itself to me, it appears. This might seem a small point, but it is of the greatest significance. If we said that appearance meant illusion, then we would immediately set out to look for the 'real' *behind* the illusion (we might be a Platonist, for instance, inquiring after the 'forms' of things). But, for Kant, the real is what appears. To investigate appearances means to investigate the empirically real. This is discussed in more depth at the end of the 'Transcendental Aesthetic', at A45–6=B62–3. There, Kant explains that no matter how profoundly we probe the real, what is revealed is still appearance. So, *within* appearance we can distinguish between 'mere appearance' (Kant's example is a rainbow) and the thing itself (light refracted by water droplets) – but both these are, again, *within* what is here called 'appearance'. The second possible misunderstanding lies in Kant's claim here that 'appearance' means an empirical intuition before it is recognised as some type of object. Now, Kant does not always use the term appearance in this specific way, but also this definition might lead us to think of appearance as 'raw' data of the senses. We will see shortly why Kant cannot mean this.

The object appears as empirical intuition through sensation. The terminology might be different, but an empiricist such as Locke would otherwise have little to argue with here. However, the implication here is that, in contrast to empirical intuitions, Kant will be searching for evidence of a priori intuitions (which would then be qualified to serve as a transcendental condition of a priori cognition). And that, obviously enough, would be anathema to Locke. Kant makes this search clear in the next two paragraphs.

'Matter' is defined as whatever, in an appearance, 'corresponds to sensation' (A20=B34). In other words, matter is what is sensed: what is smelled, touched, seen and so on. Despite the language, this is not a metaphysical claim about the nature of objects – that they are made up of matter. The distinction between matter and form is Aristotelian. Rather than a claim about *things*, Kant is rather talking about the presentations of things. Kant is making no assumptions about stuff, substance, elements or whatever. Sensation is an effect of an object; matter is whatever is presented through the simple event of that effect. What, in a presentation, is presented merely through the sensation of red is a red something; what is presented merely through a shrill sound is a shrill-sounding something. This is the 'matter' of the intuition.

The idea of 'matter' becomes clearer in its contrast with 'form'. Form is that by means of which matter comes to have order. Suppose I hear the shrill sound, and afterwards see the red something; then these sensations are in order in time. Suppose I hear the sound as located within the red something; these sensations are in order in space (that is, they are arranged or located in space). The matter of sensation is always formed in this way. Thus, sensation is not raw 'sense data', not a private mental content, but rather arises because I am in relation with something. That is why Kant speaks of sensation as affection: in this relation, I am affected by something, and this affection is the redness of the red something. Moreover, the matter of my intuitions, Kant seems to assume, will always be multiple: we never *just* encounter one red something in temporal and spatial isolation. He thus refers to the notion of a 'manifold' of intuition, meaning the stream of different presented qualities. This manifold will come to have an order or arrangement.

Kant then writes, 'that in which alone sensations can be ordered and placed into a certain form cannot itself be sensation again' (A20=B34). Now, one thing Kant is asserting here is that it is difficult and perhaps impossible to identify through which of our senses is sensed the ordering of sensations. There seems to be no sensation (no sound, no colour, etc.) that presents 'is afterwards' or 'is located within'. These features of order or arrangements are certainly part of an intuition, but are not its matter, they are its form. This is already an important issue, but it is not the one Kant wishes to highlight here. It would be easy to say that this particular order of a manifold is just what Kant means by 'form' (and sometimes he says something very similar to this, for example in the phrase 'certain form' above). But here he calls form that which 'brings about the fact that' manifolds can and do have order. That is, the condition of the possibility of such order. For convenience, we can call the particular order and arrangement of manifolds 'empirical form' and the condition of any such order, 'pure form'. Pure form is what makes it possible that (is the transcendental condition of) manifolds have order or (as we have termed it) particular empirical form.

The clue to discovering this distinction lies in the phrase 'that in which'. He is not concerned here with the problem of how we arrive at the presentation of any particular order ('afterwards', 'located within'). Rather, he is concerned with the presentation of the pure form – let us say the 'framework' or 'medium' – within which any such order is possible. To use the language with which we are becoming familiar, Kant is looking for the transcendental condition for the possibility of the ordering of sensations. In short, with the presentation of space and time. So, the quotation with which the previous paragraph began means something like 'the frameworks, within which sensations could possibly become ordered, cannot be sensation'.

And yet the matter is the only part of an intuition that is clearly a posteriori or empirical; that is, which arises from the effect of things upon us. So, Kant concludes, the form in general of intuitions (even empirical intuitions) must not be empirical. It must 'lie ready for the sensations a priori in the mind' (A20=B34), a priori. It follows from this that the form of intuition must be 'capable of being examined apart from all sensation'. That is, critique is able to isolate and investigate this transcendental condition. We don't have to analyse statistically significant numbers of empirical examples; we can simply focus on the form that lies 'ready in the mind'.

Insofar as this form can be isolated from everything empirical, Kant calls it 'pure'. In the B-edition, Kant has already defined this notion of the 'pure' (B3, see above). Here, we read: 'all presentations in which nothing is found that belongs to sensation I call *pure*' (A20=B34). There follows an odd example. I start with a presentation (intuition) of a body (by which Kant does not mean necessarily a living body, but pretty much any physical thing). Let us say, a copper kettle. From this presentation I remove the contribution of my concepts – that is, I no longer consider it as a substance of this or that type, or indeed of any type; I no longer think of it as the kind of thing that exerts force; or being a divisible or not divisible sort of thing. And again, from out of this presentation I remove also whatever belongs to sensation: hardness or softness, colour, etc. Kant then writes 'I am still left with something from this empirical intuition, namely, extension and shape' (A21=B35).

Extension and shape, Kant is claiming, are not concepts with which I identify the class of thing. Extension and shape (both *this particular* kettle-shape, and extension and shape in general) are entirely different types of presentation from concepts. They are intuited form. Moreover, extension and shape (considering now only extension and shape *in general*) are not sensations, not the matter of intuition, and are thus also not empirical. Again, they are different types of presentation from the matter of intuition; they are form. But more, they are pure (that is, non-empirical) form. Kant also calls such forms the 'mere form of sensibility' (A21=B35), because they are our sensibility (our ability to present things) separated from both concepts and from the matter of intuition.

The 'science' of all the principles of a priori (here, equivalent to 'pure') form is 'transcendental aesthetic' (A21=B35). 'Aesthetic' is derived from the Greek word for 'to sense'. So, although within philosophy we are used to using the word 'aesthetic' in a narrower meaning (those particular sensed things that are called 'beautiful' or 'sublime'), Kant is using the term in the broader, Greek meaning. Kant clarifies this in the long footnote here. (Kant does also use the narrower meaning later in his career, in his *Critique of Judgement*.) 'Transcendental aesthetic', then, means 'the study of the a priori conditions of possibility of sensing'.

Section 2

After a brief, general introduction, the bulk of this section is taken up with four numbered arguments (five in the A-edition) concerning space. These arguments provide a 'metaphysical exposition' of the 'concept' of space (A23=B38). Kant explains this as meaning a clear presentation of the contents of the concept. Then, in section 3, he follows this up with a transcendental analysis (determining what space is the transcendental condition for) and stating general conclusions or implications. Starting in section 4, the procedure repeats itself for the form of inner sense, time. The arguments and analyses given to time are strikingly similar to those given for space. For this reason, below, we will dwell at length on the analyses of space, and only briefly on time. Nevertheless, there are some revealing and helpful differences in expression, so it is well worth reading the space and time arguments side by side. We will be dealing with all four arguments contained in the B-edition.

The first paragraph of section 2 distinguishes between 'outer sense' and 'inner sense'. By outer sense, Kant means that part of sensibility by means of which we are in relation to things outside us. The form of outer sense is space. Since our own body is an object in space (even if not, strictly, 'outside' us), the body is primarily an object for outer sense. By inner sense, Kant means that part of sensibility by means of which we are in relation to ourselves insofar as we have what is broadly often called a 'mental life': my thoughts, emotions, memories, etc. The form of inner sense is time. What kinds of things are space and time, though? Historically, there are two dominant answers to this question. First, space and time might be considered some genuinely existent object or substantive container of physical objects and events. This position, roughly, was held and defended by Newton and his followers. Second, as put forward by Leibniz and the German rationalist school, space and time are nothing in themselves, but only the relations between substantial objects (which objects are thus not essentially spatial or temporal). Kant's arguments subtly work against both of these, aiming to establish a new, third account which will be an important element in what Kant calls 'transcendental idealism'.

The first argument commences 'Space is not an empirical concept that has been abstracted from outer experiences' (A23=B38). This is the statement of the conclusion of an argument. (Except for the last argument, all the others also begin with a statement of the conclusion.) The conclusion is expressed negatively; we need to understand what Kant is arguing against. The target is an empiricist position in the spirit of Locke, one that maintains that our concept of space is a posteriori, derived from our observation of spatial relations. There are two types of such relations: first, the relation in space between an observed object and me (the place where I am); second, the relation in space between two observed objects (say, a kettle and a teapot). Kant reasons that, in order for this empiricist position to be coherent, it must not be in any way circular or 'beg the question'. That is, if the empiricist is trying to understand how we come about the concept of space, he or she cannot assume that we already have that concept. And this is just the problem, Kant thinks. In order to observe the first type of relation, I have to assume space in order to present the object as *outside of me*. Similarly, in order to observe the second type of relation, I have to assume space in order to present two objects *alongside one another*. Space, then, cannot be an empirical concept because it is necessary that I present space itself in order to present empirical instances of spatial relations.

We can now understand more fully why appearance, and more specifically the matter of intuition – sensation – is not isolated sense data. Sensation occurs as the affection of something that is in relation to me. But this relation must already be spatial. Being spatial is thus a condition of being able to say that something 'affects' me. Thus, 'That which affects me is located in space' is a synthetic a priori judgement, and not a posteriori. Even an 'inner' sensation, such as feeling sad (assuming emotion can be classed as a sensation), is located in space in a not quite trivial sense: I am affected by myself, here. Thus, Kant will shortly talk about this self-affection as '*inner* sense', the form of which is time.

The second argument is similar, aiming to prove that 'Space is a necessary a priori presentation that lies at the basis of all outer intuition' (A24=B39). The argument is similar to the sample analysis of 'body' in section 1. It is possible to present (in imagination) any body in space, or even space empty of bodies. It is impossible, though, to present the absence of space. Perhaps we could even describe conceptually a universe that was purely temporal, but could this universe be intuited? Kant believes not. The fact that the presentation of space cannot in a presentation be eliminated shows it is necessary. And, again, the fact that it rests upon no empirical presentations show it to be a priori. Finally, the expression 'lies at the basis of' is meant to indicate that space is a transcendental condition of possibility of any outer intuition. Kant provides a more sustained argument later for a related (but not identical) proposition in the section 'The Refutation of Idealism'. But the argument here seems rather weak. Indeed, it either looks like little more than a tautology (a spatial intuition cannot not be of space), or it is a differently expressed version of the first argument.

In the A-edition, Kant follows this argument with one concerning the transcendental possibility of geometry. In the B-edition, however, he chooses to discuss this in section 3.

In the first argument, why does Kant write 'not an empirical concept' rather than just 'not empirical'? In other texts, both before and after the *Critique of Pure Reason*, Kant proposed a different argument that, just like the first argument, concerns spatial relations. However, its conclusion had less to do with whether space is empirical or not, but rather what kind of presentation space is. The argument is usually called the 'Incongruent Counterparts' and can be found fully expressed in the *Prolegomena to Any Future Metaphysics*.

Kant's argument goes something like this: one of the relations of 'alongside one another' (the expression Kant uses in the first argument above) will be *left* and *right*. This is significant both in the sense of 'to the left of', and in the sense of 'left-handed (glove, shoe, etc.)'. There are objects (such as my left and right hands) that are similar but not congruent, that is, which cannot be reoriented in space so as to correspond. Such objects are called enantiomorphs, or just 'incongruent counterparts'. If, however, I describe such an object conceptually (in terms of the concepts of number and order of its parts), I can find no concept that distinguishes the left from the right version. This is what we mean by saying that they are similar. Only by referring to intuition can their non-congruence be discovered, and the distinction between left and right be made; that is, only by actually being in immediate relation to some one example (real or imagined) of a left- or right-handed object. Therefore, something is given in intuition which determines what is possible in space (left- and right-handed things), but which cannot be translated into conceptual terms. Thus not all relations are conceptual, as Leibniz thought. Kant at first (in work in the late 1760s) concluded from this that Newton must be correct (that space exists in itself as an absolute framework for movement). But, if we accept the Newtonian view, then space can again be understood abstractly (that is, conceptually) by mathematics and the laws of mechanics. Everything there is to know about space can be expressed by an abstract mathematical concept. (Thus a basic thesis of classical empiricism: that there is no essential difference between sensible impressions and conceptual ideas.) Kant's argument, fully developed, must also prove that this complete abstraction from intuition is impossible. In fact, as we shall see below (for example, in the discussion of section 3), it leads Kant to claim that all mathematics is ultimately based upon constructed intuitions of space and time. For the moment, the conclusion of the 'incongruent counterparts' argument is that there is an important and irreducible difference between intuitions and concepts – and that space is originally an intuition. This takes us to the territory of the third argument in the B-edition 'Transcendental Aesthetic'.

The third argument begins: 'Space is not a discursive or, as we say, universal concept of things as such; rather, it is a pure intuition' (A24–5=B39). Kant puts forward two propositions. First, space is always one in its presentation. The space inside your home, for instance, and the space inside mine, are different parts of the same continuous space. Moreover, we can imagine fantasy worlds, but if we posit these worlds as existing, then the question must arise: *where*? (At

A31=B46, speaking about time, Kant says that 'All actuality of appearances is possible only in time'. It is a necessary part of the meaning of saying that something is 'actual' that it is in the one, continuous time. Similarly, we can say here, that it is a necessary part of the meaning of saying that some body is 'actual' that it is located in the one, continuous space.) However, it is not immediately clear how this oneness of space proves anything about Kant's target conclusion.

The second proposition provided is that the parts of the one space cannot 'precede' space, as its 'constituents'. Rather, the parts are presented as already 'in' space. Suppose that space were like a wall, and the parts of space different sized bricks in the wall. Then it would make sense to say that the wall is made up of bricks, and the bricks precede the wall, that space is made up of parts that are prior to it. In that case, it would be possible to present this part separately from that part; but this violates the first proposition. Talking about separate parts, in this sense, assumes a space in which they are separate. So, space is originally presented as unitary, and parts of space are subsequently presented through 'limitations'; analogous to the way in which a fence draws limits on a landscape, creating individual fields.

'Space is essentially one', Kant continues, 'the manifold in it, and hence also the general concept of spaces as such, rests solely on limitations' (A25=B39). This quotation divides into two: 1. the manifold in space (its various elements) rests upon limitations; 2. *hence* the general concept of spaces does also. The first of these is another way of talking about the whole prior to the parts. But why does the second follow? One way of interpreting this obscure argument would be as follows. If there is going to be a concept of spaces (plural) – the concept of the volume of this thing, the shape of that, the inside of the other – then that concept is only possible because original space can be divided. The concept of spaces, then, must be subsequent to limitation of some original space. 'It follows', Kant says, that any concept of space must be grounded upon the original, a priori intuition of space.

But why could not 'original space' be a concept, of the higher generality, that is then limited in order to determine concepts of this or that space? That is, granted that all concepts of this or that space are derivative, why must they be understood as derivative *from an intuition*? The answer is not yet clear. However, in the parallel argument in section 4, writing about time, Kant adds that 'the kind of presentation that can be given only through a single object is intuition' (A32=B47). A concept is a presentation, but it is 'given' through (that is, the concept is instantiated in) multiple possible objects. And this is in part what Kant has in mind in speaking of 'discursive' in the first sentence. My concept of a kettle is fulfilled through this kettle, or that one, or many others. But an intuition, whether of a kettle, or the pure intuition of space, is always of *one*. If, then, space is 'essentially one', then it is presented only in intuition.

The fourth argument continues this contrast between intuitions and concepts. Concepts, Kant says, are presentations that contain a potentially infinite set of things 'under' them. The concept of a kettle includes this brass kettle, that copper one, and this electric one and many others. By 'under' is meant that the concept is made up of a set of common or overlapping characteristics, abstracted from kettles, and by means of which a new kettle could be identified. Logically, then, individual kettles are subsumed under the concept whenever the concept is used. An intuition, on the other hand, (such as the intuition of space), contains many possible limitations 'within itself', simultaneously coexistent. The whole intuition is of the same order of thing as the limited part. This, as we have seen above, is how space is presented. Therefore, space is originally an intuition. Concepts of space, and of spaces, can be formed (for example, the Newtonian concept of mathematically homogeneous absolute space; or a photographer's concept of illuminated space, or whatever) but are derivative.

Similarly, again in section 4, Kant writes: 'But if something is such that its parts . . . can be presented determinately only through limitation, then the whole presentation of it cannot be given through concepts (for they contain only partial presentations), but any such presentation must be based upon direct intuition' (A32=B48). What is meant here by concepts containing only 'partial presentations'? Two related things: first, with respect to the concept, any instantiation (this kettle) is only partial, because the concept could also be instantiated by a different kettle. Second, the 'characteristics' we spoke about above are only partial insofar as they could never fully determine their object (the concept of kettle, for instance does not determine what colour the kettle must be); that is, *this* kettle is always contingent with respect to the concept of it. So, *this* kettle is only part of what the concept can designate; and the concept designates only part of what *this* kettle is. Accordingly, a concept could never designate a whole, unique entity, for it always says both too much and too little. As we discussed above in treating Kant's Introduction, our discursive cognition is always partial in this way. A presentation whose object is a whole, unique object is pure intuition.

What, in summary, has Kant's 'Metaphysical Exposition' sought to demonstrate?

1. Space is an a priori presentation.

2. Space is a presentation that is a necessary condition for the possibility of any particular spatial presentation.

3. The key differences between concepts and intuitions are that concepts are indirect and discursive, contain instantiations 'under' them, and thus contain partial presentations, whereas pure intuitions directly present unique wholes, the parts or elements of which are 'within' them, and given through limitation.

4. Space is a transcendentally necessary, a priori form of intuition.

Section 3
Section three consists of a 'Transcendental Exposition' and 'Conclusions'. The first was added in the B-edition to cover some of the ground Kant had originally treated in section 2. It is designed to pursue what kinds of cognition are made possible by space as the a priori form of intuition. Well, actually, of course, any outer experience is determined by this form, if Kant is right. Here, he focuses on a particular type of cognition, namely geometry. By geometry is meant the mathematical science of the properties of spatial figures.

Geometry is important to Kant for two inter-related reasons. First, more generally, there is a history of geometry being used as a model for philosophical method. Plato is one prominent example; and both Descartes and Spinoza explicitly advocated a rigorous axiomatic form of reasoning, as employed in Euclid, if philosophy was to achieve truth. Second, though, Kant has already made much of his new idea of what science is, and has taken geometry as a key example. So, in this little section, Kant is trying to ground his conception of science – in order that it can then be asked *whether* metaphysics could be a science, and *how*. The conclusions of geometry have absolute necessity and universality, Kant claims. This is only possible because geometry is synthetic a priori cognition concerning space. But from a mere geometric concept no proposition could be derived that was 'synthetic', which went 'beyond' the concept (B41). And this in turn is only possible because space is an a priori form of intuition – both necessary and universal. (Notice that Kant cannot therefore be advocating geometry in the sense that Descartes or Spinoza thought of it. For Kant, geometry cannot be understood simply as logical reasoning from concepts. So, hidden in this treatment of geometry is a critique of such philosophers who confuse philosophy and geometry. We will return to Kant's concept of geometry much later in the book.)

Note that in passing, Kant has given us a clue to the teasing question that arose in the B-Introduction section 4. In synthetic a priori propositions, cognition 'goes beyond' the concept – but to what? Kant is not concerned here to develop this general point at length, but the answer is now clear: to the forms of intuition. A synthetic a priori proposition is made when a concept is 'expanded' by reference to the pure forms of intuition (space and time).

'How then', Kant writes, 'can the mind have an outer intuition which precedes the objects themselves . . .?' (B41). That is to ask, how does it happen that there is an a priori form of intuition, such that we can philosophically analyse it independently of experience, and which forms the transcendental condition of cognitions such as geometry? 'Obviously, this can be so only insofar as this intuition resides merely in the subject' (B41). By 'subject' here Kant means two things. First, he means you and I and everyone – we are individual subjects. Second, and more importantly, he means the agent that intuits, experiences, thinks, knows or believes. The subject is the entity that 'does' such mental acts. So, to say that (the form of) intuition 'resides' in the subject means that it is 'built in' to the apparatus of intuiting. Space is a formal feature *only* of our sensibility, that is of our ability to be affected by external objects. We experience spatially because of the constitution of our sensibility. Kant pursues the implications of this idea in the second part of section 3.

The second part of section 3 comprises a set of conclusions and discussions concerning space. The first paragraph introduces, indirectly, an important distinction. Kant is writing about 'things in themselves'. A thing in itself is distinguished from 'appearances' (A26=B42). (Kant also, equivalently for our purposes, distinguishes 'noumena' from 'phenomena'.) What does this mean? An appearance, as we discussed above, is simply that which appears: what presents itself to sensibility. But we now know that sensibility has a formal constitution all of its own (this is what Kant, in this first paragraph, calls the 'subjective conditions of intuition'). If it is the case that space as the form of intuition is a feature of our subjectivity, then it would seem to make sense to ask: what are things like *in themselves*, that is, separate from the 'subjective condition' of our sensibility? The thing in itself, then, is just that which appears, but considered separate from its conditions of appearance and thus also from its actual appearance in experience.

Because space is a formal feature of appearances (or phenomena), Kant claims that 'space presents no property whatever of any things in themselves, nor does it represent things in themselves in their relation to one another' (A26=B42). The thing in itself is neither spatial nor in space in any way. Moreover, space is not itself a thing in itself (not for example an absolute 'container' of things). Kant continues, in the third paragraph:

Only from the human standpoint, therefore, can we speak of space, of extended beings, etc. If we depart from the subjective condition under which alone we can acquire outer intuition . . . then the presentation of space means nothing whatsoever. This predicate is ascribed to things only insofar as they appear to us, i.e. only insofar as they are objects of sensibility. (A26=B42)

Human beings have in common the structure of sensibility. We know this, presumably, partly because we have little difficulty conversing about and working together in shared space. However, it is not just the case that appearances *can* appear spatial; rather, certain types of appearances *necessarily and universally* have spatial form. Because it is a condition of my (human) sensibility, the form of space is the necessary condition of things appearing outside me. But it is not the condition of all things whatsoever (that is, including things considered as things in themselves) (A27=B43). Accordingly, as the a priori form of my sensibility, space can be studied independently of experiences. That is why geometrical propositions (and synthetic a priori propositions concerning space) carry necessary and universal certainty – provided, of course, we consider these propositions as applying only to appearances. Thus Kant writes about 'limitation on a judgement' (A27=B43): the judgement is universally true only when limited to spatial appearances. This idea of limitation preoccupies Kant throughout the rest of his book, and has enormously important implications for the range of validity of critical metaphysics.

What appears to me in space empirically is the real. (Remember, appearance does not mean 'illusion'.) These empirical spatial things are my objective world. Indeed, space itself must be considered 'empirically real' (A28=B44). Nevertheless, 'space is *transcendentally ideal*' (A28=B44); it is a function of our sensibility and not a feature of things in themselves.

The last two paragraphs in both the A- and B-editions concern sensations, the 'matter' as opposed to the form of intuitions. Kant argues that tastes, smells, colours and so forth have something important in common with the presentation of space – namely that they are subjective, a function of the subject's sensibility. A sensation arises not because of an object, but because of a *relation* between an object and my sensibility. But there the similarity ends, for while space is a necessary and a priori presentation, sensations are merely empirical. The form of space can be philosophically analysed independently of spatial objects; sensation cannot. Accordingly, Kant insists, no synthetic a priori propositions can be made employing this subjective character of sensation. (There is one important exception to this, which we will discuss in the 'Anticipations of Perception'.)

Sections 4 to 6

As mentioned earlier, the arguments and discussions concerning time are very similar to those about space. For this reason, we will here just notice a few significant deviations. Then, in the following section, we will move on to Kant's conclusions concerning the 'Transcendental Aesthetic' as a whole, in sections 7 and 8.

First of all, notice that in the third argument of section 4, and in section 5, Kant gives us key examples of how the form of time plays a transcendental role in cognition, making possible synthetic a priori propositions such as 'different times are not simultaneous but sequential' (A31=B47). A particularly important set of such principles concern change (B48–9). That one thing could have two incompatible predicates (both green and red) is, considered merely from the point of view of concepts, just an impossibility. Kant writes, 'no concept whatsoever could make comprehensible the possibility of a change' (B48). Because of time, however, we can speak of change. The two contradictory properties are possible sequentially (the traffic light changed from green to red).

Kant notes: 'These principles cannot be obtained from experience. For experience would provide neither strict universality nor apodeictic certainty' (A31=B47). ('Apodeictic' here means 'necessary because firmly demonstrated'.) This is a familiar claim in the history of philosophy (sometimes going under the heading of the 'problem of induction'). We have seen Kant discuss similar issues in the Prefaces and Introduction when writing about science. Generalisations from the experience of instances (induction) could only show that something always has been true, as far as we know – experience cannot demonstrate that something always must be true, here and everywhere. A synthetic a priori proposition has universality and necessity, which show that experience is not its provenance.

Kant then says something very important: 'These principles hold as rules under which alone experiences are possible at all' (A31=B47). This takes us to the idea of a 'transcendental argument'. How can Kant demonstrate the universality and necessity of a principle? His solution is to develop arguments that show that without it *no experience or science would be possible at all*. This move takes two forms: first, Kant moves 'regressively' from some experience or science (such as Euclidean geometry) to what its underlying conditions must be. Since experience X or science Y is evidently possible, and with it our sense of our world and of ourselves, the principle must be a priori necessary. Second, sometimes Kant moves 'synthetically' to analyse the necessary conditions of any experience. Both are versions of the transcendental argument. (The first version, however, seems to assume without argument the validity of, say, geometry. As we shall see shortly, this would appear to be a weakness.) In any case, we have seen several examples of such transcendental argumentation already. For example, when Kant argued that without the a priori presentation of space it would be impossible to present things as outside me or alongside one another. Or again, just above, when Kant showed that without the presentation of time, it would be impossible to present change. However, these are partial examples. They refer to the transcendental conditions of this or that *type of* experience, not to all experience. This entirely general transcendental argument only appears in the infamous section entitled the 'Transcendental Deduction', to which we will turn in due course.

The bulk of section 6 is taken up with drawing the same conclusions regarding time as we saw regarding space: time is not a self-subsistent thing, nor can it be ascribed as a determination to things in themselves, it is merely a subjective condition of inner intuition, time is empirically real but transcendentally ideal, and so on. All the conclusions concerning space can be carried over to time. This is by now familiar.

In the third paragraph, Kant makes a new claim. Space is the form of all outer intuition, but 'as such it is limited' (A34=B50). Thinking back to our discussion of the first argument about space above, even inner sense is 'inner' and thus in space. However, inner objects are not distinguished one from another in terms of space. Saying they are spatial presentations is important, for otherwise saying 'inner' would have no meaning, but is otherwise trivial. But time is not so limited. Not only are inner intuitions (of my thoughts, emotions, memories) presented in time, but insofar as outer intuitions are *also* presented internally, all outer intuitions are also temporal. More importantly still, the presentation of the manifold of space happens temporally; and the synthesis of this manifold is thus a synthesis of time. Time is therefore the universal form of intuition. This turns out to be hugely important. When Kant later makes the most general transcendental arguments, it is the form of time that takes clear precedence. This generality is made very clear at A36=B52: 'since our intuition is always sensible, no object that is not subject to the condition of time can ever be given to us in experience'.

Why, though, in the quotation just given, does Kant write 'our intuition is always sensible'? Is there some other (non-human) type of intuition (immediate way of presenting things) that is not sensible (dependent upon an object affecting us)? Kant addresses these questions among others in the next two sections.

Sections seven to eight

Within section 7, we will look at just the first two pages or so, for here Kant is adding something interesting to what we have seen already.

'Against this theory', Kant writes (A36=B53), meaning his account of time as an a priori form of intuition, an objection has been raised: namely, that 'changes are actual' (A36=B53). Since changes are only possible in time, this must mean that time is also actual. If time is actual, then it cannot be merely ideal, as Kant claims. Kant concedes this 'whole argument. Time is indeed something actual' (A37=B53). It is actual as the form of intuition. Time 'therefore has subjective reality in regard to inner experience; i.e. I actually have the presentation of time . . .' (A37=B53–4). In other words, Kant is insisting on the claim (which we first saw in regard to space), that time is 'empirically real' but 'transcendentally ideal'.

There follows a curious thought experiment:

Suppose, on the other hand, that I could intuit myself without being subject to this condition of sensibility, or that another being could so intuit me; in that case the very same determinations that we now present as changes would provide a cognition in which the presentation of time, and hence also that of change, would not occur at all. (A37=B54)

What is actually empirical change in my inner state would appear, to this hypothetical other type of intuition, in some other way – but not as change, because not as time. This other way of intuiting would have a different necessary form. (Note that this passage is not yet addressing the questions we asked at the end of the previous section concerning a non-sensible intuition. The other form of intuition described here is not said to be non-sensible – rather, just a differently constituted sensibility.) Perhaps we should not make too much of this thought experiment, for it is only being used to illustrate the difference between what is empirically or subjectively real as opposed to the idea of transcendental ideality. Nevertheless, it is also foregrounding the fact that, for Kant, the forms of space and time are transcendentally necessary for human experience but, beyond the human (if there are such beings), are contingent.

In the next paragraph, Kant asks why this objection should have arisen with respect to time, but not space. It is because within the history of philosophy (most obviously in Descartes) there has long been a problem with outer objects – there seems to be no way of conclusively demonstrating their existence. By contrast, inner experience has been considered immediately certain, 'directly evident through consciousness' (A38=B55). Accordingly, the actuality of time as the frame or container of our inner sensing seems obvious. Kant writes that, according to this way of thinking, 'External objects might be mere illusion; but the object of inner sense is, in their opinion, undeniably something actual' (A38=B55). Those who think this way, however, have failed to consider that both space and time, although undeniably actual as forms of presentation, are the forms of presentation *of appearances*. Just as space is the form in which objects appear to me so *time is the form within which I appear to myself*. The implication here is that, although intuition is defined as an immediate relation to a sensible object, nevertheless this immediacy is not the same as is required for Descartes to prove that 'I think, therefore I am'. Here we find the beginnings of a really interesting and far-reaching critique of Descartes; Kant will add to this critique throughout his book (and again already in section 8), but it all comes together much later in the 'Paralogisms of Pure Reason'.

Here, we will skip the remainder of section 7 and move on to section 8. This last section was considerably extended in the B-edition, at which point Kant also divided it up into four subsections with roman numerals. The first of these subsections is the part originally published in the A-edition. It is principally a restatement of the main points already covered, although in its third paragraph Kant addresses himself more particularly to the philosophies of Leibniz and Wolff (the tradition in which he had previously worked for most of his career). For these philosophers, there was no essential difference between sensible presentations and 'intellectual' presentations of things in themselves. Rather, sensible presentations were considered simply 'confused' and 'partial' images of things in themselves. For Kant, of course, the sensible presents that which appears; and this is wholly different from the thing in itself which is considered insofar as it does not appear at all. Just as, above, we had a taste of Kant's critique of Descartes, so here is a fragment of the critique of Leibniz. Again, battle is resumed periodically throughout the book; but the 'Amphiboly of the Concepts of Reflection' is particularly significant. There Kant will argue that Leibniz makes one and only one basic mistake upon which his whole philosophy rests: the confusion of intuitions and concepts.

Towards the end of subsection I, Kant discusses the example of geometry (although it is of course much more than an example) in more detail than in section 3 (A46–9=B64–6). If space were a property of things in themselves, then the propositions of geometry could only be known empirically, and thus lack that certainty that attaches to them as synthetic a priori. Or, likewise, starting with the mere concepts of geometry, it is impossible to demonstrate by logical analysis any of the *synthetic* claims that make up geometry. More generally, if space were a concept, and the propositions of geometry could somehow be teased out of it analytically, then the question of how and why these propositions actually apply to (that is, have validity for) appearances in space could not be answered. Thus geometry is 'compelled to have recourse to (a priori) intuition' (A47=B65). Kant is discussing this here because he believes it is his strongest single argument to convince the doubters of his treatment of space. For in no other way can one account for the most (and most obviously) successful science as Kant sees it in human history.

Historically, the problem Kant's philosophy faces is that, at the beginning of the nineteenth century, mathematicians began to devise internally consistent axiomatic geometries using non-Euclidean axioms. These were exercises in 'pure' geometry, and initially made no claim about real space. Then, at the beginning of the twentieth century, relativity theory demonstrated that space itself had to be understood using a non-Euclidean geometry. It might appear, then, that Kant's faith both in the a priori necessity of Euclidean geometry, and in its empirical reality, were not well grounded. The Marburg group of mathematicians tried to argue that Kant's position on the a priori nature of space was consistent with non-Euclidean geometry; Rudolf Carnap, on the contrary, argued that space now had to be understood as an empirical issue. Now, this problem is exacerbated if one argues, like Guyer for example (see references at end of this section), that the nature and objective validity of geometry is the 'main argument' for the transcendental ideality of space. That is, that Kant's main argument in the 'Transcendental Aesthetic' is the regressive argument from geometry. Alternatively, even if we accepted the incompatibility of Kant's view of Euclidean geometry with contemporary physics, it remains possible to argue either that the argument from geometry is only one among other important arguments concerning space, or even that the argument from geometry is not 'from' it at all, that Kant does not assume geometry's validity using a 'regressive' form

of transcendental argument, but rather he is showing that any presentation of space is available to *some* geometry as a science.

The material added in the B-edition (subsection II and on) is quite
daunting stuff, especially coming this early in the book. Kant will be
returning to many of these themes later. Subsection II introduces a
new argument for the ideality of space and time. Our intuitions, with
respect to their form at least, contain 'nothing but mere relations'
(B66). A place in space, for example, is defined only through the relations of 'to the left of', 'above', 'five metres from' and so forth. 'Place'
only emerges from out of the manifold of such relations; similarly,
with a location in time. Spatiality and temporality, as forms, function
entirely relationally. Kant continues: Because places in space and time
are presented only through relations, therefore 'what is present in the
place . . . is not given' at all, formally and originally (B67). That is, in
our cognition of objects, the object is synthetically constructed out of
the manifold of spatial and temporal relations; the relations are prior
to the things related. But, by definition, a thing in itself could not be
cognised through mere relations – because we would not then be cognising the thing *in itself* but only the thing in its relation to other things.
Therefore, the forms of space and time contain only relations (and
ultimately the relation between a thing and our sensibility), but do not
present 'the intrinsic to the object in itself' (B67).

Now, what is translated above as 'the intrinsic' is *'das Innere'*. Kant
sometimes speaks of the opposite notion, which is the 'extrinsic' (see,
for example, the 'Amphiboly of the Concepts of Reflection' beginning at A260=B316). These are not the same notions as in 'inner' and
'outer' intuition. By intrinsic Kant means that which belongs to a
thing considered on its own, or in itself; by extrinsic, is meant that
which is only relational. Time, although the form of inner intuition,
presents the extrinsic, just as space. This means that we have a new
characterisation of the form of intuition, to add to those discovered
through the arguments sections 2 and 4. Intuition presents only relations, that is, it presents extrinsic determinations. It is sometimes suggested that even if Kant proves that appearances must be subject to
the forms of space and time, he does not prove that things in themselves must *not* be. The argument here about the essentially extrinsic
character of intuitive form is one of Kant's key proofs. (See also
Allison 2004, 125.)

Kant then turns to time, and resumes the discussion of the presentation of the self, and thus of a critique of Descartes, commenced in section 7. The form of time consists also of relations: 'of succession, of simultaneity, and of what is simultaneous with succession (the permanent)' (B67). Further, 'this form does not present anything except insofar as something becomes placed [or 'posited'] within the mind. Therefore this form can be nothing but the way in which the mind is affected by its own activity – namely, this placing of its presentation – and hence affected by itself' (B67–8). This is not terribly clear, and the rest of the paragraph is not going to get much better. What Kant seems to be saying is that, whatever content the mind may have, this content can only be sensed insofar as it is acted upon ('placed' or 'posited'). Just as objects outside us are sensed insofar as they act upon our senses, so within us the mind (and its contents) is sensed only insofar as it acts upon itself. What is presented in inner sense, then, is not the original 'contents' of the mind, still less the mind itself, but only the effect of this activity. Or, put into the language we just learned, what is presented is not the intrinsic of the mind, but rather the extrinsic: the action of the mind on itself, expressed as a manifold of temporal relations.

Towards the end of this long paragraph, these points are repeated again, but this time accompanied by the theme of the consciousness of oneself – what Kant normally calls 'apperception'. Apperception, Kant insists, is the simple presentation of the 'I' (as in 'I think' or 'I believe') (B68). In this simple presentation, I make explicit my possession of my thoughts; I place or posit them as mine. 'If the power to become conscious of oneself is to locate (apprehend) what lies in the mind, then it must affect the mind; and only in that way can it produce an intuition of itself' (B68). The activity of 'locating' (as though finding where one is on a map) should remind us of Kant's discussion of 'placing' earlier in the paragraph. Place emerges from out of the order of spatial or temporal relations. I can become conscious of myself, Kant is claiming, to the extent that I act upon myself so as to determine the order of the manifold of 'what lies in the mind'.

In inner sense, then, I (the mind, the self) becomes aware of itself only insofar as, through its activity, it affects itself. Moreover, this activity consists of a determination of order from a manifold. (This notion becomes one of the key ideas in the 'Transcendental Deduction' below.) Inner intuition arises from this effect, for sensibility is our ability to be affected. Since inner intuition has as its necessary, a priori form, time, I become aware of myself only as in time. Accordingly, self-consciousness only 'intuits itself according to the way in which it is affected from within, and hence intuits itself as it appears to itself, not as it is' (B69). This has two important implications: first, as we shall see much later, it creates problems for Descartes's attempt to put the cogito at the foundation of philosophical knowledge. Or, more generally, it creates problems for any attempt to know the inner nature of mind or soul. Second, Kant takes up the analysis of apperception as active self-affection in the 'Transcendental Deduction', where it has a pivotal role in his argument.

We should notice that through this discussion of the priority of time and the nature of time-relations, the whole problem of the *Critique of Pure Reason* has been clarified. What was originally (in the Prefaces) the problem of a science of metaphysics, and which in the Introduction was recast first as whether metaphysics is a science of cognition, and then again in terms of the possibility of synthetic a priori judgements, is now the following: 'What are the a priori conditions of the cognition of temporal relations?' This way of understanding Kant's project remains unchanged now throughout the rest of his discussion of cognition.

We are going to skip subsection III, since it adds little new.

Subsection IV continues a discussion that was commenced in subsection II, but which we haven't looked at yet. The notion of inner intuition requiring the mind to act upon itself is contrasted with a hypothetical different type of mind. Now, again, the human mind intuits sensibly, insofar as it is affected by something. The key feature of this capacity to be affected is the form of intuition. But Kant now asks us to contemplate the possibility of a different kind of mind, with a different type of intuition. This possibility has already been raised twice. First, at A35=B52, when Kant says 'our intuition is always sensible' – he implicitly asked us to consider a non-sensible intuition. Second, at A37=B54, in the thought experiment. This second instance does indeed raise the possibility of a different type of intuition, but one that is still sensible.

But what about that first possibility of a non-sensible intuition? Kant has been talking about it all the way through section 8, subsection II, but we have so far looked the other way. Kant writes: 'The conscious-ness of oneself (apperception) is the simple presentation of the "I"; and if, through this consciousness by itself, all the manifold in the subject were given self-actively, then the inner intuition would be intellectual' (B68). We have already talked about the first part of this sentence. What, now, does the second part mean? An 'intellectual intuition' is non-sensible. That is, it does not have to, so to speak, wait passively to be affected by something (an external object, or an activity of the mind). Rather, the intuition *is itself active*, it is 'self-active'. The reason why Kant is broaching this topic is immediately clear at the start of subsection IV. 'In natural theology', he writes, 'we think an object that . . . cannot in any way be an object of sensible intuition even to itself' (B71). This 'object' is God. God's 'experience' is omniscient (all-knowing), and it would seem absurd for God to experience either cre-ation, or Himself, in terms of fragments of space or time. But Kant argues, if we do not accept the ideality of space and time, but instead suppose them to be things in themselves, then we must also consider them to be the 'conditions of all existence in general, [and accordingly] they would have to be conditions also of the existence of God' (B71). This, Kant believes, is nonsense; and its being nonsense demonstrates, once again, the viability of his own account of the forms of intuition.

So, then, the mind of God must have a non-sensible intuition. One that is not passive (or as Kant says also 'dependent' or 'derivative', B72) but is rather 'self-active' (or 'original', 'intellectual', B72). Kant writes: 'Our kind of intuition is called sensible because it is *not origi-nal*. I.e., it is not such that through this intuition itself the existence of its object is given (the latter being a kind of intuition that, as far as we have insight, can belong only to the original being)' (B72). Rather than being dependent upon the existence of the object intuited, orig-inal intuition gives that existence – that is to say, creates, or sustains in creation. All that God surveys, God created. This idea of 'intellec-tual intuition' is a fascinating aside within the main thrust of Kant's book: that main thrust being the exploration of specifically human cognition.

Notice, however, in this last quotation the phrase 'as far as we have insight'. What limits human insight other than human cognition – of which human, sensible intuition is a part? Sensible intuition not only means that our intuition is limited to appearances and we cannot 'get to' things in themselves, but equivalently also that our metaphysical or theological understanding must also be limited. (Not only are we different from God, but our difference from God affects the way we understand our difference from God!) So, that phrase takes us right back to the question with which Kant started: how, and to what extent, is metaphysics possible? Kant's strategy for answering that question was to claim that properly scientific or critical metaphysical propositions would have to be synthetic a priori. So, he then needed to investigate the possibility of such judgements. The final paragraph of the 'Transcendental Aesthetic' reminds us of this. The notion of a pure a priori form of intuition has now supplied 'one of the components' (B73) needed to solve the riddle of synthetic a priori judgements. Kant writes, 'When in an a priori judgement about space and time we want to go beyond the given concept, we encounter . . . the intuition corresponding to that concept and [which] can be combined with it synthetically' (B73). Intuitions are 'beyond' the concept by being essentially different kinds of presentations, but also having a priori form.

The last sentence of the 'Transcendental Aesthetic' reads: 'Because of this [dependence of synthetic a priori judgements upon sensible intuition], however, such judgements can never reach beyond objects of the senses, and can hold only for objects of possible experience' (B73). Just as, indeed because of the fact that, intuitions are presentations of appearances and not things in themselves, so all judgements that rely upon intuitions are also judgements of appearances. Thus, such judgements are restricted in their validity to the sphere of what can be experienced (what appears). This doesn't worry us in a posteriori judgements, because we don't normally feel the need to make transcendent, metaphysical claims about, say, kettles. But, the restriction also applies to synthetic a priori judgements – that is, to all metaphysical claims. The restriction now bites: there can be no valid metaphysics of that which exceeds the bounds of human experience. (Thus the significance of the phrase 'as far as we have insight' a few paragraphs ago.) This is one of Kant's most far-reaching claims, and a severe blow to many traditional philosophical pursuits. To take just one example we have already introduced, it interrupts Descartes's attempt to discover the intrinsic essence of the mind. This general claim about the limits of possible metaphysics also led some of his contemporaries to label him 'Kant the all-destroyer'.

Let us summarise the major results of the 'Transcendental Aesthetic'.

1. A priori knowledge of the forms of intuition is possible; that is, space and time can be studied independently of experience; equivalently, synthetic a priori judgements can be formed on the grounds of pure intuition.

2. The forms of intuition are 'subjective' in one sense (that is, they belong to the subject: you or me as the entities that act cognitively and thus have experiences) but are the condition of *all* intuiting and are therefore also both necessary and universal (in other words, are also 'objective'). An important part of Kant's work is to try to discover and describe what we could call *transcendental subjectivity*: those necessary and universal structures that belong to the subject and which uniquely make possible its experience and even self-consciousness.

3. The notion of an appearance as opposed to the thing in itself does not equate to illusion versus reality. Thus space and time are *both* empirically real and transcendentally ideal.

4. If all knowledge consists of intuitions synthetically combined with concepts, then all knowledge (even and especially a priori knowledge) is limited to what can be intuited (things within space and in time). This is a major restriction on the possibility of metaphysics.

5. But within these limits, there is also no possible radical scepticism: a priori knowledge of the basic structure of reality is entirely possible. Indeed, for example, our shared and communicable understanding of space and time is an everyday example of this.

This is the proper place to try to understand the meaning of Kant's 'Copernican' revolution and its relation to the 'Transcendental Aesthetic'. At the time Kant introduced this notion, we did not yet have a full enough picture of transcendental thought; now we do. A number of possible alternative interpretations have been suggested by recent commentators; we will here briefly sketch out three of the most commonly encountered. Peter Strawson argues that Kant's real contribution is to make possible an empiricism that is not naive, but rather one that recognises a 'limiting framework' of conditions for thoughts or language through which objects can be made intelligible to us. This he terms the 'austere' interpretation of Kant. Strawson explains this further in making a very sharp distinction between 'spec-ulative' and 'descriptive' metaphysics; Kant is doing the latter. However, in speaking of subjects, or also of 'faculties' or 'powers' of the mind, Kant is in constant danger of falling into a 'psychological idiom' (Strawson 1966, p. 38). This idiom in turn leads to transcen-dental idealism, which is incoherent because the notion of affection becomes impossible. Strawson argues that Kant's understanding of space and time as a priori elements of this framework depends upon his faith in the validity of Euclidean geometry, which has been shown to be contingent.

Paul Guyer is not interested in revisions to retain some more modest validity for Kant's thought, but rather criticises a version of Kant taken at his word. According to Guyer, Kant means to argue that universal and necessary truths about objects can be discovered by an analysis of the synthetic activities of mind, but this is only because these objects are to be understood as appearances and not things in themselves. Guyer criticises what he sees as the 'bizarre' first move in transcendental idealism, which is to distinguish between spatial and temporal appearances and things in themselves which Kant, he believes, positively asserts are not spatial or temporal. Guyer argues that nothing in Kant's analyses of logic, mathematics or physics could lead either to his claims about the constituting activity of the mind, or to this distinction between appearances and things in themselves. The real source of the latter distinction is the contrast between our human and limited cognition that is dependent upon representation, and (in the notion of intellectual intuition) a theolog-ical notion of a mind that was not so dependent. Kant's transcen-dental idealism, he concludes, rests upon a particularly 'pessimistic' theology. Of the arguments in the 'Transcendental Aesthetic', he con-siders the argument from geometry the most important and, like Strawson, argues that it no longer holds water. The other arguments, even if valid, would not provide a demonstration of the transcen-dental idealist thesis that space and time *cannot* be features of things in themselves. Guyer thus argues that Kant has not successfully elim-inated the possibility of a transcendental realism.

Henry Allison, by contrast, defends Kant on these points. Kant's project as revealed through the Copernican revolution is not primarily an account of knowledge, an epistemology, but rather a metaphysical analysis of human cognition. The revolution marks a move from an essentially intuitive to an essentially 'discursive' (requiring both concepts and intuitions) model of cognition (Allison 2004, p. 12). Allison defines discursive cognition with three 'bedrock' assumptions: that cognition requires objects be given; that human minds are receptive rather than creative; that sensible intuition requires the spontaneity of the understanding (Allison 2004, p. 77). The third of these is an attack upon both empiricism and also an attack upon a theocentric view of knowledge according to which mediated presentation is a 'second class' mode of presentation (Allison 2004, p. 79). Kant's transcendental idealism considers the human mind as the source of rules (and, with space and time, also *content*) under which there can be a cognitive presentation of the objective world. Accordingly, the distinction between appearances and things in themselves is not a distinction between two *things* but rather a distinction between two *views of things*. The thing in itself is only a problem – as something really out there but also unattainable – within the realist view of mind and reality. Allison argues that the argument about space, specifically, does not rest solely upon the assumption of the validity of Euclidean geometry. Moreover, Kant is not offering an alternative ontology of space (and time) but rather an 'alternative to ontology' (Allison 2004, p. 98) focusing instead upon epistemic functions, and forms as the 'pre-intuited framework' that conditions any actual spatial presentation.

Transcendental Logic – Introduction and Transcendental Analytic

We are now into the second part of the 'Doctrine of Elements' – the elements that synthetically make up cognition. The first dealt with pure intuitions; we are now turning to concepts. The Introduction to this part, though, concerns itself with 'logic', specifically with 'transcendental logic'. As we shall see, Kant defines logic as the 'science' that deals with the rules of the understanding (A52=B76). Since the 'understanding' is Kant's name for our ability to employ concepts, logic comprises then the rules that govern concepts.

The first paragraph summarises what Kant had already said in the opening pages of the 'Transcendental Aesthetic'. There are two sources of cognition, first our ability to be affected by things, and second our ability to think them through concepts, and so forth. The only substantially new point Kant makes is to identify the capacity to think with concepts as 'spontaneity'. (Not to be confused with the idea of 'self-activity' which Kant had raised in the 'Transcendental Aesthetic' as part of the discussion of intellectual intuition.) The contrast is between the passive 'receptivity' or 'dependence' of intuition, on the one hand, and the independent activity characteristic of thought. Thought can proceed without having to 'wait' to be affected by its sensible object.

The second paragraph begins likewise as summary, but here Kant is stressing a point made previously but much less forcefully. Cognition has two key elements, and synthetic cognition is impossible without both. Kant famously writes: 'Neither of these properties is to be preferred to the other. Without sensibility no object would be given to us; and without understanding no object would be thought. Thoughts without content are empty; intuitions without concepts are blind. . . . Only from their union can cognition arise' (A51=B75). The thoughts without content – without any relation to intuitive givenness – would be either tautological analytic truths, or those metaphysical questions that perpetually 'trouble' reason (Avii). But in either case, despite occasional illusions, 'empty'. In 'intuitions without concepts are blind', sight (or the lack of it) stands in for all sensory relation to objects. Having eyes but no capacity to identify what is being seen, is functionally equivalent to blindness.

It is important, Kant continues, to distinguish between these two 'elements' of cognition. The 'science' of sensibility is called 'aesthetic' (as we have seen); the 'science' of the rules of the understanding is 'logic' (A52=B76). In the next paragraph (the third), Kant begins to distinguish among various types of logic. We are going to skip much of the rest of section I. All we need pay attention to is the idea of a 'general' logic. Such general logic concerns the rules of thought 'without regard to the difference among the objects to which the understanding may be directed' (A52=B76). In other words, without any concern for what kind of object is in question: a particular thing, a class of things, a mathematical equation, a memory, a moral rule, God, or whatever. The fourth paragraph makes it clear that Kant is speaking of 'pure' rather than 'applied' logic: abstracted from sense, from imagination, memory, prejudice, etc. (A53=B77). The kind of formalised logic typically taught as part of philosophy courses would be equivalent to what Kant means by pure, general logic.

It is in section II that Kant makes an all-important distinction. Pure general logic abstracts from all content of thought, dealing only with 'relations' among thoughts (A55=B79). Normally, we would think of this 'content' as empirical. But, from the 'Transcendental Aesthetic', Kant takes the idea that there are pure as well as empirical intuitions. In parallel, can we speak of pure thought that is not indifferent to objects but which has a priori content? That is, are there pure concepts that 'refer' a priori to objects (A57=B81)? If so, there must be a logic that abstracts from all *empirical* content of thought, but not from pure content. Moreover, general logic is indifferent as to the origin of the pure thought it considers. However, this new type of logic would also concern itself with the origin of cognitions of objects insofar as that origin was not from the objects (not empirical, that is) (A55–6=B80). By 'origin' here Kant is drawing our attention to two things: first, that intuitions and concepts are both origins of presentations but that it is important not to fall into the trap of confusing them. Second, he defined 'transcendental' knowledge as knowledge of the conditions of possibility of ordinary cognitions; thus, transcendental knowledge must be concerned with origins.

Kant calls this new type of logic 'transcendental logic'. He tells us again that by 'transcendental' is meant not that which is merely a priori or pure, but rather cognition that is knowledge of the constituting role played by such a priori or pure presentations. So, to take his example, the presentation of pure space is not a transcendental presentation. Transcendental cognition is rather cognition concerning the role of space as the condition of possibility of outer experience.

So, Kant frames the hypothesis that there are indeed a priori concepts of objects: 'Not being pure or sensible intuitions, but being merely acts of pure thought, they would be concepts, but such concepts as originate neither empirically or aesthetically' (A57=B81). The science of cognitions founded upon such concepts will have two branches, Kant implies (though it is not stressed here): that concerned with the understanding, and that concerned with 'rational cognition' (A57=B81). Kant will carry out the first of these in the 'Analytic', and the second in the 'Dialectic' (we'll turn to this distinction in a moment). This science would 'determine the origin, the range, and the objective validity' of such cognitions', and 'would have to be called *transcendental logic*' (A57=B81). Again, the 'origin' is the question of how a priori cognition is possible – where does it come from? The 'range' is the *critical* question: where can these cognitions legitimately be employed, and where must they not be? The 'objective validity' is the *transcendental* question: in what way do these concepts make possible, a priori, both cognition and ultimately our experience?

We will skip section III, which although interesting is a detour, and go straight on to section IV. The purpose of this last section of the introduction is to justify the key structural division in the 'Transcendental Logic' (most of the rest of the book by page count). The first division of the 'Transcendental Logic' Kant calls the 'Analytic'. It 'sets forth the elements of understanding's pure cognition, as well as the principles without which no object can be thought at all' (A62=B87). It is, so to speak, building up a picture of how (from the side of thought, rather than intuition) cognition is possible. Kant then adds:

> On the other hand, there is great enticement and temptation to employ these pure cognitions of understanding and these principles by themselves, and to do so even beyond the bounds of experience, even though only experience can provide us with the matter (objects) to which those pure concepts can be applied. (A63=B87–8)

(Note that 'matter' is used here more broadly than in the 'Transcendental Aesthetic', where it means the sensation in intuition. Here it means any intuitive content whatsoever: i.e. objects.) This temptation is again a reference to reason being 'troubled'. Each time Kant has described this 'temptation' or 'troubling', the picture gets a bit clearer. The issue goes back to the proposition that 'thoughts without content are empty' (A51=B75). Cognition requires both concepts and intuitions. So when, in his discussion of transcendental logic, Kant spoke of concepts that refer a priori to objects – concepts that have a pure content, instead of simply being formal and empty structures of thought – he was not giving the full picture. If there are such concepts, then they have that content and thus 'refer' *only under the condition of pure, sensible intuition*. 'Hence', Kant writes, 'we misuse transcendental analytic [the first, building up, part of transcendental logic] if we accept it as the organon of a universal and unlimited use' (A63=B88), that is, as a system whose use is without conditions.

Accordingly, the *second* division of the transcendental logic serves as a diagnosis and corrective to such errors that arise specifically in rational cognition. Significantly, Kant calls these errors 'illusions' (A63=B88). (This notion is to be sharply distinguished, as we have seen, from 'appearance'.) A transcendental illusion, then, will be an illegitimate attempt by reason to use pure concepts beyond the bounds of experience. This second division Kant names the 'Transcendental Dialectic'. Its purpose is to 'uncover' illusion wherever it is found, and 'downgrade' reason from a faculty of 'hyperphysical' (what above we called uncritical) metaphysics to a faculty that judges and guards the understanding (A63–4=B88).

Transcendental Logic, Book I, Introductions and Chapter I ('Metaphysical Deduction')

The first division of the 'Transcendental Logic' is the 'Transcendental Analytic'. It is divided into three main parts: Book I, Book II and an Appendix. Book I has two chapters. We will be touching only lightly on the first chapter 'On the Guide for the Discovery . . .', but spending a great deal of time on the second 'On the Deduction . . .'.

The first paragraph of Division I is another mini-introduction. Kant is trying to identify potential candidates for a priori concepts. Here he lists the key criteria: they cannot be empirical, obviously, nor derivative. Moreover, our list (Kant will call it a 'table') of such concepts must be 'complete' (A64=B89). Not, Kant hastens to add, complete in the sense of an 'aggregate' to which, after a long search, we cannot find anything to add. Rather, 'this completeness is possible only by means of an *idea of the whole* of understanding's a priori cognition . . . through the *coherence* of these concepts *in a system*' (A64–5=B89). The basic notion here is that if we can describe the nature and structure of the understanding as a faculty and as a whole – resulting in an idea of the whole – then the complete 'table' of its pure concepts should follow. Once we have the 'whole', then we can perform a 'dissection' (A64=B89) to see exactly what it contains. This is just what Kant aims to do. This idea of the whole is what is meant by the 'guide' in the title to Chapter I. The short paragraph introducing Book I says much the same thing, even including the metaphor of dissection. Likewise the first short paragraph prefacing Chapter I.

Very briefly, Chapter I 'On the Guide . . .' lays out the following analysis. First, 'All our intuitions, as sensible, rest on our being affected; concepts, on the other hand, rest on functions. By *function* I mean the unity of the act of arranging various presentations under one common presentation' (A68=B93). So, for example, if I have several presentations and mentally bring them together under the notion 'kettle', then the unity of that act is a 'function'. Because thought acts, rather than being affected, Kant calls it a spontaneity. Now, Kant also says, later in this same paragraph, that a judgement is a function (A69=B94). A judgement is a complete and unified mental act: I judge that these three presentations (copper coloured, hot, whistling) go under the notion of 'kettle'. A concept is the 'one common presentation' of the judgement.

To give an idea of the whole of the understanding, Kant claims, would be equivalent to providing a structural diagram of all the basic or pure types of function or judgement of the understanding; that is, all the basic ways in which a mental act can be a unity (A69=B94). This Kant does in section II, A70=B95. It is a table of twelve functions or judgement types, divided into four groups of three. Kant claims that this table does not differ significantly from the standard ways of talking about judgement in general logic. Since, as we have seen, he considers general logic to be a complete a priori science, so this table must be complete (and not an 'aggregate'). The way in which these twelve are grouped has considerable significance for Kant later, and we shall return to it when necessary. For the moment, it is only important to notice that it is *structured* as a table, and this is indicates its role here as an idea of the whole operation of the understanding, and not a mere aggregate of abstract notions.

Several pages later, in section III, Kant makes the essential move. Transcendental logic is not just a set of conceptual functions, for it was originally posited as having content. But it has content only under the condition of sensibility and thus it has to deal with the forms of intuition. Accordingly, Kant writes, 'Transcendental logic . . . has lying before it a manifold of a priori sensibility, offered to it by transcendental aesthetic' (A77=B102). We know this manifold is essential and without it transcendental logic (and the judgements within it) 'would be completely empty' (A77=B102). This manifold rests upon what Kant has called receptivity, the ability to be affected. He continues, 'Yet the spontaneity of our thought requires that this manifold, in order to be turned into a cognition, must first be gone through, taken up, and combined in a certain manner. This act I call synthesis' (A77=B102). This synthesis is a function of the 'imagination' (A78=B103). We will talk about this first going-through and taking-up in more detail shortly, in treating the 'Transcendental Deduction'.

However, 'Bringing this synthesis *to concepts* . . . is a function belonging to the understanding' (A78=B103). Concepts are what give unity to the synthesis of the manifold; and, accordingly, pure concepts are what give unity to the synthesis of the pure manifold (A79=B104). 'Hence', he continues, 'the same understanding [that was analysed to discover the pure types of judgement] . . . also brings into its presentations a transcendental content, by means of the synthetic unity of the manifold in intuition as such' (A79=B105). That is, the understanding's function of bringing unity to a judgement in general logic (these functions are the pure types of judgement) is the same as its function of giving unity to the synthesis of pure manifolds. Because of this sameness, Kant is able to conclude: 'Thus there are precisely as many pure concepts of understanding applying a priori to objects of intuition as such, as in the preceding table there were logical functions involved in all possible judgements' (A79=B104). For every pure function of judgement there will be a concept that describes how that function applies to pure objects. Or, expressed differently: under conditions of pure sensible intuition, the pure functions of the understanding correspond to pure unity-giving concepts. The table of logical forms of judgement, then, has served its purpose as a guide: it can now be reinterpreted as the table of pure concepts.

Following terminology first introduced by Aristotle, Kant calls these pure concepts 'categories'. The table of categories is supplied at A80=B106, and it indeed has the same structure as the previous one. This table completes the 'elements' of cognition: we had pure intuitions, and now we have pure concepts. As a set, these categories are a complete description, so to speak, of the pure object – the form of any object of judgement whatsoever. Although not using the phrase here, Kant later calls this section the 'metaphysical deduction' of the categories (as opposed to the transcendental deduction to come) (B159), and this name has stuck.

For Strawson, Kant's insight is that, 'for experience to be possible at all, we must become aware of particular items and become aware of them as falling under general concepts' (Strawson 1966, p. 72). This 'austere' version of Kant must be detached from transcendental idealism. The metaphysical deduction, he believes, is an an attempt to abstract the categories from actual procedures of judgement; but, first of all, Kant's table of categories should but does not properly correspond to the table of judgements and second, more recent developments in logic question whether it is even possible for Kant's table of judgement forms to be essential in character. Bennett argues similarly about probabilistic judgements (Bennett 1966, pp. 79–80); and in general questions about Kant's claims of completeness in the metaphysical deduction are very common in the literature. Allison defends Kant on this point, arguing that the 'logical forms' in Kant's sense cannot be confused with how modern logic talks about form (Allison 2004, p. 146). When a judgement is made about a subject and its predicate, it is necessary to treat the object of the subject concept *as if* it were a substance. The judgement forms are 'clues' to the categories because of this 'hypostatisation' of the subject, or 'isomorphism' between activities (Allison 2004, p. 149). Longuenesse argues that Kant's concern in the metaphysical deduction is not with logical judgement forms considered as products of judging activity (that is, as a set of the types of judgements that can be formed), but with the forms of activity themselves (Longuenesse 1998, p. 5).

But Kant still has a long way to go in the 'Transcendental Analytic'. First of all, he does not yet feel he has sufficiently demonstrated the necessary validity of these concepts. This challenge is next in the 'Transcendental Deduction' in Chapter II of Book I. Second, he needs to explore the basic synthetic a priori judgements that these pure intuitions and pure concepts make possible (these are the 'principles', in Book II).

Transcendental Logic, Book I, Chapter II, Section I

Chapter II, section I is mostly common to both editions (A84–95 = B116–29). Thereafter, Kant completely rewrote the 'Transcendental Deduction'. We will look at a couple of key passages from this common part first; then we will deal with the A and B versions of the rest separately.

The section opens with a famous passage in which Kant explains the term 'deduction' (A84=B116). He is *not* using it in the familiar sense of a type of logical argument or inference. Rather, he is using this term in the sense ascribed to it by 'teachers of law'. There are two things that must be proved in a legal case, Kant says. First, the 'question concerning fact (*quid facti*)'; that is, what are the facts about what happened? Second, the 'question regarding what is legal (*quid iuris*)'; that is, the applicability of laws or precedents to these facts. For example, in a case concerning an alleged theft, it is one thing to establish what X, the accused, did that night; it is another to show that what X did was actually in violation of the law. Or, to express this latter point differently, it is another thing to show that the laws (and indeed the court) have *jurisdiction* over what X in fact did.

Kant continues: in just the same way it is one thing for me to prove that, in fact, a concept is being used in a certain way. That is the easy part, and Kant seems to feel this job has been accomplished in the 'metaphysical deduction' above. It is another thing entirely to prove that I am right to use this concept, or that the concept has jurisdiction over all such instances. For empirical concepts, however, this is no problem: the question of fact and the question of right are the same: 'we always have experience available to us to prove . . . objective validity' (A84=B117). But this is not always so easy. To take Kant's own example, many people make liberal use of the concepts of 'fortune' or 'fate'. These concepts 'run loose', he writes, and only occasionally come across the question of their legality: are they legitimate or justified concepts? Showing their legality, Kant believes, will prove difficult, as these concepts are neither justified by experience nor by reason. But such troublesome concepts as 'fate' are not at all what Kant is interested in. Rather, the question of 'legality' is most important for a priori concepts. Kant writes:

For proofs based on experience are insufficient to establish the legitimacy of using them in that way; yet we do need to know how these concepts can refer to objects even though they do not take these objects from any experience. Hence, when I explain in what way concepts can refer to objects a priori, I call that explanation the *transcendental deduction* of these concepts. (A85=B117)

Let us summarise how Kant elucidates this line of thought in the rest of this section. He is attempting to show: 1. that such a deduction must be transcendental in nature (and not empirical, as in Locke); 2. that the performance of such a deduction is 'inescapably necessary' (A87=B119).

Concerning this latter point, Kant makes two observations based upon his essential distinction between intuitions and concepts. First, the use of a priori concepts is not confined to the conditions of sensibility, so a deduction would be required to justify a valid employment, and distinguish it from an invalid employment, of such concepts. (The invalid employment is the topic of the second division of transcendental logic, which Kant gives the title 'Transcendental Dialectic'.) Second, our sensibility can be affected without cognition – or, as Kant puts it, somewhat ambiguously: 'For appearances can indeed be given in intuition without functions of the understanding' (A90=B122). ('Appearances' being used here in the same narrow sense as at A20=B34, the 'undetermined' object of intuition.) It is possible, then, to wonder whether a priori concepts are in fact 'empty' (A90=B122) – whether they simply loiter ineffectually in the mind. Notice that Kant is admitting this grudgingly; it 'could' or 'might' be the case. As we shall see, what he will end up demonstrating is that, while appearances can be given separately from the action of the understanding, this *on its own* is of trivial importance epistemologically; moreover, little sense can be attached to the scenario in which the categories do not have universal legitimacy. But these doubts are why a transcendental deduction is necessary.

Accordingly, the purpose of the transcendental deduction is to show that the categories have 'jurisdiction' over appearances. The basic strategy Kant will employ to show this is outlined in the next subsection, the 'Transition' (A92=B124). This begins with a discussion that should remind us of the second 'Copernican revolution' passage at Bxvi. Kant states that there are two ways in which a synthetic presentation and its object can 'concur' or 'meet each other'. Namely, 'either if the object makes the presentation possible, or if the presentation alone makes the object possible' (A92=B124). The first of these possibilities (the object makes the presentation possible) is Kant's summary of the standard route of seventeenth- and eighteenth-century empiricism. And, indeed, this subsection carries on with brief discussions of Locke and Hume. Scattered throughout the book so far have been the reasons why

Kant feels this approach is insufficient to account for experience, much less science.

Now, in the latter case the presentation does not *produce* the object, for 1. I am not an intellectual intuition; and 2. the issue of my *willing* to make something actual (in the way that I would will to make pancakes for breakfast) is not relevant. However, the presentation makes the object possible in the sense that '*cognising* something *as an object* is possible only through it' (A92=B125). Note, then, that we have a distinction here between the presentation of an 'object' in intuition alone as mere appearance, and the experience, through the activity of cognition, of the 'object' *as an object*. The presentation that makes possible the object rests on two elements: the a priori forms of intuition, and a priori concepts. The first is not a problem: insofar as the object is given *at all*, it is given in space or time. Space and time as forms of intuition therefore do not need further deduction at this stage. (But Kant will return to space and time in the full account of the deduction.) However, 'the question arises whether concepts do not also a priori precede [objects], as conditions under which alone something can be, if not intuited, yet thought as object as such' (A93=B125). This is important, 'For in that case all empirical cognition of objects necessarily conforms to such concepts, because nothing is possible as *object of experience* unless these concepts are presupposed' (A93=B126). This is the key move. Kant has turned the problem of deduction on its head. In order to demonstrate the validity of the categories with respect to experience, he will seek to show that they make that experience possible in the first place. If that is so, then the question of validity is of course also answered.

Accordingly, he writes, the deduction is 'directed' towards a principle: 'these concepts must be recognised as a priori conditions of the possibility of experience' (A94=B126). Kant immediately points out that the phrase 'possibility of experience' must be understood correctly. Just to show that this or that experience includes or requires a priori concepts would be insufficient. It would make their reference to experience merely 'contingent' (A94=B126), because our happening to have that experience is contingent. What must be shown in the transcendental deduction is not, then, how the categories relate to experience, but how they relate to any possible experience – that is, how they make experience as such possible. Thus, Kant appears to be rejecting as insufficient a 'regressive' transcendental argument that argues *from* some experience. Let us briefly leave the letter of Kant's text to talk in general about some key ideas.

Notice that a transcendental condition of possibility is not a cause (it is a condition of *possibility of*, not a cause of the *reality of*, something). Nor is it temporally prior (the 'prior' in a priori is not temporal: for example, intuition of time is not 'before' the intuition of temporal things – that would be absurd!). Nor again is this condition to be thought of as some thing or organ in the brain that acts in this way ('where' in the brain is space situated? – the question makes no sense, because the brain is a *phenomenal object*). Nor finally is it merely required as a *logical* condition (the relation between the a priori intuition of space, and an intuition of a spatial thing, would be ill described as logical entailment). The relation between transcendental condition and conditioned appears to be a *whole new type of relationship* not reducible to the other metaphysical/natural/scientific/logical relationships discussed in philosophy.

So, then, what is meant by the condition of 'possibility'? Let us distinguish between three meanings of this word. First, logical possibility is anything the concept of which is not contradictory. So, it is logically impossible that A not equal A. There are many things that are logically possible, but are utterly alien to our experience of the world. Second, phenomenal possibility concerns things which fit in with the web of empirically established truths about the world. So, it is not phenomenally possible that I sprout wings and fly out of the window, that is just not how the real world works; but it is possible that I chose a bacon sandwich for lunch rather than cheese. Third, transcendental possibility concerns the a priori structure of experience. It is not transcendentally possible, for example, for a left- and right-hand glove to coincide – because space doesn't work like that. (What we have called 'transcendental possibility' Kant sometimes terms 'real' possibility – see Bxxvin.) These types can be seen as nested one inside the other, as in Figure 1.

This gives us four classes of things: the logically impossible (A not equal to A); the logically possible but transcendentally impossible (the gloves); the logically and transcendentally possible, but phenomenally impossible (wings); and the phenomenally possible (sandwich). *Kant almost always uses 'possibility' to mean 'transcendental (or real) possibility'.*

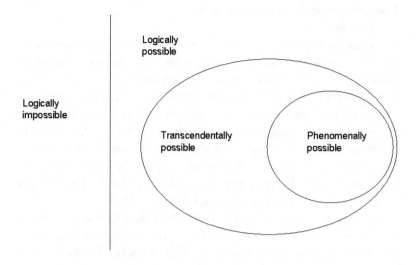

Figure 1. Types of possibility and impossibility

Now, the above figure may be helpful, but it makes it appear that being a transcendental condition is just a logical thing after all: a dealing with what is or is not included in a set. In part, this appearance arises because we are viewing these 'sets' from the outside. That is, not thinking them from the point of view of an intuiting and experiencing human being, but rather from the point of view of some super being, for whom our forms of intuition and pure concepts are just arbitrary limitations that can be dispensed with at will. If Kant is right, then this view from the outside is rigorously impossible, and these 'sets' or 'classes' are anything but arbitrary. That this is the case can be shown if we try to add in one further 'class'. In the 'Dialectic', the objects of ideas of reason are said to be possible because they do not contradict real possibility. For example, using reason, one can neither prove the existence of a God, nor disprove it. But not contradicting does not mean that such objects agree with real possibility, but rather that the question of their existence lies outside the range of the legitimate application of the principles of experience. Intelligible possibility (let us call it) has no location in Figure 1.

Transcendental Deduction in A

The Three Syntheses

As we saw briefly in the 'metaphysical deduction', Kant understands the categories as functions for the synthetic unification of pure manifolds. So, we said there by way of anticipation that in the 'Deduction' he will be trying to demonstrate, for any possible experience, the transcendental necessity of an act of synthesis achieved through a priori concepts. In fact, Kant believe he needs to distinguish three syntheses. Since 'synthesis' cannot be understood otherwise than as an activity, all these are based on 'sponteneity' (A97). The three syntheses form the topics of the first three subsections of the 'A-Deduction'. Let us go directly to the first of these, starting on A98.

The first paragraph reiterates that time is the absolutely universal form of intuition (space applies only trivially to inner sense); consequently, all intuitive givenness is subject to the form of time. But, to be presented simply as formed by time, on the one hand, and to be presented as a single presentation that contains a manifold, on the other, are two different things. The difference to which Kant is pointing takes the form of a paradox: how can one presentation nevertheless also be manifold? He explains it this way: 'although intuition offers a manifold, yet intuition can never bring this manifold about as a manifold, and also as contained *in one presentation*, unless a synthesis occurs in this process' (A99). This synthesis is called the 'synthesis of apprehension'.

Accordingly, time must be 'distinguished' (or 'differentiated') and also 'gathered together' (A99). What this means is not clear; perhaps something like this: 1. the homogeneous dimension of time must be presented (gathered together) so that 2. given temporal relations can be disentangled (from other presentations) in order to lay them out as a manifold (distinguished). The manifold thus becomes presented as a *temporal* manifold. Empirical intuitions present relations as their content. This content needs to be presented as actually manifold *in time* (one presentation, though manifold) and thus ready for synthesis. But in order for that presentation of a manifold to happen, what we called the 'dimension' of time must first be given. This latter aspect concerns the pure intuitive presentation, and is thus a 'pure synthesis of apprehension'. Pure time as a single, unitary and homogeneous dimension of presentation, requires such a synthesis in order to be presented. This is because the original form of time contains nothing but relations (extrinsic), as we saw. In the synthesis of apprehension, this original form is transformed into a dimension. The contents (what is presented in appearance) of this homogeneous dimension will now be of a type that is available to synthesis under a concept. The pure synthesis makes possible the empirical synthesis. Because of these syntheses we are presented with intuitions as temporal manifolds. Evidence for and further discussion of this interpretation of what Kant means in this abnormally dense passage can be found in the parallel passages in the 'B-Deduction' (see B160n especially) and in the Axioms of Intuition (see our discussion below, p.).

The next synthesis Kant calls 'reproduction'. Kant begins speaking in a Humean vein: He writes, 'presentations that have often followed or accompanied one another will finally associate, and thereby enter into connection with one another' (A100). This is a 'natural law', but an empirical one. Really, it is a law of empirical psychology: when we see something happen several times under similar conditions, we come to expect it. Indeed, we reproduce its effects even in the absence of the thing itself (we flinch at all the surprises in a horror film, even the ones that are harmless red herrings). That is why Kant calls it a 'law of reproduction' (A100). This type of pattern recognition, according to Hume, helps make up the intelligibility of our world. Kant agrees but adds that this empirical law 'presupposes, however, that appearances themselves are actually subject to such a rule' (A100). Thus, the problem of induction is a more statistical, not an ontological, issue.

In the second half of this paragraph, Kant imagines empirical presentations so disordered that no empirical law of reproduction could get a grip on them. The point, however, is not the order or disorganisation of experience. After all, empirical experience *can* be or appear chaotic. So, the issue is not what makes experiences ordered but rather *what makes it possible for experiences to be ordered*. How, that is, is any empirical synthesis possible?

Kant's solution first looks back to the synthesis of apprehension. Therein, presentations were laid out in a homogeneous time; as Kant says it here: 'I must, first of all, necessarily apprehend in thought one of these manifold presentations after the other' (A102). However, he

continues, 'if I always lost from my thoughts the preceding presentations . . . and did not reproduce them as I proceeded to the following
ones, then there could never arise a whole presentation' (A102). In
other words, in order to cognise some relation between A and B, it
must be the case that in considering time B, I must hold in my
thought, or 'reproduce' at its most basic, time A.

This synthesis of reproduction holds true for all empirical presentations, but also, Kant maintains, for pure presentations of time (and
space) as wholes. Since the pure presentations of space and time are
the conditions of the possibility of any intuitive presentations whatsoever, so then the pure synthesis of reproduction must likewise be a
requirement of any act of presentation. More particularly, since there
is a pure, a priori synthesis of reproduction, then (with respect to any
a posteriori synthesis) there will be an a priori presupposition 'that
appearances can be reproduced' (A101). This is the necessary presupposition that the manifold laid out in the synthesis of apprehension can, in some way or other, be brought together. It is the
presupposition that synthesis is always possible. Thus our problem –
how can the mere possibility of the reproduction of appearances be
known a priori – is solved. The ability to perform this synthesis Kant
calls the 'transcendental power of the imagination' (A102).

Kant's analysis of the third synthesis builds on the second. Kant
writes:

Without the consciousness that what we are thinking is the same as what we
thought an instant before, all reproduction in the series of presentations
would be futile. For what we are thinking would in the current state be a new
presentation, which would not belong at all to the act by which it was to be
produced little by little. Hence the manifold of the presentation would never
make up a whole . . . (A103)

To paraphrase: it is one thing to reproduce A when B is being presented, it is another to be able to recognise that A and B are the same
(or in some other definite relationship) – that is, A and B have a conceptual relationship, such as being the same thing at different times,
species of the same type, or being cause and effect. Without that
recognition, B would be always new with respect to A, always be
different and without unity. Therefore, the presentation would remain
manifold and not 'make up a whole'.

That is most of the story. However, the quotation above (A103) begins with consciousness, and also finishes with 'because it would lack the unity that only consciousness can impart to it' (A103). Kant then briefly considers the example of counting. It is a rather obscure example, however. Suppose in counting we are moving from five to six – we are producing the presentation of six, 'little by little'. The concept of the six is, in part, that it is the number reached by counting through and beyond five. So, in order for me to count to six, I need to recognise its continuity or unity with the number five before it. That is, the concept of counting to six consists of the consciousness of the unity in the synthesis of the five followed by six. Without this concept, and thus without this unity, the presentations of five and six have no relation – and the presentation of six (which again consists in part of 'following five') could not happen. Kant is claiming that we do not understand the cognitive act properly if we just talk about bringing a manifold to a synthetic unity, and stop at that; for what could this mean if not the *consciousness of unity*?

Moreover, it is not just consciousness of the unity of five and six. Although Kant does not stress this point yet, I need equally to be aware that it is the same counter that is counting – that is, I must be conscious of my own continuous identity across the act. The identity of the self is also a condition of any particular concept bringing unity to a manifold. Again, a concept is required for 'recognition'. But more than this, *so is the unity of consciousness*. We can see that some level of consciousness is a condition of recognition, even if 'only faint' (A103). Kant writes, 'without this consciousness, concepts, and along with them cognition of objects, are quite impossible' (A104).

Why does Kant introduce 'consciousness' here? Notice that for each of the previous two syntheses he has analysed, Kant has moved from an 'empirical' requirement back to a pure or a priori requirement. For example, in the synthesis of apprehension, from the 'differentiation' of particular temporal relations to the differentiation of pure time. This is a general argumentative strategy that involves recognising a relationship of dependence, of some X on a synthetic act B. But B is a particular or empirical synthetic act, that in turn rests upon some pure, a priori synthesis A. Thus, *all* X must be conditioned by A.

Just so here in the third synthesis: recognition requires some concept or other, but the employment of *any* concept requires consciousness as its transcendental condition. So, the natural next problem must be: what are the transcendental conditions of *any* consciousness? This problem Kant will address shortly.

The Transcendental Object

First, though, he returns to issues relating to the thing in itself. What is meant by the expression 'an object of presentations' (A104), he asks.

Here, Kant is concerned with a related distinction. We have first of all an object in the sense of an ordinary, particular object (a kettle, say). Such an object, as we have seen, appears as an object because it is cognised, rather than (as in empiricism) the other way around. What appears, however, when separated from *particular* conditions of appearance, that is as considered 'distinct from all our presentations' (A105), is the 'object as such = x' (A104). This algebraic-looking expression is meant to signal that this object is (and must remain) an unknown; not because it is unknowable in some mysterious sense, but because any cognition of it would be to determine or limit it to some particular thing. Kant a few pages later calls this object as such the 'transcendental object' (A109). This x becomes presented in some particular way, and only *as* it is presented can it be cognised and known.

Now, let us imagine an empiricist philosophy that argues that the unity of my presentation of the kettle comes about because of the kettle itself. That is, the kettle as a real object in the world has unity (that is, it is a real, distinct thing), and it affects my senses accordingly. The elements of my presentation necessarily agree with one another, and hang together, because of this unity. Now, empirically or phenomenally, Kant is happy to agree with this. However, transcendentally, the unity of the real object is itself dependent upon the synthetic unity of consciousness. Maybe, then, it is the unity of the transcendental object that affects us sensibly and is the ground of the unity of consciousness? But this transcendental object (the x) is by definition a sensible unknown for us, and so could not be a ground. Kant thus writes:

Clearly, therefore, the unity that the object makes necessary for us can be nothing other than the formal unity of consciousness in the synthesis of the manifold of the presentations. When we have brought about the synthetic unity in the manifold of intuition – this is when we say that we cognise the object. (A105)

When we say 'transcendental object', in other words, we mean nothing more than the correlate or counterpart to the pure unity of consciousness. It is a notion of object as projected by nothing more than the synthetic functions of the mind. The concept of the transcendental object is thus actually a concept of the synthetic unity 'which must be encountered in any manifold' (A109).

As if things were not complicated enough, we need to realise that what is translated by 'object' here could be one of two German words. Your translator will hopefully have marked each of these. Kant generally (though not entirely consistently) uses the term 'Gegenstand' for object in the sense of intuitable object or object of experience (in the discussion above, the kettle). However, he generally uses 'Objekt' to mean object in a more general sense, as an object *of a concept*, and thus as an object of knowledge, where the notion of it actually being given in intuition is not directly at issue. So, for example, at B137, Kant writes: '[A]n object [*Objekt*] is that in the concept of which the manifold of a given intuition is united . . . Consequently, the reference of presentations to an object [*Gegenstand*] consists solely in this unity of consciousness.' Here in the 'A-Deduction', Kant is able to distinguish in this way, in the same sentence, between 'the concepts of objects [*Objekte*] in general' and 'objects [*Gegenstände*] of experience' (A106). Thus this terminological distinction (especially were he more consistent!) allows Kant to capture part, although by no means all, of the transcendental argument of the 'Deduction'.

In other words, there are in fact *four* notions of 'object': 1. the object as that which appears; 2. the object as an object *of a concept*; 3. the thing in itself as that which appears but considered separately from its appearance; and 4. the transcendental or pure object which is the correlate of pure synthetic unity. We mustn't confuse 3 and 4; the fact that we can think (though not cognise) the transcendental object is quite different from knowing, cognising or intuiting the thing in itself. (See below, the section on 'Phenomena and Noumena'.)

Unity and necessity are discovered in objects because of the synthetic unity of presentations. This synthetic unity (and the necessity it makes possible), Kant continues, requires a concept, as we have seen (A106). But in turn, the act of synthesis according to a concept requires the unity of consciousness. So, we are back to the question: what is the transcendental basis of the possible unity of consciousness?

Before trying to answer this question, Kant gives the answer a name: 'transcendental apperception' (A107).

Let us look again at the last sentence of the above, extracted quotation: 'When we have brought about the synthetic unity in the manifold of intuition – this is when we say that we cognise the object.' This can be expressed differently: it is one and the same act that brings about the unity of consciousness, on the one hand, and brings about the unity of the presentation of an object, on the other. This is the case even at the level of pure, a priori synthesis. Kant explains it in this way: 'Hence the original and necessary consciousness of one's own identity is at the same time a consciousness of an equally necessary unity of the synthesis of all appearances according to concepts' (A108). The former (original and necessary consciousness) is transcendental apperception. The latter (the unity of all appearances according to concepts) is the concept of the transcendental object. Only because objects can be cognised a priori, then, is transcendental apperception possible.

Although Kant says he has hardly begun the 'Transcendental Deduction', in fact all the ideas would seem to be in place. What Kant believes he has shown thus far in the discussion of the third synthesis of recognition, is the following. First, that any empirical act of recognition requires a concept. Second, that any such act further requires a unity of consciousness (the consciousness of the presentations as unified, and also the consciousness of the 'I' as unified). Third, as a condition of any particular consciousness, there must be the possibility of the pure synthetic unity of consciousness (transcendental apperception). Fourth, that the synthesis of presentations in a concept in order to present an object happens at the same time and in the same way as the synthesis of consciousness to achieve self-identity. Thus transcendental apperception can be achieved in particular consciousness only insofar as the absolutely a priori cognition of objects is possible.

Recall that the aim of the 'Deduction' is to show the necessary validity of the categories with respect to any experience. The strategy was to show that the categories were in fact conditions of any possible experience – and for that reason must also be valid. That is why the reference to the unity of consciousness is so important. The categories could be a priori concepts that aid experience, so to speak, here and there, but not everywhere. Only by speaking of the necessary unity of all consciousness can Kant move from this contingent role to a necessary one (see, for example, A111). However, he has also tried to show that the synthetic act of the unity of consciousness and the synthetic act of presenting an object through a unity of presentations are the same. If Kant can show that the categories are the necessary condition for either of these 'sides', then the 'Deduction' will be complete.

But, in fact, he has already done so in the 'Metaphysical Deduction', where the categories were derived as the concepts of the pure object – that is, they were the functions that brought unity to any possible judgement. Collectively, then, they must be the concept of the transcendental object – although of course this object is 'nothing to us' (it is the field of possible things to be experienced or known, rather than something that itself is experienced or known). The transcendental object is equivalent to the pure synthetic unity of consciousness. This addition (the categories as concept of the pure object) would, apparently, allow us to complete the 'Transcendental Deduction'. So, to summarise this version of Kant's argument: the categories are the concepts that serve as the functions of unity for the pure object. This unity is correlated to the pure synthetic unity of consciousness (transcendental apperception). In turn this unity of consciousness is an absolute and necessary condition of all synthesis of recognition – and finally, this synthesis is a requirement of any experience. Therefore, it follows that the categories are the condition of all experience. In turn, their validity with respect to experience has been conclusively demonstrated.

The Transcendental Power of the Imagination

Why, then, does the 'A-Deduction' go on for another fifteen or so pages? There are a number of reasons, some easy to understand, others not so easy. First, and very simply, Kant is clearly trying out a number of different ways of explaining the argument we gave above. Second, equally simply, he is using the occasion to pursue some of his main philosophical themes: above all the distinction between the thing in itself and appearance, which makes the whole 'Deduction' possible. But there are at least two other reasons, more complex and interrelated. A third reason is that the argument of the 'Deduction' as we presented it above relies entirely on Kant's analysis of the third synthesis of recognition. This raises the question of how the first two syntheses contribute to the 'Deduction'. Fourth, Kant places a great deal of stress on the transcendental power of the imagination, a theme we mostly ignored above. These last two change the nature of the 'Deduction', meaning the summary argument above is rather a mis-representation than a 'summary'. Let us now turn to these changes.

'Let us now', Kant writes at the beginning of section III, 'present in a unified and coherent way what in the preceding section [section II] we set forth separately and individually' (A115). Cognition, he continues, has three 'sources', and these correspond with the three syntheses discussed above: sense, imagination and apperception. Each of these can be considered empirically, in reference to ordinary acts of cognition; each of these also has a pure, a priori dimension upon which the possibility of the empirical function rests.

Kant says he now aims to 'pursue the inner basis of this connec-tion of presentations' (A116), beginning with pure apperception. All intuitions 'are nothing for us' (A116) if they cannot be taken up into consciousness. Our a priori consciousness of the 'thoroughgoing identity of ourselves' with respect to any presentation is a condition of the possibility of any presentation. 'For', Kant argues, 'any such presentations present something in me only inasmuch as together with all others they belong in one consciousness; hence they must at least be capable of being connected in it' (A116). (This statement should also be compared to the notion of 'whole of experience' first introduced at B12.) It is this last statement that is the key: presenta-tions must belong together therefore it must always be possible to connect them together – that is, to perform synthesis. *How* presenta-tions are connected together – even if this how is a function of a pure concept – is a secondary issue at the moment. This is because no analysis of any particular 'how' of synthesis will show it to be univer-sally necessary for all presentations – that is, to be a transcendental condition of presentation as such.

This 'must at least be capable of being connected' is an a priori principle of the synthetic unity of pure apperception. But this syn-thetic unity presupposes an act of synthesis – a pure, a priori synthe-sis. Kant writes, 'Therefore the transcendental unity of apperception refers to the pure synthesis of imagination as the a priori condition for the possibility of all assembly of the manifold in one cognition'

(A118). The 'pure synthesis of imagination' refers us back to the 'synthesis of recognition'. As we have seen, while it is a concept that serves as the rule of unity in the synthesis of recognition, it is the synthesis of reproduction that guarantees the mere possibility of any synthesis whatsoever. Only because of the pure synthesis of reproduction could one presentation be connected, in any way, with another – thus making possible any synthetic unity of manifolds or consciousness. The imagination, in the pure synthesis of reproduction, however, because it is not 'reproducing' anything actually given before (it is thus pure), Kant terms 'productive'. It produces rather than re-produces. Therefore, 'the principle of the necessary unity of the imagination's pure (productive) synthesis prior to apperception is the basis for the possibility of all cognition' (A118). Accordingly, 'the transcendental unity of the synthesis of imagination is the pure form of all possible cognition; and hence all objects of possible experience must be presented a priori through this form' (A118). All objects, considered merely as the formal possibility of any object – that is, what Kant has also called the pure or transcendental object – are presented in this synthesis. This pure form of the object is described by the categories. So, Kant then argues that the categories are 'pure a priori cognitions that contain the necessary unity of the pure synthesis of imagination in regard to all possible appearances' (A119).

Accordingly, our first misrepresentation of Kant's full argument was to focus exclusively on the third synthesis of recognition. To be sure, it is here that particular concepts (empirical or pure) are put to work, as the unity of *this or that* synthesis. What Kant needs to show, however, is that certain concepts have validity for all synthesis of appearances (at least insofar as they are brought to cognition). In order to prove this he turns not to this or that synthesis, but to the possibility of any synthesis. This is the pure synthesis of the productive imagination (the synthesis of reproduction), which provides the form of all objects of cognition. The categories – as collectively the concept of the pure object – 'contain the necessary unity' of this synthesis. Consequently, through the categories, not only is the notion of the pure object possible, but *any cognitive synthesis whatsoever* becomes possible. It is this richer picture that Kant had in mind in saying that the transcendental object is nothing more than the correlate of the necessary unity of presentations in consciousness.

Kant then (A119) starts a new analysis that works from the bottom (empirical appearance) up. Very briefly, Kant's objective is to show that the first synthesis (of apprehension) is also a function of the imagination: for, if the imagination is to synthetically take the manifold up into an 'image', first it must 'apprehend' that manifold as such (A120), that is, lay it out as a homogeneous manifold ready for synthesis. This, again, must happen both at the empirical and a priori level. The spontaneity of human action (here in the form of the imagination) thus goes all the way down, so to speak, to the most basic sensible contact with objects, which Kant had called the synthesis of apprehension.

As a consequence, the imagination becomes the keystone of all cognition: 'By means of pure imagination we link the manifold of intuition, on the one hand, with the condition of the necessary unity of pure apperception, on the other' (A124). Imagination, that is, forms a bridge (so to speak) between mere sensibility and the understanding. This bridge not only makes it possible for cognition to happen, but makes it necessary that these 'two extreme ends . . . cohere' (A124). Speaking in terms of 'bringing together' and making 'cohere' explains why Kant needs the imagination. He is troubled by the same problem that disturbed Plato, and which led Aristotle to reject the theory of forms. (See the so-called 'third man argument' in Plato's *Parmenides*.) If an appearing thing is mere appearance, and a 'form' or 'idea' pure thought, then how do they connect together? – how, for example, are we to explain how an appearing thing is an imitation of, or a participation in, its form? The imagination, as 'always in itself sensible' (A124) – and yet also spontaneous, productive and enacting the rules of the understanding – is indeed a suitable bridge, touching both 'extreme ends'. Kant makes this point again, although without much additional clarity, in the chapter on the Schematism which follows close on the 'Deduction'.

It is important to point out just how strange Kant's claim is. As he frequently notes (see A120n or A123), in the history of philosophy the imagination has always been given a subsidiary role, a function of the mind that merely passively associated presentations together, or brought images to mind. Indeed, imagination was often associated with the body and thus the passions more than with the mind (as in Descartes; see the beginning of *Meditation* VI) – in other words, it was not properly part of reason or cognition at all. Here, Kant is not only putting imagination centre-stage, but even speaking of a pure, transcendental and productive power of imagination. This account of imagination has been enormously influential; it is for example the starting point of Martin Heidegger's interpretation of Kant (see Heidegger 1990).

Kant's summary presentation, at the end of the 'A-Deduction', should now make sense to us. He begins by reiterating that we are not concerned with the cognition of things in themselves, but with appearances. As all appearances are 'in me' (presented in inner sense, A129), and thus in connection with my self-identity (unity of apperception), there must accordingly always be possible a synthesis of them in one consciousness. 'But the form of all cognition of objects . . . likewise consists in this unity of possible consciousness' (A129). That is, again, the pure object exists merely as the correlate of apperception's necessary unity. Therefore, the manner of this pure synthesis, and thus the form of all cognition, must precede 'all cognition of the object' (A129). The synthesis of pure imagination and the synthetic unity of 'original' apperception 'precede all empirical cognition' (A130). The categories comprise the pure form of the synthetic cognition of objects. Accordingly the categories, the pure forms of the understanding, have not only a possible but also a necessary relation to all experience, by virtue of making experiences possible.

Transcendental Deduction in B
The Original Synthetic Unity of Apperception
However, Kant decided that the above way of presenting his 'Deduction' was in some way deficient. So, he scrapped every word of it and began again for the second edition. Some commentators believe that the 'A-Deduction' was a 'patchwork' of notes that Kant had written over the previous few years, and therefore that Kant's rewriting of the chapter was designed to make it more orderly and coherent (see Kemp-Smith 1930, Wolff 1963). Above, we argued that the 'A-Deduction' in fact has a beautiful, symmetrical structure. In any case, the 'B-Deduction' is no less difficult.

The first paragraph of section 15 is about 'combination' of manifolds. The manifold is given in sensible intuition; that is, given passively or receptively. And the form of this intuition is given a priori. But what is not and can never be given is combination. The manifold in sensibility is always given as uncombined, and an act of spontaneity is required for combination. This combination Kant commonly calls 'synthesis', and here he claims it is an act of our power of understanding, as distinguished from the sensibility. At the end of the paragraph, Kant adds that the act of analysis is the opposite of synthesis, but that synthesis must always come first: only something already combined can then be analysed.

In the next paragraph, Kant makes a new and very important move. In order to bring about combination we need a general 'concept of the manifold's unity' (B130). This concept cannot arise from combination, because combination presupposes it. Moreover, this concept cannot be the category of unity (one of the twelve categories Kant discussed earlier). For the categories arise from logical functions, Kant argues, and this whole notion of function again presupposes unity. A still 'higher' unity must be found that is the absolutely general concept of the synthetic unity of a manifold. The unity in question is not named here, but the title of the next section gives it away: the unity of apperception.

Section 16 begins with a famous analysis. Kant writes, 'The *I think* must be *capable* of accompanying all my presentations' (B131). By 'I think' is not meant the words, nor a proposition, but rather the presentation to myself of the fact that I am thinking something. That is, every presentation I have can, by having 'I think. . .' added to it, become self-conscious. (This whole discussion of what is contingently not an object of explicit self-consciousness is, in part at least, Kant's response to the notion of petite perceptions in Leibniz. See, especially, his *New Essays*.) Not all of my presentations become objects of explicit self-awareness, of course. I was just tapping my foot to some music, quite without thought. But it is one thing to say that a particular mental act happens to be 'unconscious', and quite another to say that it *must be* unconscious. Thus, Kant's writing 'capable of' indicates that all presentations *can* become self-conscious. Otherwise, they could not be thought at all, and that means either they are impossible or at least 'nothing to me' (that is, irrelevant). This 'nothing to me' is explained at the end of the paragraph. Presentations 'surely must conform necessarily to the condition under which alone they *can* stand together in one universal self-consciousness, since otherwise they would not thoroughly belong to me' (B132). Whatever I think must be something that I think – which 'belongs' to me. This claim, Kant will say a couple of paragraphs from now, is just analytically true. In this, Kant agrees with Descartes. But, as we shall see, the claim may be analytically true, but the act by which presentations come to belong to me is synthetic.

The presentation 'I think' is an act of spontaneity – it is an *act* of becoming aware of my own thoughts. Therefore, it cannot belong to sensibility. Kant calls this mere 'I think' pure and original apperception, and its unity is 'transcendental'. Pure, because distinguished from any particular (empirical) act of 'I think this or that'. Original, because self-consciousness is always the same and thus cannot be doubled up. To say 'I am conscious of the fact that I am conscious of. . .' is just to say 'I am conscious of. . .' So, apperception is the original source of 'I think', because there could not be some other or higher condition. Transcendental, finally, because a priori cognition can be obtained from it, as Kant hopes to show. The unity in question (the original synthetic unity of apperception, as the title of the section names it) is the 'higher' unity Kant posited at the end of the previous section.

The next paragraph (B133) contrasts 1. the empirical consciousness of individual, uncombined presentations with 2. the act through which it becomes possible for 'I think' to accompany a unified manifold. Empirical consciousness is 'in itself dispersed' [*an sich zerstreut*] (B133) (Kant may mean 'extrinsic') and has no 'reference to the subject's identity'. These two points are linked. For, without the ability to recognise that the 'I' that thinks A is the same as the 'I' that thinks B, and so on, 'I would have a self as many-coloured and varied as I have presentations' (B134). (An interesting question arises here: is 'empirical consciousness' here some real state of consciousness, or is it a *hypothetical* mode of consciousness assuming *per impossibile* one could separate consciousness from the condition of the unity of apperception? Kant provides an answer shortly.) Synthetic acts acquire a reference to the identity of the subject not just because the act is 'accompanied' by consciousness, but because the synthesis happens in and across consciousness. (This is the same point we made above in discussing Kant's counting example at A103.) 'Hence', Kant writes, 'only because I can combine a manifold of given presentations *in one consciousness*, is it possible for me to present *the identity itself of the consciousness in the presentations*' (B133). The act of combining individual presentations into one, within consciousness, means that through the unity of these presentations I can present the fact that 'I' is one. Accordingly, the analytic principle that whatever I think must be something that I think, is in fact founded on the synthetic act that is the unity of apperception. Indeed, I could only be conscious of individual elements of a dispersed manifold retrospectively, so to speak: 'I' can be conscious of one element (as opposed to another, or the whole) only if it is already clear that the 'I' is in fact identical across all these presentations.

The last paragraph of this section (B135) returns to the idea of intellectual intuition, which we discussed above at the end of our treatment of the 'Transcendental Aesthetic'. We'll skip to section 17.

The first paragraph of section 17 repeats the results so far in the form of an analogy. Just as the basic principle of the possibility of intuition, in so far as it is *given in sensibility*, was that it was subject to space and time, so here the basic principle of all intuition, insofar as it is *combined for the understanding*, is that it is subject to the original synthetic unity of apperception. The next paragraph makes an important new move. The understanding is the ability to produce cognition; cognition is the determinate reference of presentations to an object. Cognition, that is, occurs when we can say 'that is a presentation *of X*' (even if, in fact, we are mistaken). This is already an important claim: through the understanding, objects become presented. But what is meant by an object, speaking as generally as possible? Will Kant try to define 'object' in terms of matter or substance, perhaps? No: an object 'is that in whose concept the manifold of a given intuition is *united*' (B137). In other words, an object is presented to us as the manifold of intuition unified under a concept of that object. 'Object', most generally, is defined by the act of synthetic unity of a manifold; object is defined *from the point of view of mental acts*. Kant's point here is that since objects are presented only through the unity of cognitive acts of the understanding, the understanding itself is only possible if unity is possible. Thus, the original synthetic unity of apperception – which Kant claims is the highest possibility of unity – is the condition of the possibility of the understanding. (Recall in this connection the terminological distinction that Kant often seems to be making between *Gegenstand* and *Objekt*. The former refers to the object in experience, the latter to the object of a concept and thus of knowledge. We discussed this above in treating of the notion of Transcendental Object in the 'A-Deduction'.)

This is just what the third paragraph says: the principle of apperception is the 'primary pure cognition of understanding' – it is the first or most basic act of the understanding. The mere form of intuition, space for example, is not yet cognition – it becomes cognition insofar as the understanding acts upon it to bring its manifold to unity. Kant's example is of drawing a line, which he considers an act of presenting a pure, unified, spatial object. In drawing a line I synthetically combine the manifold of space into a single object, according to the concept of a line, and thereby also unify consciousness. To become an object for me, 'every intuition' (and that must include pure intuitions) must be subject to the unity of apperception. Kant seems in a hurry just here, but he is working on the same ideas as in the syntheses of apprehension and reproduction in the 'A-Deduction'. He will return in section 25 to the synthesis of space and time.

Section 18 distinguishes this original unity of apperception from any empirical unity: Kant's example of the latter is word association which might reveal something subjective about the person associating them, but reveals nothing about the objects referred to (accordingly, word-association became for a time at least a standard psychologist's instrument). Only the original unity of consciousness is objectively valid, because only through it are objects presented. Significantly, the empirical unity of apperception is not *another* way in which consciousness is unified; rather, it is 'derived from the original unity under given conditions *in concreto*' (B140). That is, it occurs only against the background of the necessary unity of consciousness. This seems to answer the question we posed above about the actuality of something called empirical consciousness. Empirical consciousness, like word-association or any other act where a synthesis occurs apparently without reference to self-consciousness, occurs only within the horizon of an always possible objective self-consciousness. Thus, Kant argues, it is a derivative or reduced state, rather than (as for many empiricists) an original one.

Section 19 continues to elaborate this distinction. A judgement is not to be defined as the positing of a relation between two concepts; this doesn't say enough, Kant argues. Instead, a judgement is 'a way of bringing given cognitions to the objective unity of apperception' (B141). In other words, judgement is the act by which cognition arrives at a consciousness of the unity of a manifold through a concept. This new way of thinking about judgement also gives us a new way of thinking about the above distinction between subjectively or objectively valid states of consciousness. When I use the 'little relational word' *is*, I refer to some objective necessity that *this is that*. I don't mean that it just looks like it, or feels like it. Rather: *it* the object *really is* something, independently of how it looks or feels to me. The necessity is derived, Kant claims, from the necessary unity of original apperception. 'Looks' or 'feels' is a derivative, subjective type of thinking that does not make the claim about the object. However, as we saw above, such thinking occurs against the background of the objective type. For example, although in saying 'this feels heavy' I am not making an objective claim about the object, but I am (implicitly) making an objective claim about myself: I am, really and objectively, experiencing the feeling of heaviness. Only because of that objective claim can I go on to make a merely subjective one.

There is a significant consequence to defining judgement in this way. The notion of judgement was used in the so-called 'metaphysical deduction'. Judgement acted by way of what Kant called a 'function'. Logic provided a table of functions of judgement: these were the ways in which presentations of whatever type could be brought together. These functions, insofar as they must also apply to the pure manifold of intuition, were the categories. Now we see judgement as bringing the manifold to the objective unity of apperception. So, in general, it is the functions of judgement that bring any manifold to the objective unity of apperception. One more step and we can see that *the categories are the means by which any pure manifold is subjected to apperception*. Which is exactly the argument Kant makes in section 20.

Section 20 is where it all starts to come together – where Kant shows the relevance of the analysis of the original unity of apperception to his basic problem of a deduction of the validity of the categories. The argument appears simple, and the section is brief. The manifold of intuition is necessarily subject to the original synthetic unity of apperception (this was the main result of the first few sections of the 'B-Deduction'). The act of the understanding by which a manifold is brought under one apperception is the logical function of judgement (this is the result of the so-called metaphysical deduction, combined with Kant's definition of judgement in section 19). Therefore, all manifolds, insofar as they can be apprehended as one in consciousness, are determined with regard to one of the logical functions of judgement. The categories are just these functions of judgement considered as determining pure intuition. Thus, 'the manifold in a given intuition is subject necessarily to the categories' (B143). That is, the categories have necessary validity with respect to any intuitive manifold.

The Figurative Synthesis
However, this proof has a limitation, to which Kant turns in section 21. Recall the 'A-Deduction', where the argument seemed to be complete, and yet there were fifteen pages to go. Kant had demonstrated the validity of the categories with respect to the third synthesis of recognition, but he had not yet brought all three syntheses together within the framework of the spontaneity of the understanding. So, again, here we have a very similar problem. The categories arise in the understanding alone, independent of sensibility, Kant claims (B144). In section 20, then, when Kant writes 'intuition' he can only mean 'wherever manifolds come from, and whatever they may be'. Everything so far said has been at the level of the understanding with respect to *any sensibility*, or 'sensibility' as the understanding on its own conceives it, and not yet at the level of *our human sensibility*. So, the above argument abstracted from the question of how manifolds of intuition are actually given to us, and how their unity is possible. This is just what happened in the 'A-Deduction': Kant had to move backwards from the third synthesis (which concerns concepts of the understanding) to the first two syntheses (which are more closely tied to sensibility).

Section 22 distinguishes between thinking and cognition. The former is the employment of concepts; the latter is the employment of concepts *with respect to given intuitions*. We can then also distinguish between pure cognition and empirical cognition. Here, Kant makes this distinction by contrasting the employment of concepts with respect to the pure forms of intuition (thus pure cognition), as opposed to with respect to 'objects of sense' (empirical cognition). An example of the former employment is pure mathematics; Kant calls the latter 'experience' (B147). However, Kant insists that the pure form can be called cognition only because it has also a possible application to experience. We can determine a priori the form of any possible object (later in the 'Analytic', Kant will talk about the *principles* of possible experience); however, we can only cognise an *object* if it is given. Kant writes, 'Consequently, the categories cannot be used for cognising things except insofar as these things are taken as objects of possible experience' (B147–8). Possibility is being used in the sense of 'transcendentally possible' (see above, Figure 1. Types of possibility and impossibility), namely what is made possible a priori through the categories and forms of intuition. However, Kant is adding a new restriction (this is made more clear in the next section): our intuition is *sensible*, able to present objects *only insofar and as they are given to us*. So, the limits of possible experience are what above we called the transcendentally possible, but with two added caveats. First, that what can be experienced are not things in themselves, but only appearances, given to us in our sensible intuition. Second, a category can only be used to determine an *object* (as opposed to the pure form of an object, or the principles that legislate for our possible experiences of objects) in *empirical* intuition; only, that is, if an instance is given.

Kant further explains the significance of the first result in section 23. The validity of the pure categories extends 'to objects of intuition as such' (B148) – that is, to any *sensible* intuition whether of the forms of human intuition or not. This does us no good, of course, because these cognitions could never present objects; so, they may be valid in that sphere, but useless. 'Solely *our* sensible and empirical intuition can provide them with meaning and significance' (B148–9). I can, Kant continues in the second paragraph, think of a nonsensible object, an object whose properties are defined negatively as *not* belonging to sensible intuition. Can I make any headway towards cognising the thing in itself this way? No, I have no proper cognition because I have (by definition) no intuition. Moreover, I cannot even apply a category, because the categories again have meaning only with respect to *our* sensible intuition.

Sections 22 and 23 were important clarifications. With section 24, Kant returns to the central problem of the 'Deduction'. The categories, Kant observes, are 'mere forms of thought' (B150), and not yet cognitions. The synthesis of the manifold to achieve the unity of apperception, which they make possible, is related to sensible intu-ition in general. Thus, it is 'purely intellectual only' (B150). However, the issue of how the understanding relates to *our* sensibility is solved virtually at a stroke by the fact that the forms of our sensible intuition lie 'in us' (B150). It is not a question of asking how the categories apply to things in themselves, but only how they apply to things as they appear. Appearances are conditioned by the forms of sensible intuition: space and time. These forms are part of the a priori struc-ture of our sensibility.

Kant clarifies this distinction between the sensible and intellectual in the second paragraph. The 'figurative synthesis' is this synthesis of the manifold of our sensible intuition. The 'intellectual' combination, or 'combination of understanding' is more general, the synthesis as the understanding alone conceives it. The problem of the second half of the 'Deduction' is to show that the figurative synthesis must be such as to fall under the intellectual. Now, both of these have as their highest principle the original unity of apperception, which is the 'transcendental unity thought in the categories' (B151). In other words, apperception is 'intellectual', it is of the understanding, too. So, if both syntheses are in fact intellectual, what is the difference between them? Kant answers this question by returning to an impor-tant theme of the 'A-Deduction': imagination. The figurative synthe-sis, insofar as it concerns apperception, is called the 'transcendental synthesis of imagination'.

'Imagination', Kant writes, 'is the power of presenting an object in intuition even *without the object's being present*' (B151). Kant doesn't make it explicit here why we must consider this 'power' under the name 'imagination'. However, the working definition of imagination in general is the same as in the 'A-Deduction' (A100–2), and moreover the description there of a 'transcendental power of imagination' has much in common with this 'B-Deduction' passage. There seems to be good reason, therefore, to read this whole passage as Kant's rework-ing of what he had earlier called the 'synthesis of reproduction'.

Recall the limitation Kant discussed concerning the first part of the 'Deduction'. The argument abstracted from the question of how manifolds of intuition are actually given to us, and how unity of actu-ally given manifolds is possible. Expressed in the language Kant has just introduced, the first part of the 'Deduction' concerned itself with 'intellectual synthesis', and must now look to figurative synthesis. Imagination, Kant here claims, both belongs 'to *sensibility*' and yet also is an 'exercise of spontaneity' (B151). The imagination, that is, is in part that which is determined in synthesis, and in part what is 'determinative' – it is a bridge so to speak between the understanding and sensibility. (Just so, in the 'A-Deduction', by working back from the synthesis of recognition to the synthesis of reproduction, Kant was able to connect the activity of concepts with sensible intuition.) Insofar as the transcendental synthesis of imagination is spontaneous – indeed, the 'action of the understanding upon sensibility' – Kant also calls it 'productive'. The 'reproductive' imagination is simply contingent, empirical, association (as in the word association Kant discusses at B140).

The transcendental synthesis of imagination (pure figurative synthesis), in short, is the first synthesis of the manifold of intuition 'in accordance with the categories' (B152). Through imagination the principle of the unity of apperception is the principle not just of 'intellectual' synthesis but also of 'figurative' synthesis – the synthesis of intuition in its human type: the forms of space and time. So, the figurative synthesis falls under the same conditions as the intellectual. But even this new addition to the argument does not complete it. Something is still missing, and Kant will address it when the 'Deduction' resumes in section 26.

The rest of section 24 and all of section 25 concern generally important notions, but with respect to the main argument of the 'Deduction' they are an aside. These passages aim to clear up what appears to be a paradox entailed by the 'Deduction' thus far. Kant writes: '[W]e intuit ourselves only as we are inwardly *affected*; and this seems contradictory, because we would then have to relate to ourselves as passive' (B153). I, as active, have an effect upon myself; the same I, as passive, is affected. Is not passive inner sense (my sensible awareness of myself) the same as active apperception (self-consciousness)? How can the I be both active and passive at the same time?

The solution, Kant claims, is in fact to distinguish between inner sense and apperception. Inner sense is the means by which we are affected; it 'contains' the form of intuition (time) but is not a combining power. It merely presents manifolds of temporal relations. Apperception, on the other hand, is the first principle of the synthetic activity of the understanding, and its unity applies to intuitions as such, and thus also to objects as such, that is without reference to the particular human forms of sensible intuition. Inner sense, then, presents a manifold, but does not yet present *something*: e.g. a thought or memory. Apperception is the original act by which the manifold is unified, and thereby becomes both an intuition of something and connected to the 'I think'. Our understanding is sensible, and cannot produce intuitions itself (see the discussion above of intellectual intuition). That is, apperception synthesises but does not *give* the manifold. Therefore, my self awareness must proceed through the detour, so to speak, of inner sense and the form of time. Not only are my cognitions of the world discursive (are always mediated) but so are my cognitions of myself.

Once that distinction is made, Kant claims, the paradox (nearly) disappears. At least, it is now no worse a difficulty than that faced by any philosophy confronting the question of how I can be an object for myself. Kant concludes by writing: '[A]s far as inner intuition is concerned, our own subject is cognised by us only as appearance, but not in terms of what it is in itself' (B156). At the end of section 24 Kant states that the determination of time (inner sense) relies upon features exhibited by outer sense. Here this claim is employed to try to explain the possibility of self-affection. Just as we cognise objects insofar as we are outwardly affected by them, and not as they are in themselves, so we cognise ourselves only insofar as we self-affect, and not as we are in ourselves. This apparently simple claim turns out to be very important later for Kant: it provides him with the tools he needs to defeat the idealism of Descartes or Berkeley. This is made explicit in a later passage entitled the 'Refutation of Idealism'.

Section 25 pursues the distinction between apperception and inner sense a little further. In intellectual synthesis, 'I am not conscious of myself as I appear to myself, nor as I am in myself, but am conscious only that I am' (B157). This is in full agreement with Descartes's 'I think (therefore) I am'. But this existence is as yet undetermined: *how* I exist cannot even be raised as a question. My self-awareness is pure and empty, because apperception does not itself provide a manifold. In order to raise the question of how I exist, who I am, what am I doing – to have cognition of myself as this or that – requires an intuition. My *mere* existence, then, is not an appearance, but it is *determined* as an appearance. Kant accordingly can distinguish between consciousness of oneself as a mere intelligence or power of combination (B158–9), on the one hand, and cognition of oneself. The distinction between my mere awareness of my existence and its determination through inner sense is the subject of a much more sustained discussion later in the 'Paralogisms of Pure Reason'.

Transcendental Apprehension

The central argument of the 'Deduction' resumes and indeed concludes with section 26. The 'metaphysical deduction' (the derivation of the categories from the table of the logical forms of judgement) showed that the table of the categories was complete and a priori. But it did not show that these categories have any objective validity. In the first part of the 'Transcendental Deduction', Kant claims to have shown their necessary relation to 'intuition as such'. That is, to intuition as the understanding alone conceives it, separated from the condition of human, sensible intuition. Then, we argued, the first part of section 24 had provided the categories with a bridge or access, so to speak, to human intuition. However, Kant now claims, this was access only to the *forms* of intuition. Not yet, that is, access to 'whatever objects *our senses may encounter*' (B159). This is the limitation of the argument so far. It relates to the forms of human sensible intuition, but not to the actually, though purely, given manifolds of space and time in their presented unity. Again, we are reminded of how in the 'A-Deduction' (A119ff) Kant, having already moved backwards from the third to the second synthesis, then moves back again to the first.

So, there is good reason to believe that this last, third phase of the 'B-Deduction' will parallel the 'A-Deduction' treatment of the 'synthesis of apprehension'. And, indeed, Kant even employs that phrase in the second paragraph of section 26. However, here, 'synthesis of apprehension' names a mere empirical phenomenon: that empirical combination of the manifold such that what Kant here calls 'perception' becomes possible. Perception is 'empirical consciousness of the intuition' as appearance. Perception is something like, then, the empirical consciousness that *something has appeared to me*. This takes us back, of course, to the beginning of the 'Deduction' and the claim that the 'I think' must be capable of accompanying all presentations. Such merely empirical consciousness on its own, Kant has already argued (B133–4), would be inherently dispersed. Such empirical consciousness is a kind of minimum condition of any cognition that even an empiricist would recognise. But what Kant did not argue earlier was that such dispersed consciousness was strictly impossible *in isolation*. So, the force of the argument here will be to link the possibility of even this last, minimal, bastion of naive empiricism to the universal and necessary legitimacy of the categories. The argument proceeds by showing that such empirical perception has its possibility and indeed its necessity guaranteed by a transcendental synthesis. For once, Kant does not assign a new name to this new synthetic activity. Following the structure of the 'A-Deduction', and given that Kant uses the term here, we will call it 'transcendental apprehension'.

This last phase of the 'B-Deduction' commences in the third paragraph. Space and time are the formal structure of intuitions; these forms lie 'in us' a priori. Thus, in the transcendental synthesis of imagination (or transcendental figurative synthesis), Kant was able to show above that the same conditions of the unity of the purely intellectual manifold must also apply to the pure forms of intuition. That was in section 24. However, the a priori presentations of space and time are not only forms of intuition, but presented as themselves intuitions. Space and time are themselves presented as given unities. This Kant takes from the last of the arguments in the 'Metaphysical Exposition' of space and time (A25–6, B39–40, A32–3=B47–8): e.g. 'we present space as an infinite *given* magnitude'. But more: space and time are also *dimensions*, presented as the space and time *within which* objects are or events happen. Or, using a Newtonian language, he claims that space and time are presented *as themselves a type of object* (Kant uses this language in the footnote to B160). Accordingly, space and time are not just the structure of manifolds but themselves presented as unified manifolds. (This transformation from pure form to presentation is shown to have still further important consequences in the 'Axioms of Intuition', A162–6=B202–7.) How does this happen, and why is it important?

The examples Kant gives at B162–3 are extremely helpful. The first example is spatial, the second, temporal. I have an 'empirical intuition of a house' and 'turn' it into a 'perception' by 'apprehending the intuition's manifold'. That is, I have a manifold of spatial relations (and their sense-contents) that *will eventually be recognised* as a house. Through the empirical synthesis of apprehension, I grasp this manifold not yet as a house, to be sure, but at least as *a something that appears to me*. Accordingly, Kant says, I can perceive (become aware of having) the intuition: I can *see* (or otherwise sense) *something*. But, Kant continues, in order to achieve even this much, I must lay at the basis of the apprehension 'the *necessary unity* of space and of outer sensible intuition as such'. Why is this at the 'basis'?

If we go back to the beginning of the 'A-Deduction' and the 'synthesis of apprehension' as discussed there, the reason becomes clear. Space and time must be laid out as a dimension – as a unitary and unique dimension. Otherwise, I can have no reason for even assuming that the door to the house not only belongs with the window, but *even exists in the same space*. If not in the same space, the parts of the house wouldn't be *parts of* anything, and accordingly I would not have that basic, elemental perception of a *something*. So, at the 'basis' of that perception lies the unity of space. The synthetic unity of space is a necessary requirement for even the *empirical* synthesis of apprehension. Moreover, this synthetic unity makes it possible that the relations of door to window, and of window to roof, are of the same type (spatial extensions), and can thus be compared and *ordered* in empirical synthesis, and it becomes possible to present at least *something*. Back at B162, Kant writes, 'But this same unity [of space as an 'object'], if I abstract from the form of space, resides in the understanding, and is the category of the synthesis of the homogeneous in an intuition as such, i.e., the category of *magnitude*.' In other words, thought of as the intellectual synthesis, the particular unity in question is 'magnitude' or 'quantity'. The spatial relation between door and window must be determinable, be a quantity that can be determined, and this means that all relations *are the same but differ in quantity*. For this to be the case, they must appear against the background of the unitary dimension of space – which, as we have seen is 'an infinite *given* magnitude' (B39) and is thus the dimension of presented extension as such. Even empirical synthesis of apprehension requires the category, for the category gives the unity of a dimension of presentation to the pure manifold of space and time in an act we have called transcendental apprehension.

The temporal example adds little new. In order to perceive the freezing of water, the prior and subsequent states (liquid and ice) must be assumed to appear in the same, unique dimension of time.

Otherwise their relation is indeterminable, and nothing strictly speaking has appeared at all. Moreover, through this synthetic presentation of the dimension of time, '*everything that happens is, in terms of its relation, determined* by me *in time as such*' (B163) and temporal relations of happening can be compared and ordered. Again, abstracting from time and returning to the intellectual synthesis of 'intuition as such', the unity of this dimension is the category of cause. The transcendental apprehension of time through which time appears as the dimension of happenings as such, occurs synthetically through the category of causation. We shall have much occasion, in the 'Analytic of Principles', to discuss causation in more detail.

With this, the 'Deduction' is finished. In its first part was demonstrated that the unity of apperception is an absolute requirement of experience, and that this unity is achieved with respect to 'intuition as such' through a synthesis according to the categories. In the second part (section 24), the form of human, sensible intuition was shown to also fall under this (otherwise merely intellectual) notion of 'intuition as such'. Spatial and temporal form are necessarily subject to the principle of apperception and thus also to synthesis under the categories. Finally, in the third (section 26), Kant moved from the form or structure of intuition to the presentations of space and time as what we called dimensions of appearances. Space and time are originally extrinsic, 'nothing but relations'; for empirical perception to be possible, these relations must be reformed, so to speak, as a 'composite' (B136n) or manifold within a unitary dimension that is space or time considered as an object (B160n). Kant thus showed that the presentation of such a dimension was a necessary requirement of even the most basic experience, and that this presentation assumed synthesis according to the categories (which we called transcendental apprehension). Putting all three parts together, Kant claims to have achieved the 'exhibition of the pure concepts of the understanding (and, with them, of all theoretical a priori cognition) as principles of the possibility of experience' (B168). Since these concepts make possible experience, it is obvious that they legitimately apply to experience – and that was what Kant set out to prove in the 'Deduction'.

The last part of section 26 returns to the broad theme of transcendental idealism and the Copernican revolution, of which Kant wrote way back in the B-Preface. Kant was able to explain how appearances must 'agree' with the forms of intuition by distinguishing between appearances and things in themselves. Appearances do not exist in themselves, and therefore do not have any intrinsic sensible form; they exist only relatively to a sensible subject, and this relation gives them their form. So, similarly, the *laws of* appearances (that is, their presentation as necessarily orderly or predictable) are not intrinsic to appearances, but are a product of their relation to an understanding. 'As mere appearances . . . they are subject to no law of connection whatever except the one prescribed by the connecting power' (B164). Accordingly, there is no real puzzle in thinking how it is possible that we 'prescribe laws to nature, and even make nature possible' (B159). That would only be a puzzle if it was not nonsense to say that nature as mere appearance had laws in and of itself. The categories are the 'original basis' of the law-governedness of '*nature as such* considered as law-governedness of appearances in space and time' (B165). Notice the inclusion of time here, the form of inner sense. It is very easy to assume that when Kant speaks of nature he means trees and rocks and stars. But of course the human body is a part of nature too. And, moreover, so is the appearance of the self in inner sense. *Insofar as it appears*, my mental life is a part of nature.

However, it is important we realise that there is a built-in limitation to this otherwise bold conclusion. The metaphysics as a science that Kant spoke of in the Introduction is, certainly, only a metaphysics of nature as appearance. But more: it is a metaphysics only of the absolutely universal conditions of any appearance. More particular laws or concepts, governing this or that type of natural phenomenon (for instance, magnetism, bacteria, the emotions) are empirical. To be sure, without the a priori law-governedness, no empirical law could be discovered. The pure concepts are the ground of particular laws as they are the ground of objects of experience; that is to say, an empirical law is only a law because nature is constituted a priori as a place of laws. But transcendental philosophy is, as Kant insisted early on, a critique and not a 'doctrine'. It is now clear that it *could not be* a doctrine, in the sense of a complete account of the laws of nature. Kant had made this point earlier (sections 22–3), in a different form. He said that the categories were valid only as the conceptual form of any possible experience. This meant that through the categories only the possibilities of objects could be thought, but objects themselves could not be cognised; rather, objects still have to be given empirically.

IMPORTANT NOTE: The governing principle of this book is that it will serve to aid its readers in becoming confident readers of Kant. To this end, we said at the beginning that we would start slowly, working carefully through Kant's text. Then, we would accelerate, such that the whole span of the Kant's book is covered, but not in the same detail. Having spent a long time on the 'Deductions', this is the point where the acceleration begins. We will no longer proceed section by section and paragraph by paragraph; now, some sections will be discussed more briefly, and some skipped.

The 'Deduction': Some Views
If the Copernican revolution is the place where many commentators find the sense of what Kant's philosophy means overall, the 'Transcendental Deduction' is equally a key place for understanding how Kant could possibly prove his claims. The fact that the whole passage was rewritten, and that even in its rewritten form it is neither easy nor clear, means that it is also a focus for major disagreements. For Strawson, the 'Transcendental Deduction' is concerned with asking the question of how objects must be conceived if it is to be possible for us to form judgements about them that are determinable as true or false (Strawson 1966, 83). Kant's analysis, however, also asks us to believe in an 'imaginary subject of transcendental psychology' with its doctrine of the faculties (Strawson 1966, 97). This is especially true of the 'A-Deduction', Strawson thus belongs to the tradition of commentators who prefer the 'B-Deduction' on the grounds that it more successfully avoids falling into the trap of mere psychologism. Kant is successful in proving, however, that experience would be impossible on the basis merely of 'sense data' – merely of what 'seems' – without adequate criteria for judgements about what 'is' and does not merely 'seem'.

Bennett sees Kant as taking up the issue in Hume considering whether there is any necessity to the fact of order in the world. Kant sees the basic error here as the empiricist assumption that disorder in experience is inconvenient, rather than the undermining of all thought. Kant wishes to show that such a 'nightmare' of chaos is impossible (Bennett 1966, 100–2). Kant's point is not to remove fear of what might be, but to describe what is the case; that is, to provide a description of cognition. Kant is committed to a 'phenomenalist' account of objectivity, according to which objects are not noumenal but rather logical constructs from the data of experience (Bennett 1966, 127). The argument involves, centrally, an analysis of self-consciousness. This is not just a 'glow' that accompanies mental states, is not something mystical or unanalysable, but rather involves an intellectual capacity, specifically the capacity for forming judgements about memory (Bennett 1966, 117).

Guyer criticises the 'Deductions' on a number of fronts. The 'Deductions' (and especially the first), Guyer argues, have two distinct strategies – to address judgements of objects, and to address the unity of apperception – and these are never properly integrated. Moreover, Kant throughout is assuming the validity of necessary synthetic truths about either objects or apperception, and *from* these arguing to some a priori ground (Guyer 1987, 77). These assumptions cannot be upheld and the 'Deductions' as a whole are a failure. However, Guyer sees here a trace of a valuable argument – one that does not rely upon a priori knowledge of a necessary unity of the self, but rather upon knowledge of the mere possibility of an empirical unity – but this argument is only stated in full in the 'Refutation of Idealism', to which we will return (Guyer 1987, 149–50).

Henrich (1982) famously argues that the 'B-Deduction' divides into two parts, the first concerned with sensibility in general as already unified, the second removes this restriction by addressing itself to human sensibility. (Above, we argue that the 'Deduction' in fact has a *three*-part structure, paralleling the 'A-Deduction' more closely than other commentators would have us believe.) He further argues that Kant's overall goal is to refute a position of global scepticism that is akin to the scepticism that Descartes worked through in the *Meditations*. Allison follows Henrich in regarding the 'B-Deduction' as falling into two halves; but disagrees about how these should be interpreted. The 'spectre' of scepticism is not removed, as Henrich thought, by the first half of the argument, but rather by the second. This is because the first is concerned only with the conditions of *thoughts* of objects, Allison argues. Allison concludes that the 'Deduction' is incomplete and that one must look to the 'Schematism' and the 'Analytic of Principles' to 'complete the account of the connection between the intellectual and sensible conditions of human cognition' (Allison 2004, 201).

The Analytic of Principles
Introduction and Schematism
Following the 'Transcendental Deduction', we find the 'Analytic of Principles', the second book of the 'Transcendental Analytic'. This has the job of showing 'how', 'in what way' and 'with what critical implications' the categories have legitimate application. The 'how' is the 'Schematism' chapter, which provides a way for pure categories to apply to objects. Kant subsequently must show exactly 'in what way' each of the four sub-classes of categories functions within our experience, and what synthetic a priori judgements (here called 'principles') become possible thereby. This section is called the 'System of the Analytic of Principles'. Subsequently the 'Phenomena and Noumena' section gives the critical implications of the necessary validity of categories within experience – or, as we now know, the constitution of experience through categories.

What Kant calls the 'principles of understanding' is in fact a 'doctrine of the power of judgement' (A132=B171). Accordingly, he writes, 'If understanding as such is explicated as our power of rules, then the power of judgement is the ability to subsume under rules, i.e. to distinguish whether something does or does not fall under a given rule' (A132=B171). Now, we know from section 19 that 'subsuming' is not the most fundamental characterisation of judgement for Kant, for it ignores the much more important task of bringing about the unity of apperception. Nevertheless, this notion of 'subsumption' serves Kant as a convenient short-hand for the more elaborate analyses. Here in the 'Analytic of Principles', Kant now addresses directly the question: 'How are synthetic a priori judgements possible?' At stake are no longer the *elements* of our experience (intuitions and concepts), and the question is no longer their legitimacy. Rather, the question is *how* must these elements 'come together' such that judgement happens.

The 'Schematism' section is among the most controversial in the whole of the book, partly because it is also one of the most obscure.

At first glance, at least, the problem Kant is addressing in this section is straightforward: how do categories apply to intuitions? In every judgement, Kant insists, the presentation of the object must be 'of the same type' (or 'homogeneous') with the concept. He glosses this by saying the concept must 'contain' what is presented, and thus the presentation is said to be 'subsumed under' the concept. The sentence about the plate and the circle that follows is very obscure indeed, and no two translators or commentators agree even on what it says. The sense would seem to be, roughly: a concept of a circular plate is homogeneous with the presentation of a plate insofar as the concept contains the roundness presented. In other words, the concept 'fits' in the way a concept of, say, a cardboard box, being rectangular, would not. So far, this seems pretty innocuous.

Now, there are two ways in which the presentation of something could fail to 'fit' with a concept. First – as in the plate and the concept of a cardboard box – by the fact that what the concept contains is not found in the presentation. The plate is not homogeneous, but something else could easily be. Second, however, if what is contained in the concept *could not in principle* be found in *any such* presentation. This latter problem arises with pure concepts or categories. Precisely because pure, such concepts are originally unrelated in any way with intuition, through which objects are presented. Now, this looks like a very similar problem to that which Kant encountered, and claimed to have overcome, in the 'Deduction'. There the solution was the productive imagination, and here in the 'Schematism' Kant relies upon the imagination; this is why some commentators argue that the 'Schematism' is redundant. However, it does have something to offer if we think of it, first, as at least adding detail to the earlier analysis; and, second, in particular answering the following question, which Kant did not even raise earlier: what does a conceptual rule 'look like' when it is considered as a rule for the synthesis of an intuitive manifold?

In any case categories and intuitions have to 'fit', if Kant is correct that *both* form the conditions of any and all sensible experience. Indeed, on the previous few pages, Kant had argued that transcendental philosophy has a particular virtue and task in that it not only discovers universal rules but can also indicate the cases to which these rules apply (A135–6=B174–5). That is, we must be able to see how the categories find their intuited objects. This requirement is reiterated here (A139–40=B178–9). The 'Schematism' aims to do just this – but even on Kant's own terms, only partially succeeds. He will infamously say that schematism is a 'secret art' in the depths of the human soul. This is hardly a satisfactory explanation. However, what Kant *is* able to do here is to introduce the schema as a third term. The schema is both law-like ('intellectual' as the category) and intuition-like (or sensible). It is thus the third term that mediates between these two sources of cognition, making pure synthetic judgements possible.

Once Kant sets up the nature of schematism in this way, however, it becomes clear that even in the case of ordinary concepts and presentations (the plate from earlier; his new example is a dog), schemata are required. For, 'in themselves the images are never completely congruent with the concept' (A142=B181). That is, where the first paragraph of the 'Schematism' seemed content to obscure the fundamental difference between concepts and intuitions, the notion of schematism allows us to see it again. We see, then, that all synthetic cognitions rest upon schematism, and thus the problem of how *transcendental* schematism is possible – the third term between pure categories and pure intuitions – becomes all the more pressing. Kant will conclude that schematism is a procedure for judgement. Transcendental schemata provide the minimum framework of procedural rules for any application of empirical concepts in judgement. Just as in the two Deductions, this role is attributed to the transcendental imagination (A142=B181).

All presentations are temporal – all presentations are in 'inner sense'; only some presentations are spatial. Therefore, time is the most universal medium of presentation. A schema is first defined as a 'transcendental determination of time' (A138–9=B177–8), and is contrasted with an 'image'. An image is any particularly determined shape of time – for example, five seconds. It is, in other words, a particular presentation. A schema cannot be identified with an image because that would just be reasserting the problem that schematism is supposed to be solving.

Instead, Kant experiments with the notion of schema as a 'procedure' for time determination; let us say, a rule for the synthesis and determination of time. This notion of a 'procedure' is the answer to the question above about how we should understand a concept in its role as a rule of synthesis of an intuitive manifold. In the second half of the section, he very briefly (and often obscurely) runs through each of the categories. Some of these are enlightening. For example, the schemata of the categories of reality and negation are the procedures by which time is recognised as either having content, or being empty. Or, the schema of the causality of a thing involves 'the real upon which, whenever it is posited, something else always follows. Hence this schema consists in the manifold's succession insofar as this is subject to a rule' (A144=B183). That is, the schema of causality is the procedure by which a succession of events is determined to be rule-governed as to its order.

There are a number of important results to be taken from this discussion. First of all, Kant in the schematism reiterates the significance for his philosophy of the basic difference between concepts and intuitions as types of presentation, or the understanding and sensibility as conditions of cognition. One implication of this is the discussion at the end of the schematism chapter of the limits of categorical application – a theme we have seen before often enough. '[H]ence', Kant writes, the categories are restricted by schematism and 'have, in the end, no other use than a possible empirical one' (A146=B185). Notice the word 'possible'. As we have seen, it is a characteristic of transcendental philosophy that it investigates the possibility of cognition. The schema, again, is not an image because it is not *actual* cognition; rather, it is a procedure or function by means of which sensible cognition becomes possible.

Second, we have already mentioned Kant's assertion that it is the transcendental imagination that produces schemata. Philosophers who take the 'Schematism' chapter very seriously are thus often led to take the role of the imagination very seriously. The schemata 'realise' the categories (which are otherwise merely logical functions of unity) (A146=B186). This verb has at least two meanings here. First, the categories are brought to the real through schematism: they come to have a relation to possible experience and thus things that may be said to be 'real'. Second, however, the categories are themselves *made real* as concepts, are given transcendental objects, are fulfilled as such. The categories, as a type of presentation of real things, are not just given (they are not innate ideas, then) but are made real in a spontaneous synthetic act of the imagination.

On the other hand, schemata are said to 'produce' time, give it possible content, order and totality (A145=B184–5). What exactly all this means is obscure. But there is likely a relation to the kind of analysis that Kant put forward, for instance, at the beginning of the 'A-Deduction', and in the last stage of the 'B-Deduction'. There, time itself as a pre-sentation that contains a manifold, is produced by an act of synthesis that Kant calls 'apprehension' from out of the a priori form of time which is 'nothing but relations'. In short, time too is 'realised' by the schematism of the transcendental imagination; the time we recognise as being time is not original, but the product of schematism. Thus, the 'Schematism' is seen as a supplemental investigation of what Kant in the 'Deductions' called the synthesis of apprehension.

The third major conclusion that we can draw from the 'Schematism' chapter is a sense of the necessity with which Kant makes his next move. The schemata are the third thing that is able to bring together intuitions and concepts, which are otherwise utterly heterogeneous. It realises the categories, giving them meaning (A146=B186). Or, in other words, through schemata pure, a priori judgements become possible. But in each case, what is this meaning, and what are these judgements? This Kant will turn to next, providing for each class of category a transcendental argument aiming to show the validity of some a priori judgement by describing how experience becomes possible through it. In addition, we know that schemata are procedures for the determination of time. Each of the arguments to follow, not surprisingly then, will comprise an analysis of time-determination.

Some commentators argue that this section is the key to the whole critical philosophy; others argue that the schematism is quite irrelevant. In the latter category one will find Prichard, Geoffrey Warnock and Bennett, all of whom argue that Kant's basic error is to imagine that one could meaningfully 'have' a concept, and yet be unable to apply it. Allison defends Kant here, claiming the problem of the schematism is a real one. The issue is not, he argues, about the applicability of the categories, but rather a description of the sensible conditions under which that applicability can happen. Considering a concept as a rule for the subsumption of a particular case meets the problem that cases are infinitely variable. Allison's analogy is with chess: there are a finite number of rules defining a 'legal' chess move, but if one tried to describe the rules of a 'good' chess move, these would have as much variation as there are possible games of chess. Therefore, recognition of a case falling under a concept is a matter of 'imagination' and 'interpretation'. A schema is a 'perceptual rule' that *guides* perception in this imaginative act. Bell's account has a broadly similar starting point, insofar as he too sees the schematism as a response to the problem of an infinite regress of rules. Bell compares schematism here with creative or aesthetic response that forms a judgement immediately, in accordance with Kant's notion of spontaneity. Guyer's account of the schematism argues that it should be understood as a an attempt to dissolve the problem of abstract ideas that was inherited from from the empiricists. First, ordinary empirical concepts are their own schemata, and we are not confronted by two ontologically distinct types of entities, the general and the particular. Second, schematism explains how the categories are instantiated or manifested in sensible intuition, solving Hume's problem of what 'impression' corresponds to our supposed idea of causation.

The Supreme Principle, Axioms of Intuion and the Anticipations of Perception

In 'The Supreme Principle of All Synthetic Judgements', we should notice two things. First, the claim at A155=B194, that 'time' is now named as the 'third thing' that permits synthetic judgements, and it is thus also the 'medium' of all synthesis. We should not confuse this idea of the 'third' with the 'third man' problem of bringing together the understanding and sensibility, which Kant discusses in the 'Deductions' and especially in the 'Schematism'. Here, Kant is referring back to the notion of synthetic judgements requiring a reference to something outside the subject and predicate terms. For synthetic a posteriori judgements, the third thing is experience, specifically; for a priori judgements it is space and time as the pure forms of intuition. But, at its most general, the third thing will always be time. This also means that even the categories (insofar as they apply to experience, and we now know in general that they do) will have to become subject to time; or equivalently, we must understand the manners in which time itself becomes presented synthetically through the categories. The 'Schematism' chapter began this task.

Second, Kant writes: 'If a cognition is to have objective reality, i.e. if it is to refer to an object and have in that object its signification and meaning, then the object must be capable of being *given* in some way' (A155=B194). That is, if our judgements are to be about the real, then what is judged (the object) must be *capable of being* given – and that, as Kant quickly makes clear, means subject to the possibility of experience. (Note that Kant has two words which are generally translated as 'object'. Obviously, here, Kant is concerned with the first of these. See our discussion above in the treatment of the 'A-Deduction'.) 'Object' [*Gegenstand*] means object or event in intuition – in general, something given to us for our experiential judgement. To experience means to experience objects. So: 'the conditions for the *possibility of experience* as such are simultaneously conditions for the *possibility of the objects of experience*' (A158=B197). Or, to put it another way, the supreme principle of all synthetic judgements is that 'Every object is subject to the conditions necessary for synthetic unity of the manifold of intuition in a possible experience' (A158=B197). The 'Transcendental Deduction' had as its purpose the demonstration of the necessary validity of the pure concepts of the understanding with respect to all experience. Subjectively, the categories are the rules of synthesis that realise the transcendental unity of apperception in empirical consciousness. Objectively, these same acts of synthesis are also the manner in which intuitions are brought to cognition, and thus the same acts that make it possible for presentations to be *of objects*.

The next section, 'Systematic Presentation . . .', examines the categories according to the headings under which they were originally derived, back at A70ff=B95ff. For each of these headings, (and in two cases, for each of the three individual categories), Kant will provide a transcendental argument that demonstrates its particular role and validity with respect to experience. In brief, he is demonstrating what objects are made possible a priori through the category. The role and validity is always expressed as a synthetic a priori proposition, a principle. Kant explains, 'these principles are nothing but the rules for the objective use of the categories' (A161=B200). There are, obviously, four sets of these principles, as the categories are organised into four groups of three. The category sets Relation and Modality have three principles each; the category sets Quantity and Quality only one each. We shall be discussing only four of these principles, starting with Quantity and Quality. We will then briefly discuss Kant's arguments for the first of the categories of relation: substance. However, only the last will be dwelt on at length, for it is the most famous and often taught: the second principle corresponding to the categories of relation, the principle of cause and effect.

The principles that correspond to the category groups labelled Quantity and Quality are, here in the 'Analytic of Principles', called the 'Axioms of Intuition' and the 'Anticipations of Perception'. The first principle is expressed (in the B-edition) as 'All intuitions are extensive magnitudes' (B202). The question is: what can be said a priori concerning the role that the categories of quantity have in the constitution of objects of experience? All objects are given in the form of space and time, and are given in an act of synthesis whereby a determinate space and time are produced. As we saw at the beginning of the 'A-Deduction', one absolute condition of such an ordinary act of synthesis is the prior synthesis by which space and time are given as homogeneous dimensions of presentation (see our discussion above of A98–A100). The mere forms of space and time, through this synthesis, become *presented as* the dimensions of presentation for objects and events. Thus, in the 'Transcendental Aesthetic', Kant argues that space is not originally a concept; while later in the 'Transdendental Deduction' he claims that the 'Aesthetic' contained a simplification, and the unity of space and time are products of synthesis (B160–1n). (For this latter point, see our discussion above of the 'B-Deduction'.)

The concept of this homogeneous dimension, Kant claims here in the 'Axioms of Intuition', is 'magnitude'. Accordingly, in the 'Transcendental Aesthetic', Kant wrote: 'We present space as an infinite *given* magnitude' (B39). 'Given' is italicised because of this transcendentally prior synthesis. It is given to us insofar as, first, sensibility is always characterised by receptivity; and yet also, second, the product of a synthesis. The type of magnitude that these presented forms have is 'extensive'. Kant writes, 'Extensive is what I call a magnitude wherein the presentation of the parts makes possible (and hence necessarily precedes) the presentation of the whole' (A162=B203). A figure, which with respect to the pure form of space is relational and a limitation on the whole becomes presented (through the transcendental synthesis that Kant earlier called the synthesis of apprehension) as an aggregate made up of parts. (This is also part of the point Kant was trying to make way back at A25=B39.) That is, a determined 'shape' of space or time, and indeed space or time themselves, must be presented as an 'aggregate'. From this basic principle of how spatial or temporal quantity must be presented, Kant claims, follow a number of basic axioms of mathematics. That is why the title of this section is the 'Axioms of Intuition' instead of, say, the 'Principle of Extensive Magnitude'.

The rest of this section concerns itself with Kant's account of mathematics, a subject we have already addressed, and to which we shall return at the end of the book.

Let us turn to the 'Anticipations of Perception' where Kant argues as follows: the chief distinction between empirical and a priori presentations is that the former involves 'sensation' or 'the matter of perception' (A166–7=B208–9). We saw Kant speak of sensation as 'matter' earlier, at the beginning of the 'Transcendental Aesthetic'. Sensation, moreover, is chiefly characterised by quality: the colour blue, the sound of a flute playing a high C, the coolness of water in a lake. If we use the term 'anticipation' to designate any a priori cognition of what is or can be encountered empirically, then Kant's question is: what anticipations can be made concerning sensation? The answer is: absolutely nothing, since sensation is precisely what distinguishes that which is empirical. However, the answer is different if we focus not on sensations as particular qualities but on 'sensation as such' (A167=B209). Kant finds, rather to his surprise, that sensation as such can be 'anticipated', that is to say, has an a priori principle through which it is made possible. Still more surprising, perhaps, is that the principle corresponding to the category heading of Quality should be about quantity. The principle corresponding to this heading is 'In all appearances the real that is an object of sensation has intensive magnitude, i.e. a degree' (B207).

Sensation is our sense being affected; sensation is of the (empirically or phenomenally) real. This corresponds to the brief discussion at the end of the 'Schematism': the schema of the real is the presence of sensation. Sensation occurs in a moment, although it may also occur over time (be sustained). So it cannot be presented as a quantity by a synthesis of a temporal manifold; that is, as an extensive magnitude. Nevertheless, a given spatial-temporal figure can be filled with sensation, or it can be empty. We can, for example, contemplate a painting (that is in fact filled with colours) just in terms of the shapes it contains and, ultimately, the shape of the frame. This contemplation treats the sensation as null, as if the colour had been 'turned off' and thus literally treating the painting as unreal. By intensive magnitude is meant something that is presented as a simple unity (the quality complete and whole and in a moment), but yet can present a manifold by progressively reducing it towards zero.

The whole treatment of intensive magnitude takes place at the level of empirical consciousness – that is, at the 'naive' level where we are embodied, sensible beings being affected by a universe of material things – and is only incidentally concerned (as the previous section was) with the transcendental constitution of appearances. This passage thus appears rather atypical of Kant. This is because the notion of sensation already has built into it, so to speak, a certain idealism. Kant had to provide arguments in the 'Transcendental Aesthetic' that space and time are forms of our sensibility and thus are empirically real but transcendentally ideal. Few philosophers, however, would argue that the colour blue is anything but an effect of something (something that in itself is quite different from blue) on our eyes. That is, no one confuses sensations with things in themselves (although one can certainly focus on sensations as themselves types of objects). Accordingly, there is no need to provide a transcendental account of sensation becoming presented as phenomenon, in order to critically limit metaphysical claims about 'sensation in itself'.

Now, in the previous section on extensive magnitude, Kant proved the principle in question by reference back to the necessity of synthesis in all presentation, and specifically to the synthetic production of space and time as homogeneous dimensions of presentation. That is, the principle that all intuitions have extensive magnitudes is proved by the fact that extensive magnitudes are 'already' involved in the possibility of the experience of anything in space and time. Here, though, such argument is missing. Instead, the argument turns on the *possibility* of a synthesis, by which the given sensation would be reduced to zero (or, presumably, increased from zero to its givenness, or higher). Perhaps, working a little against the grain of Kant's presentation, it is the fact that we are never without this possibility that serves as the transcendental demonstration of the validity of the principle. In other words, the *necessity of the possibility of* progressively 'tuning out' sensation, and of consciously focusing on formal structures in space and time, is the experience made possible by the principle of intensive magnitudes. If, the argument runs, sensations were not intensive magnitudes then it would not always be possible to move from 'empirical' to 'pure' consciousness. Kant's argument hinges on whether we accept this move as itself involving a change of degree.

It is worth pointing out that the measure of intensity was a hugely important practical problem within eighteenth-century physics. Astronomers hunted for techniques of measuring the brightness of stars without relying upon subjective assessments such as 'that looks about as bright as that other one'. The mercury thermometer was only recently invented and in wide use. And Kant himself here raises the more theoretical problem of whether the specific gravity of things (that is, the intensity represented by the mass of something per unit volume) varies because the underlying types of matter in fact have variable specific gravities, or whether it is because a uniform type of matter is spread more or less thinly throughout the volume. In the former case, specific gravity would be an intensive magnitude, in the latter it would be extensive but masquerading as intensive. Kant's work here is not by any means meant to be a contribution to this whole domain of research. Rather, Kant is concerned to open the mere possibility that there might be intensities of the real, along specific dimensions such as luminosity or specific gravity.

The First Analogy of Experience
The 'Analogies of Experience' investigate those principles corresponding to the three categories of relation. The first analogy concerns substance; the second, causation; the third, interaction. As stated above, here we will deal briefly with the first, at greater length with the second, and skip the third. This is because although the arguments Kant gives are different, the type of argument and the kinds of basic moves he makes are very similar throughout. The same holds for a passage Kant added to the end of the 'Analytic of Principles' in the second edition, the 'Refutation of Idealism'. When we look at this passage, we will quickly see its close relation to kinds of arguments in the analogies, and especially the first analogy.

But first of all, why are they called 'Analogies' at all? (This whole discussion takes place at A178–80=B220–3.) An analogy is when we say that a relation between a first pair of things has structural similarities with a relation between a second pair of things. So, here Kant is claiming that these principles (for example, of cause and effect) govern the relations between objects or events according to an analogy with the way logic governs the relations between concepts in a relational proposition. 'If A then B' expresses a relation of logical consequence between A and B. 'Alcohol causes drunkenness' expresses an analogous relation of causation. Kant calls the 'Analogies' 'dynamical' principles because they concern relations between things, rather than 'mathematical' principles that concern, and constitute, the structure of empirical intuition. Kant's proofs here all involve the notion of *order of succession in time*. Now, this should not surprise us: first, because Leibniz made spatial and temporal relations matters of order; also, Hume saw that one of the principal ingredients of making sense of our experience was order. Second, because we saw just above that time is the universal 'medium' of synthesis. And finally, because in the 'Schematism', *time order* was the schema of the categories of relation.

Some commentators see the 'Principles', and especially the 'Analogies', as directly continuing the work of the 'Deduction', but with greater specificity. Strawson, for example, views the 'Analogies' in this way. In addition, he is concerned to defend them against historicising accounts that see the 'Analogies' as only relating to a particular eighteenth- and nineteenth-century concept of physics; rather Kant's point must be to work out the ahistorical conditions of any objective experience. Allison, too, wants to treat the 'Analogies' as a whole, arguing that only together do they provide a defensible position on time-determination (Allison 2004, 229). Guyer goes further; in his interpretation of the 'Analogies', we need to start by skipping over them to the 'Refutation of Idealism', where the notion is found that no time sequence, even the merely subjective, is given passively. Only this idea rescues the 'Analogies' from the standard objections to them (we will bring up some of these standard objections later). As a whole, the 'Analogies' are not concerned with arguing for the necessity of principles for ordering or measuring objects and events; rather, they are necessary for determining that our subjectively fleeting presentations stand for any objects at all (Guyer 1987, 207–9).

Considering the importance attached to them by recent philosophers, it is surprising that Kant's treatments of the three 'Analogies' are so brief. The proof and discussion of the principle of substance is only about five pages long; for Kant, that is little more than a footnote. The statement of the principle was rewritten for the second edition, and Kant replaced the first five lines with a new first paragraph. But the clearest statement of the principle at issue is in a parenthetical comment at the beginning of the second 'Analogy': 'All variation (succession) on the part of appearances is only change' (B233). By variation [*Wechsel*] he means that some accident of substance goes out of, or comes into, existence; variation only concerns accidents. By change [*Veränderung*] he means that a substance will now have one accident, and now another; it is substance that changes. A substance, Kant is trying to demonstrate, is the permanent. The particular ways in which that substance exists (that is, the phenomenal properties it exhibits and which can vary) are called 'accidents'. Our discussion here will distinguish three arguments (although they may in fact be variations on just one), which we will call the 'time substrate argument', the 'duration argument' and the '*ex nihilo* argument'.

Time substrate argument. This argument is found several times, for example, in the new first paragraph (B224–5), and at A183=B226. Things in time may change, but time itself does not change. If it did, then, first, we would have to posit another time 'behind' it as the condition of the presentation of the change in time; and, second, we could not experience ordinary changes, since the succession of changes requires an enduring time as its condition of presentation. Moreover, time itself cannot be perceived – that is, my experience is always of a time determination attaching to an object or event. (These two premises show up frequently throughout the 'Analogies' and the 'Refutation of Idealism'.) So, the enduring of time as such is not directly presented in experience, and yet this enduring must be presented if the succession of changes is to be experienced; that is, if it is to be possible to determine time. That in appearance which is the presentation of the enduringness of time, and which is the substrate of time determination, we call 'substance'.

The duration argument. This argument is found at A183=B226–7. Time is the form of experiences insofar as we can say they are successive. Some successive things are experienced as having a type of magnitude: duration. But, 'in mere succession by itself existence is always vanishing and starting, and never has the least magnitude' (A182=B225). As we discussed in the 'Deduction', the manifold itself does not and cannot contain combination. Only insofar as there is something in appearances that is permanent is it possible for duration to be presented. This permanent in appearance cannot be time, but must be 'the object itself, i.e. the (phenomenal) substance' (A183=B227).

The ex nihilo *argument. Ex nihilo nihil fit*, out of nothing comes nothing, is a classic metaphysical proposition to which Kant refers at A185=B228. The argument concerning substance is a bit later at A188=B231. Now, obviously, things appear to come and go from existence. Let us say I buy a new car, which officially came into existence on 1 May. The substance (the enduring substrate) has changed. The particular manner of its existence, which for a time will be this car, has varied – indeed, it has popped into being. Kant's argument here is a *reductio ad absurdum*. I hypothesise the only alternative to the claim I am trying to prove, and then show that this hypothesis leads to a contradiction; this proves my claim. So, Kant hypothesises that there is no permanent substance; this would be equivalent to saying that there is no real difference between change and variation. Kant argues as follows:

> Suppose that something absolutely begins to be. If you suppose this, then you must have a point of time in which it was not. But to what will you fasten this point of time, if not to what is already there? For an empty time that would precede is not an object of perception. (A188=B231)

This is clear enough though still cryptic. Recall that time itself is not an object of our experience; we only experience things as having time determinations. The time before the 'absolutely' new thing would however be empty of things; nothing would be there that would be able to carry a time determination. However, perhaps the previous point in time was not empty, things were there to bear time determinations, but just not this new thing. Kant's argument accordingly continues: 'If some substances arose and others passed away, this would itself annul the sole condition of the empirical unity of time; and appearances would then refer to two different times wherein existence would be flowing by concurrently – which is absurd' (A188=B231–2). Kant is here assuming substance against his hypothesis. He should have written 'If some things arose absolutely, and others passed away absolutely'. One time would be that time the determination of which was grounded upon substance A; the other time, substance B. It is absurd because two 'concurrent' times would, by that very fact, be located in one time. Kant's arguments prove the hypothesis (that there are no permanent substances) false and thus prove his claim that substance exists and does so as the permanent substrate of time determination in appearance.

On Strawson's reading of the 'First Analogy', Kant's move is from the need for a permanent background, to a substance characterised by a fixed quanta. This move is historically contingent to a Newtonian conception of the principle of conservation of matter. Strawson thus argues Kant's principle is defensible only if it is taken to prove that some objects must be perceived as permanent, but not the principle of absolute permanence (Strawson 1966, 128–9). Bennett argues that Kant should have distinguished between two meanings of 'substance'. First, what he calls S1, substance as a thing which has qualities; second, S2, substance as a thing which can neither arise nor be destroyed. According to Bennett, the second meaning of substance can be dispensed with. Our use of the concept of substance is pragmatic; a thing is said to be substance insofar as it lasts long enough for its qualities to be 'useful' for a certain cognitive purpose (Bennett 1966, 181–99). Allison claims that Kant, in the 'First Analogy', should not be understood as primarily concerned with the conservation matter (this Kant deals with in *The Metaphysical Foundations of Natural Science*); here, rather, the concern is with absolute persistence. Allison then defends Kant's argument for substance in its 'full blown ontological sense' of absolute permanence, against those (such as Strawson and Bennett above) who believe a relative permanence suffices (Allison 2004, 236–46). Guyer argues that Kant's argument here has nothing to do with the measurement of duration of substances, but rather concerns the presentation of the permanent duration of time itself; however, he believes that little sense can be made of this notion. Guyer's argument here is based upon an analysis of the pragmatics of the use of 'overlapping' clocks. Kant does succeed in showing that I could never have adequate empirical evidence of the annihilation of a thing; but this does not lead to a metaphysical thesis about substance. Rather, it leads to a conception of substance as a regulative notion. What is substance is not given in perception nor absolutely determined metaphysically; rather what is assumed to endure is the object of current theory and subject to revision (Guyer 1987, 207–34).

The Second Analogy of Experience

The text of the 'Second Analogy' falls roughly into four parts. First, a series of proofs, with variations and discussions, of the main thesis of the section. This takes us up to A202=B247. Second, the discussion of the case of simultaneous (or near-simultaneous) causation (A202–4=B247–9). This leads, third, onto a treatment of the concept of the action of a substance, which continues until A207=B252. Then, from this analysis of action, Kant derives the law of the continuity of change, which takes us to the end of the 'Second Analogy'. Here, we will discuss only the first and second of these parts.

Notice that Kant rewrites the principle of causation for the second edition. The second edition also adds two new paragraphs to the beginning of the section. Originally, he wrote 'Principle of Production. Everything that occurs (i.e. starts to be) presupposes something that it succeeds *according to a rule*' (A189). In the second edition, this changes to 'Principle of the Temporal Succession According to the Law of Causality. All changes occur according to the law of the connection of cause and effect' (B232). The new version drops the language of 'starts to be' in favour of 'change'. This is explained in the first of the new paragraphs. Substance changes, meaning that its *properties* change, but substance itself does not come into or out of being. This new version allows Kant to bring the language he uses in the first two 'Analogies' closer together. The new version of the principle also replaces the 'rule' with the 'law of causality'. This is to stress that it is not just any rule, in particular any *empirical* rule, that is at stake.

According to the 'Supreme Principle', the possibility of objects is also the possibility of experience. Here in treating causality, Kant will give us a very clear guide to what that supreme principle means. He invites us to consider a series of presentations of objects or events, spread out in time. Now, sometimes these series have an arbitrary order to them, as in Kant's own example of looking at a house. I could look at the roof first, then the door, then the window; or any other order. The order has nothing to do with the house as an object. Other times, the order does concern the object, as in the example of a boat floating down river. The order of events – first I see the boat up here, and then down there – is necessary. If things *did not* happen in that order, then it *could not* be a boat floating down river. The key question is, how am I able to distinguish between the two cases (house and boat)?

One obvious answer would be that we compare the order in which we experience things (subjective order) to the order in which they really happen (objective order). This comparison reveals which experiences are only subjective in their order, and which ones are objective. But this answer will not do. We know, transcendentally, it is inappropriate to talk about 1. an object existing separately from me, and then also 2. the presentation of that object to me. This would be a kind of naive realism. The fact that such a realism is valid empirically is an effect of the transcendental constitution of knowledge. For Kant, speaking transcendentally, the presentation *is the object*, and what it is 'in itself' is an unanswerable (and here irrelevant) question. So, the above 'obvious' answer misses the point. The real issue is how, transcendentally, we come to be able to distinguish empirically between these two orders in the first place.

Analogously, we can think of the manifold of presentation as 'flat'. It has no depth, nothing behind it; or, at least, it has no depth that is relevant to our experience and knowledge. One result of the 'Transcendental Deduction' – drawn to our attention by the 'Supreme Principle' – was that only through the work of categorical synthesis does this flat manifold come to have the *appearance of depth*. Saying that a presentation is 'of' an object, then, is saying something about the presentation itself, rather than about something beyond or outside the presentation. Specifically here, Kant insists, it can only be saying that the order is necessary according to the relation of cause and effect. It is because the water causes the boat to move that the boat example is objective order; it is because nothing in the house causes my experience of it to happen this way rather than that, that the house example is of subjective order. (Of course, the order of perception of the house *is* caused, by the muscles in my eyes turning them up then down. But that causation is not *in the house*. Thus, the presentation of the house to that extent is indeed a subjective order.)

Sometimes, to be sure, the sequence of events is not spread out conveniently in time but 'vanishingly brief' or even simultaneous (A203=B248). Kant's example is a lead ball resting on, and making an indentation in, a cushion. The lead ball causes the indentation, even though the events of 1. resting on and 2. indentation happen at the same time. This is not a problem, Kant insists. We are concerned with time *order*, not time *lapse*, and the order still has only one objective determination (the indentation does not cause the appearance of the ball). The problem becomes more complicated, however, when we notice that the ball is causing the indentation and the cushion is causing the ball to stop descending. That is, the causation is simultaneously *reciprocal*. This will be the case in instances of mechanical causation, as Newton described with the third law of motion. Kant topic is just such reciprocal causation in the third 'Analogy'.

Let us reconstruct Kant's argument out of the various versions presented in the first part of the section, and bearing in mind that one of his chief objectives here is to argue against Hume. Hume, a radical empiricist, famously claimed that we have no concept of causation. Instead, we have habits instilled in us by the contingent regularity of our experience, and we sometimes illegitimately claim that this regularity is necessary. Kant's argument thus looks something like the following.

1. Time itself cannot be perceived, for it is the form of intuition. That is, we perceive things in time, not time itself. (Or, time is not an 'absolute', A200=B245.)

2. My presentation of two non-simultaneous events, A and B, is encountered as being in a certain order. Let us say A followed by B, or A–B.

3. There may be a difference, empirically, between the order of my experience and the order of the events themselves. This is the difference between objective and subjective order or 'succession'. If A–B is merely subjective, then the objective order might be B–A.

4. If time itself could be perceived, then objective order could be immediately established (if events, so to speak, carried their dates with them as inner properties). But time itself cannot be perceived.

5. To be able to decide the objective order would mean to have some determination of the events in their temporal order. In our experience of order it is always in principle possible (and usually in practice too) to determine this difference as an object of knowledge. No one, not even Hume, has tried to deny that we *appear* to have something that we call knowledge of causation. In this connection, Kant writes, 'this to be sure no one will grant' (A190=B235–6). This 'knowledge' (whether apparent or real) is a phenomenon that needs accounting for.

6. Such a determination will be either directly a causal rule (A causes B, therefore A–B) or indirectly (A and B are related causally to

some third event C, which may in fact be my perception of them, and thus A–B). What we just called the *indirect* rule of cause is meant to answer an objection from Schopenhauer that there are necessary orders that are not causal (for instance, night following day); we are replying, on Kant's behalf, that all such instances will be indirect causal ordering. Thus experience of objective order always depends upon some knowledge of causation.

7. The empirically obvious difference between my subjective presentations and the object is not transcendentally original. Objective order is a claim about the presentations and not about something separate or beyond them. The possibility of talking about an objective order is constituted by the employment of the law of causation. Since the 'object' is not a thing in itself, the necessary subjection of the manifold of appearance to rules is precisely what is meant by an 'object' in experience (A197=B242–3).

8. The causal rule will be 'necessary' in several senses. For example, all other things being equal, the same order must occur at other times and places; if the order does not occur, that must be because a different causal rule has superseded it; and the objective order is cognised as strictly observer-independent.

9. Such particular causal knowledge will be at least partly empirical. (For Kant all knowledge that some actual type of thing A actually causes B will be empirical; but the necessity of their being such knowledge, the necessity carried by such knowledge, and the account of what is meant by such knowledge, are all transcendental knowledge.) Let us however form with Hume the hypothesis not only that such 'knowledge' is *in every case* empirical, but also that it is not knowledge strictly speaking but rather a habit formed by individual perceptions of contingently invariant temporal patterns. (The objection immediately arises that such empirical causal knowledge will not have the requisite necessity (step 8 above). Hume knew this, and that is why he claimed that, in fact, there is no idea of causation other than the habit itself. Accordingly, he says there is no causal knowledge *per se*.)

10. But we have two orders (subjective and objective). Which order would be taken as the invariant temporal pattern, upon the basis of which I form my habits? If the subjective, then the knowledge will not be of the objective world, and will thus not be very useful. If the objective, then by virtue of the argument above, some causal knowledge will

already be assumed. In either case our Humean hypothesis fails to account for causal knowledge, *or even the possibility of a useful psychological habit.* That is to say, following Hume, we cannot even distinguish between order in the object and order in the subject. Thus, says Kant, we would have a mere 'rhapsody' or 'play' of presentations (A194=B239).

11. This a priori principle of causation is what makes it possible for us to learn empirical laws of causation through experience, insofar as it makes possible the experience of a determinate temporal order. This a priori knowledge of causation will be equivalent to a universal assertion of the real empirical difference between subjective (arbitrary or indifferent) and objective (necessary) succession, and that this difference is a possible object of knowledge. That is, for every sequence of presentations, we can become conscious of it only insofar as there is an order by virtue of which we can say it is a presentation of an object, and this order is, in principle and in all cases, determinable and necessary according to a rule (which we call a causal rule).

Among the many highly significant implications of this section, let us single out the notion of truth. At A191=B236, Kant is discussing how the combination of the manifold according to a rule produces the empirical appearance of the object and thus also the *difference between* presentation and object. Kant writes, 'We soon see that, since agreement of cognition with the object is truth, the question [of how cognition and object come to be different so that they could, later and empirically, come to agree] can only be inquiring after the formal conditions of empirical truth' (A191=B236). Empirically, then, Kant is broadly speaking a realist holding an adequation theory of truth; much more interesting and important to him, though, is the transcendental constitution of the possibility of this realism.

In a manner that is similar to his account of the 'First Analogy', Strawson argues here that Kant has confused a conceptual with a causal notion of necessary connection. Experience requires connection – a background of regularity – but does not require a notion of necessary and universal causal laws (Strawson 1966, 133–46). Bennett argues similarly that there must be a minimum degree of temporal order so that there can be objective experience, but that our overall experience would not be threatened by 'occasional flurries of disorder'. Bennett accuses Kant of a *non-sequitur*: If XY could not have occurred in the order YX, then (to be sure) they had to happen in order XY, but this does not entail that 'given X happened, Y had to happen'. That is, it does not entail a necessary causal connection. For Bennett the problem of temporal order is not about a distinction between subjective and objective order, but rather the establishment of one's subjective temporal story. I require a causal law to establish the temporal order of my memories (Bennett 1966, 219–26). Guyer sees the 'Second Analogy' as having a double purpose: first, to replace a rationalist derivation of the principle of sufficient reason on the basis of logic; second, to refute Hume's scepticism. The key to interpreting this passage correctly, Guyer claims, is to see Kant not as providing 'a psychological model of the generation of beliefs, but an epistemological model of the the confirmation of beliefs' (Guyer 1987, 258). For Allison, what is at stake here as in the other two 'Analogies' is the conditions of possibility of the perception of an event (the coming to be or cessation of some determination of an object). Kant's argument moves from an analysis of event-perception back to its conditions of possibility; it does not assume a (transcendental or empirical) realist ontology of objects, and then seek to understand how these can be cognised. In this interpretation, these conditions first make possible any thought of an object (Allison 2004, 246–52).

The Refutation of Idealism

In the second edition, Kant adds a short section (B274–9) near the end of his presentation of the principles. This is the 'Refutation of Idealism' and it has become one of the most famous passages in the book. After the *Critique of Pure Reason* was published in 1781, Kant was attacked or dismissed as an immaterialist, like Berkeley. Berkeley's idealism was complete: there are ideas, and the notion of material things to which the ideas 'refer' is absurd.

The 'Refutation' is inserted into the end of the 'Postulates of Empirical Thought as Such'. Here Kant is discussing the synthetic a priori principles that are based upon the categories of *modality*: possibility, actuality, necessity. These categories have a special role within thought: they do not say anything about objects, but only about the manner in which judgements about these objects are asserted. For example, 'It might rain tomorrow' would normally have to be asserted in the mode of the possible; 'it is raining' normally in the mode of the actual. Something is 'actual', Kant argues, if it is materially given in sensation. But, if I dream of a chair, is my sensation of it any less actual? For this reason, Kant goes on: something is actual if, first, either it is given in sensation, or its material actuality can be inferred from some other actuality by way of the laws of the empirical world (e.g. cause and effect); *and*, second, its actuality 'coheres' with what we know of other existences and the laws that govern them. The dream does not 'cohere' in this manner, and so we can (belatedly perhaps, upon waking and reflecting) judge it to be 'only a dream'. The problem is that some idealists deny the possibility of inferring the existence of an actuality in this way. Let us call 'idealism' any philosophy that claims that knowledge of the existence or nature of things outside the mind is either nonsense, or at least is always subsequent and subordinated to the existence of ideas within the mind. This covers a wide variety of philosophies, from Plato on. Hume, Berkeley and Descartes, for example, in their different ways, deny the inferences Kant is talking of.

For Hume the sceptical empiricist, the 'laws of nature' are at best descriptive of how my presentations behave, and thus cannot authorise the above inference. Thus, there is no certain knowledge to be had of whether my sensations have to relate to something empirically actual outside of me; presentations exhibit no *internal* difference between waking and dreaming, shall we say. One would only find this situation troubling, Hume thought, if one did not know how knowledge worked. Now, we have seen that for Kant the notion of a thorough-going connection and coherence of my experience is not only possible but necessary. Thus, Kant's problem with idealism cannot be that attentive readers conflate him with Hume (not *here*, anyway; things may look different in the 'Transcendental Dialectic').

A different problem (Kant calls it 'material idealism' B274) arises via Descartes and Berkeley. For Descartes, prior to the discovery within me of the idea of God and the implications of that discovery, the actuality of sensations and thus too of any inferences involving actual sensations are one of the first things to be subjected to doubt. Berkeley, on the other hand, denies the intelligibility of the claim that ideas 'stand for' anything outside me. Matter, for Berkeley, is just an absurdity; there are only ideas. As we have just been reminded in the 'Second Analogy', Kant does argue that the distinction between presentations and their objects is an *effect* and not something originally given. So, is it the case that, for Kant, we just have presentations that behave according to laws (ultimately traced back to the categories), but cannot be known to stand for anything empirically real separate from my mind? If so, Kant would have failed to distinguish his position sufficiently from material idealism. (The reader should also look at Kant's note to the B-Preface, Bxxxix, where Kant further contextualises and discusses his 'Refutation'. It is here that he famously calls our inability to prove the existence of an external world the 'scandal' of philosophy and human reason itself.) However, this is clearly not a Kantian position. Several times now we have observed that, at a level of reflection he often calls 'empirical', Kant is a realist. Berkeley, Kant thinks, is an easy target here. If we consider space to be a property of things in themselves, then to be sure nonsense arises and material idealism starts to look attractive. Calling him a 'dogmatic' idealist, Kant accordingly claims Berkeley is refuted as soon as one accepts the transcendental ideality of space.

Kant describes himself as a 'transcendental idealist'. Kant has no problem with idealism in general, then, either. What Kant is trying to supply is a once-and-for-all counter-argument to what he calls 'problematic idealism', particularly that of Descartes. Kant's refutation will be a proof of this theorem: 'The mere, but empirically determined, consciousness of my own existence proves the existence of objects in space outside me.' If this theorem were true, then Descartes's separation between certainty within the self and doubt of the apparently external cannot be maintained. Here, we change Kant's order a bit and start with 'comment 2'.

Everything which exists as a possible object of cognition must exist as determinable in time. Time is the universal form of intuition, and existence must show itself in time if we are to be able to form inferences about it on the basis of other knowledge about the world. It makes no sense to say that something does exist, but at no point in time. Certainly, it makes no sense to say that I exist as a mind that can determine other things in time (for example, employing causal rules), but that I am indeterminate myself. I need to be able to say 'now', 'then' and 'later' to myself. A determinate position in time is part of what we mean when we say that something really exists, rather than is imaginary. But, determination of location in time requires the 'background' of something permanent. Every temporal determination of a *change* or a *motion* is possible only on the basis of something that has not moved. (Analogously, clock hands require a clock face, or at least something else to orient against, if they are to have meaning.) Now, that something permanent might be the self as a substance. However, Kant insists, the 'I think' is not an intuition of myself as I am in myself. Again, as so often, Kant agrees with Hume: we have no direct apprehension of ourselves as substantial, and thus no knowledge. Like any other intuition, the intuition of 'I' is a presentation under the form of time, and not a direct access to the thing in itself. (Indeed, Kant claims that the 'I' is not even that much, but only an intellectual presentation of my activity.) All Kant needs here is the negative point: that there is no intuition of the self as of a permanent substance underlying all my thought. If there *were* such an intuition, then we would be straight back to Descartes. However, it is well worth asking why the principle of the 'First Analogy' is not applicable here: there, too, substance is not something that can be directly intuited; it is rather constructed synthetically according to a principle. Kant, here, seems to be saying that such a presentation cannot happen on the basis of *inner sense alone*. Kant's reasoning would appear to be similar here to the reasoning in what we called the 'duration argument' above in the 'First Analogy of Experience'. This turns out to be the key move.

Since I have no intuition of myself as substance, the permanent background must be supplied from elsewhere. But also I cannot intuit time itself, Kant says. That is, time is not given as a fixed 'visible' framework within which things are in each case given along with their temporal locations. (Kant relied upon this idea in the proof of the 'Analogies' also.) And again, it cannot be a permanent *presentation*, because such a presentation could only be judged by virtue of something permanent outside it; thus, the permanent must rather be something permanent to which presentation refers. So, what is the source of this permanence? The only intuition that can fulfil this requirement is the intuition of an actual permanent something outside me. The permanence is not, of course, discovered there; it is presupposed a priori according to the category of substance, and then *found in* material objects insofar as these are presented through synthetic acts. The fact that my consciousness, empirically speaking, is itself something real and determined in time, is conditioned by the existence of real things outside of me. If I am empirically conscious at all, the external world must actually exist.

Kant calls the world outside me 'appearance' or 'phenomenon' – but, as we have had to remind ourselves several times, this does not mean 'illusion'. What appears empirically to me really exists, as material substance. Transcendentally, Kant is an idealist since he argues that the forms of intuition and the categories make it possible for a world to be presented in the first place. Even the permanence of the permanent, and its difference from presentation, are presupposed a priori. *Empirically*, however, Kant is a realist: real things are really out there, and we can have real knowledge of them. Moreover, the self as not just a mere consciousness but as able to cognise itself does not exist prior to its experiences of the world, does not stand outside that world 'making it possible'. Rather, the empirical self and its world come into being at the same time. *Consciousness and the objects of consciousness arise at the same time and through the same set of synthetic acts.* This is one of the interpretations we gave in the B-Preface of the Copernican revolution. Copernicus provided a kind of co-operative, all-at-the-same-level model of the solar system in which everything moves; so here, discursive cognition is neither an absolute sponteneity of the mind (a radical idealism) nor an equally absolute passivity (empiricism) but a 'cooperative' constitution of both mind and world.

Bennett interprets Kant's 'Refutation' as describing the conditions under which I can trust my memory, because rather than basing an individual judgement about the recollection of the past just on *other* past recollections, I can appeal to a manifold of data concerning something altogether other than memories – that is, present objective states of affairs (Bennett 1966, 203–5). Allison sees the 'Refutation' as a reflection upon what must be required for thinking *res cogitans* (the 'thinking thing' – the term is from Descartes). For one could assume it was simply and directly given, in contract to our inferential knowledge of outer things, only if one confused apperception with inner sense (Allison 2004, 287). Scepticism about outer reality, if we assume a transcendental realism, opens an 'epistemological' gap between the presentation and the purported object; transcendental idealism (with its notion of appearance subject to the forms of sensibility) alone gives us hope of establishing the reality of things separate from the self (Allison 2004, 301). Guyer sees the 'Refutation' as entirely epistemological in character, and neither an empirical nor a transcendental psychology. It establishes that spatiality is the form by which we represent things as ontologically independent from ourselves. A further entailment is that it is epistemologically necessary that our existence is embodied. 'Only as a perceiver of external objects by means of its own physical organism can the empirical self arrive at determinate knowledge of its own mental life' (Guyer 1987, 314).

Phenomena and Noumena

This section ends the 'Analytic of Principles' (and, indeed, the whole 'Analytic of Concepts'). Also, it serves as a transition to the second division of the 'Transcendental Logic', which is the 'Transcendental Dialectic'. (The first division was the 'Transcendental Analytic' which began straight after the 'Aesthetic'.) It begins with a famous florid passage about the secure island of knowledge and the tempting but stormy sea of illusion. This metaphor is a direct continuation of the first sentence of the A-Preface (Avii). Then follows a useful couple of pages of summary of Kant's basic epistemology (up to A246=B303); these are some of the clearest and most straightforward passages in the book. Not only are the categories without 'meaning' or 'sense' when separated from intuition, but so are the principles. On their own, the categories express the mere form of thought and the unity of a manifold in general, but this is in no way the presentation of an object.

Notice first of all that Kant is using the term 'transcendental' in a modified, broader sense here. Previously, the term primarily referred to the conditions of the possibility of experience, which were earlier in the book shown to be legitimate. This was how the term was used in phrases such as 'Transcendental Aesthetic' or 'transcendental knowledge'. Here, though, Kant is using it to mean something different: a use of concepts that need not restrict itself to experience. (The previous usage would be a sub-class of this broader meaning.) Here Kant talks about the attempt to put the categories to transcendental use. That is, to employ the categories to determine objects that are not under the conditions of sensible intuition. As we have known for some time now, this is impossible. Accordingly, Kant writes, 'the pure categories can *never* be of *transcendental* but always only of *empirical* use' (B303).

In this connection, he also writes of the 'transcendental object', a phrase we haven't seen much of since the 'A-Deduction' (see our discussion of A104–5). The transcendental object is the correlate of the unity of apperception (see A105 and A250), it is the 'object as such' without further determination, and without even a determinate reference to the 'kind' of intuition in question (A247=B304). In other words, it is the object projected by the synthetic function of cognition, under the conditions of 'appearance as such' (A253). (This notion should be compared with the passage above on the 'dignity' conferred on something in calling it an 'object', A197=B242.)

The next passage of this section was rewritten entirely for the second edition. Starting at the bottom of A248 and on B305, Kant turns to the distinction between phenomena and noumena. By 'phenomenon' is meant appearance with the emphasis on a synthetically constituted empirical presentation. By 'noumenon', however, is *not* meant the transcendental object, Kant insists. The latter is the object presented as such. However, the former is the presented object considered as a 'being of the understanding' (B306) and that means precisely separated from the conditions of sensible appearance. To be sure, both are 'indeterminate'. The transcendental object is indeterminate because space and time are considered merely as such, in their abstract unity, and not as a determinate shape, duration or sensible content. The transcendental conditions for determination are present, but no determinative judgement has been effected. The noumenon however is indeterminate because these very conditions are taken away.

There is an 'underlying delusion' that is difficult to avoid (B306). Precisely because the categories are separate from pure intuitions, they would seem to have potentially wider application. Moreover, we have used the terms phenomena to distinguish things presented to us from what they are 'in themselves'. From these considerations, the temptation is overwhelming to employ the categories to cognise these things in themselves. This would mean, however, treating the 'wholly indeterminate' concept of a noumenon as if it were, in fact, a fully determinate concept for use in cognition. That is, the delusion consists in failing to recognise the indeterminacy of concepts of noumena.

Again, 'indeterminacy' means wholly lacking in any capacity to determine an object. This delusion is what Kant terms the 'positive' meaning of the term 'noumena' the object of a non-sensible intuition. However, he also admits the legitimacy of a 'negative' meaning: a thing 'insofar as it is not an object of sensible intuition'. This negative meaning is legitimate, not only because it follows straightforwardly from the basic move of critique, which is to reflect upon the conditions of any possible cognition, but also because it usefully serves us as a 'boundary concept'. That is, it serves to warn us of when metaphysical nonsense is sneaking up on us. It has a legitimate *function*, though to be sure no legitimate *content*.

To understand this, we need to think more about Kant's distinction between sensible intuition (the human way of intuiting) and non-sensible or intellectual intution. We first discussed this problem in our treatment of section 8. Human experience necessarily occurs through sensible intuition; specifically within the forms of space and time. This raises two theoretical possibilities. First, a type of being with a different form of sensible intuition: experiencing in a 'space' or 'time' that are differently structured; this does not seem to interest Kant very much. Second, a type of being with a non-sensible (or 'intellectual' intuition). Although with good reason, theological issues do not impinge much on Kant's epistemology, this being with non-sensible intuition would have to be a creating God. Why? Sensibility is the manner in which we (the type of beings that we are) become affected. In our everyday empirical or phenomenal world, we generally think of ourselves as affected by that which is outside us – or indeed, as we have seen, affected by ourselves (what Kant calls 'inner sense'). With respect to this affection the sensible being is always, in part at least, *passive*. The affection could not happen without the prior and independent existence of something that is acting upon us. That is, again speaking empirically or phenomenally, if I smell something it is because there is something that is producing a smell. Even an hallucination is partly passive insofar as it is a form of self-affection. Now, transcendentally, we know that the mind is active in the constitution of any experience, even an elementary one such as smell. The smell has a place in space and time, and in the same act it is constituted as an object for me through judgement and ultimately categorial judgements (principles). Nevertheless, this activity always has some kind of relation to something other than itself (what Kant in the 'Transcendental Aesthetic' called the 'matter' of sensation). With respect to this 'other', it understands itself to be passive. Thus, the very beginning of the B-Introduction states famously that all cognition and knowledge begins with experience, but does not necessary come from experience (B1). We need to be quite cautious in formulating this passivity and this 'other', of course. Empirically or phenomenally, as we have noted, a common sense realism will not lead one too far astray: we generally understand ourselves as being affected through our organs of sense by some object outside us. But to speak transcendentally of the 'object' prior to the constitution of the object is just nonsense. Indeed, even the 'matter' of sensation is constituted through transcendental activity, given intensity and location. Thus, at A253=B309, Kant reminds us that the fact that sensibility is affected is by no means the same as an assertion about the *object* that affects it. Through reflection, we can dig into our judgements as far as we like, there will never be anything but constituted objects. Yet the basic passivity of our cognition remains, because it is *sensible*. The problem of affection in Kant is indeed a troubling one.

For a sensible being, then, cognition is not self-initiating. For a being of non-sensible intuition, however, it would be, for it does not rely upon some passivity. Indeed, for a non-sensible or intellectual intuition, cognising an object, and the object existing, would be *identical events*. The mind of God creates and sustains existence. (Metaphysical speculation of this type does no harm so long as we remember, guided by the noumenon in the negative sense, that my concept is entirely indeterminate.) Accordingly, the noumenon in the negative sense is the thought of the necessity of the structure of sensibility in all human cognition. It serves as a boundary concept, warning any line of thought that would seek to dispense with this absolute necessity. The noumenon in the positive sense, then, is not just the object separated from my forms of intuition and concepts; that's only part of it. Rather it is the *object as thought by God in the moment of creation*.

To further pursue this matter, let us appropriate an idea from another book entirely. Not long after completing the second edition of the *Critique of Pure Reason*, Kant wrote the *Critique of Judgement* (often called the *Third Critique*). This book claims to do for the faculty of judgement what the *Critique of Pure Reason* (the *First Critique*) did for the faculties of understanding and theoretical reason. In the earlier work, Kant had claimed that the faculty of judgement was essentially just a mechanism for bringing together sensibility and understanding in order to determine objects (think of the 'supreme principle') and realise the unity of apperception. In short, judgement was in the service of cognition. In the new book, however, Kant claims that judgement has a legislating principle all of its own, and thus there are types of judgement that are not reducible to cognition in this way. Late in the *Third Critique*, Kant is discussing how teleological judgements (judgements that employ the roughly Aristotelian notion of a final cause) are essential to biological science while at the same time are not a part of that science. All of this is just background; here is the important point. Kant makes a distinction between the *intellectus ectypus* and the *intellectus archetypus*, or between an intellect that requires images as opposed to an intellect that deals with originals (*Akademie* V, 405–10). This is another attempt to understand the difference between a cognition condemned to sensibility and a cognition that is intellectual intuition. The passivity (or receptivity) of the sensibility of the *intellectus ectypus* lies in the fact that its intuitions, although singular, are *images*. The terms Kant employs are potentially misleading, for they perhaps make us think of Plato, the original ideas or forms, and the *mimesis* or copy of these forms in apparent things. The danger in this way of thinking is that the two (original and copy) might be construed to be the same kind of object, just as a person and the portrait of them are both physical beings in space and time. (Problems of this type are acknowledged by Plato in his *Parmenides*, and are made much of by Aristotle in the *Metaphysics*. Indeed, we saw Kant struggle with a closely analogous problem in the 'Deductions' and 'Schematism'.) We know this cannot be what Kant has in mind. The image that we work with in cognition can become knowledge only insofar as it is subject to the conditions of possible experience; within sensibility this means space and time. But space and time are entirely relational forms (they are 'extrinsic' in structure; see our discussion in the 'Transcendental Aesthetic', and immediately below in our treatment of the 'Amphiboly of the Concepts of Reflection'). That which is presented in space and time is originally dispersed, the manifold is never in itself combined. Thus, presentations of the sensibility require the supplement of concepts to bring them to unity.

In order to help him to understand the distinction between types of intellect, Kant uses a notion from Leibniz: the 'complete concept'. A complete concept would be a perfect conceptual image of the object, in the sense that every aspect of the object, at every moment of its existence, would be determinately represented in the concept. Leibniz uses this notion to distinguish between finite minds (human beings) who could never have such a concept, and an infinite mind (God) who thinks with nothing but. The implication seems to be that the distinction between human and divine mind is one of *quantity*. God is just (infinitely) smarter. Kant rejects this. An infinitely intelligent and capacious *intellectus ectypus* would still not be an *intellectus archetypus*, because it would still be sensible. It would still be thinking through the detour of sensibility. This detour is structural (above we said 'necessary'), rather than something that could be overcome, even granting an infinite extension of our powers of thinking. An infinitely sophisticated representation is not the same as a thing. The understanding is thus also finite, and requires a supplement. That is, our understanding is 'discursive', and although spontaneous it deals with concepts that are never singular presentations. A concept requires an intuition in order for there to be cognition.

Expressed in the language of the *First Critique*, no study of the phenomenon, no abstraction from it, no reasoning concerning it, would ever yield the first iota of determination to the noumenon. The noumenon is an 'object' for God, and God alone. Thus, again, the positive conception of the noumenon can never yield anything *determinate*, and leads inevitably to metaphysical nonsense. *What* nonsense precisely is the topic of the 'Dialectic', to which we will turn in a moment.

Finite cognition (Kant's *intellectus ectypus*) means: the singularity, wholeness and immediacy of sensibility is only passive or receptive; presentations in sensibility are through and through relations (are extrinsic), and thus even subject to the transcendental synthesis of apprehension are uncombined manifolds that await conceptual unity; the spontaneity of the understanding is only discursive, and thus awaits intuition; cognition is possible *as cognition of appearances* through synthetic acts involving these two 'stems' (A15=B29).

The distinction between phenomena and noumena is one of those 'pivot' points, like the Copernican revolution, at which various commentators' interpretations of what Kant's critical philosophy really means converge or diverge. Strawson interprets Kant's transcendental idealism as positing a supersensible reality of things, neither spatial or temporal, that nevertheless exist in relations of affection. Strawson argues that this notion of affection, in particular, would be nonsensical by Kant's own criteria if employed with respect to supersensible reality. Kant's transcendentally idealist model is a perversion of a different appearance–reality distinction (found for example, in Locke). The latter is a model based upon shared spatial-temporal frameworks and cognitive standards, in which reality is a corrected account of illusion, and thus in which there is no radical dualism of appearance and reality. Strawson argues that Kant should rather be seen as arriving at an epistemological modesty wherein refusing dogmatism does not entail scepticism (Strawson 1966, 38–44, 236–69). Guyer argues that the attempt to read Kant in this epistemologically modest fashion (*à la* Strawson or Bird) is mistaken. Instead, Guyer believes, Kant wants to assert a dogmatic thesis (based, as we saw above, on a theological basis), that talking of the objects that lie outside experience in spatial or temporal terms is simply impossible. Kant wants to degrade ordinary objects to being mere representations of themselves. Guyer argues that Kant fails in this intention.

Allison argues that 'thing in itself' does not mean some special type of thing (for example, a noumenal substance) that would really exist even if there were no sensible beings to cognise them; rather it means the ordinary objects of human experience but considered as they are in themselves. The distinction between the appearing thing and the thing in itself (understood in this 'two-aspect' way) is simply a necessary procedure of transcendental reflection when we seek to avoid a transcendentally realist conception (Allison 2004, 56). The noumenon, on the other hand, is the conceptually determined object of a *non-sensible* intuition (Allison 2004, 58). Allison further interprets the transcendental object as related to what he calls the 'immanentisation' of cognition. What is new in Kant, what follows directly from the Copernican revolution, is the claim that it is impossible for us to stand outside of our presentations and compare them with some transcendental real thing. Instead, philosophy is given the task of identifying and analysing the role of the transcendental conditions of cognition; the transcendental object = x 'points' us to this task (Allison 2004, 60–1).

For other philosophers, this notion of a 'task' would suggest that philosophy requires a specifically *historical* study of the nature of its presentations, including the a priori. Just such a study is undertaken, though in very different ways, by Hegel (*Phenomenology of Spirit*), Nietzsche (in, for example, *The Genealogy of Morality*), Heidegger (in *Being and Time*), Gadamer (in *Truth and Method*) or Foucault (*The Order of Things*).

Appendix: Amphiboly of the Concepts of Reflection

The next section, the 'Amphiboly', was appended by Kant to the end of the 'Analytic'. It is in large part an attack on the basis of Leibniz's metaphysics. Although Leibniz's work predates Kant's critical philosophy by nearly a century, the dominant philosophy in Germany toward the end of the eighteenth century was still within the tradition of thought that he inaugurated. Providing a genuinely fundamental criticism of Leibniz, then, was an important job if Kant was to stake his claim as an original thinker. In this regard, the 'Amphiboly' is a breathtaking *tour de force* of philosophical criticism: Kant claims that the *whole basis of Leibniz's metaphysics* can be discovered in one error: the failure to distinguish between intuitions and concepts. As we have seen before, this distinction is necessary for us to formulate the notion of a sensible intellect: cognition, as discursive, is always subject to the 'detour' of passive sensibility. Without the distinction, one must, Kant believes, either be a naive empiricist for whom all presentations (including concepts) are intuitions; or one must be a Leibnizian, for whom all presentations (including intuitions) are concepts. Kant argues that this led Leibniz to reason from the type of presentation to the type of object presented. That is, Leibniz generates his philosophical conclusions about the nature of substance on the basis of his analysis of the nature of presentation: substance is concept-like.

We will not pursue this attack on Leibniz further, as it would take us too far from Kant's own ideas. However, the criticism of Leibniz is only one of the important things to be found in this passage. Along the way, Kant clarifies the distinction between intuitions and concepts in a very useful way. We must remember that philosophical thought begins with experience which, again, is always synthetic. Philosophy then reflects back upon the transcendental conditions of this experience. We never encounter an intuition as such, separated from all conceptuality, from which we could learn about space or time. Thus the *prima facie* 'empirical reality' of space and time within which space and time are treated as objects. Our knowledge of space and time occur via this transcendental reflection. Likewise, we never encounter a concept separated from all intuition, except within philosophical reflection. Thus, even the categories are 'realised' in sensibility, as Kant said unequivocally in the 'Schematism' (see also A310=B366). The categories as *pure* thought, separated from intuitions, are in this sense derivative or artificial, arriving through philosophical reflection on the conditions of experience. In order for philosophy to begin to discover and investigate the nature of the transcendental conditions of our experience, it must 'first' be able to distinguish between intuitions and concepts in reflection. Accordingly, Kant provides a list of four differences: these are the 'concepts of reflection'. One of these we have already come across earlier in the book. The distinction between the 'intrinsic' and the 'extrinsic' was a notion that Kant employed in the 'Transcendental Aesthetic', B66–7 (see the discussion of the 'Transcendental Aesthetic'). An intuitive presentation is comprised of relations, its determination arrives from beyond itself; a conceptual presentation is 'intrinsic' (although, for all that, discursive), and its determination is understood to be prior to any relations it might enter into with other things. (For a more thorough treatment of the 'Amphiboly' and its implications, please see Burnham 2004, chapter 1.)

Transcendental Logic – Transcendental Dialectic

The book we are reading is called the *Critique of Pure Reason*. So far, however, we have said very little about the faculty or power of reason, instead concentrating on explicating the faculties of sensibility and understanding. What, then, is 'reason'? Kant defines it according to two 'uses' (A299=B355).

First, there is the formal capacity to reach mediated inferences. A mediated inference is basically an inference that does not follow immediately from a given premise. Kant gives two examples starting at A303=B359. The second is easiest: the premise 'All humans are mortal' immediately contains the proposition 'Some humans are mortal'. However, arriving at the proposition that 'All scholars are mortal' is mediated by the requirement of further premises (for example, 'All scholars are humans'). Reason, in this first sense, is what we ordinarily mean in English by 'reasoning'. At A304–5=B360–1, Kant adds two further details to this first, logical sense. Mediated inferences are distinguished by the relation among premises; there are three basic relations, corresponding with the three basic kinds of syllogism. A categorical syllogism ('All humans are mortal; scholars are humans; therefore all scholars are mortal'); a hypothetical syllogism ('If a being is human, then she is mortal; she is a human; therefore she is mortal'); and a disjunctive syllogism ('Either a scholar is a man or woman; she is not a man; therefore she is a woman'). These three types are of importance when Kant turns to the major types of dialectical illusion. Finally, Kant notes that the logical use of reason sets itself a 'task' of reducing 'the great manifold of understanding's cognition to the smallest number of principles (universal conditions)'. That is, reason seeks to discover whether a proposition that has been established concerning a certain type of object (for example, 'All scholars are mortal') cannot by reasoning be seen as conditioned by some other proposition ('All humans are mortal'), and in this way to bring isolated bits of cognition under increasingly unified general conditions. This observation is extremely important in understanding the *second* 'use' of reason.

Reason in the second 'use' is the 'power of principles' (A299=B356); that is, the capacity to arrive at synthetic propositions entirely on the basis of concepts (A301=B357–8). (Principle is thus defined differently from the 'Analytic of Principles'.) Now, the attentive reader will have noticed a problem here: back in the Introduction, was Kant not at pains to argue that synthetic judgements were impossible without *both* concepts *and* intuitions? (Bennett 1974 and Walsh 1975 both consider much of Kant's account of reason a disaster and the above is one key reason.) Indeed, Kant's very next paragraph calls the situation 'preposterous' (A320=B358). Reason, in the second sense, is the power of 'preposterous' principles. (Kant often draws attention to this by an important distinction in terminology. 'Theoretical reason' is reason that deals with issues of knowledge; 'speculative reason' is a subclass that deals with *supposed* knowledge of unconditioned objects.)

How does the first, perfectly legitimate, type of reason fall into the second? As we saw just above, reason in its merely logical use has the 'subjective law' of managing the many materials of the understanding (A306=B362). But this 'law' or 'demand' for unity of principles has nothing to do with objects; it is rather an obvious rule of thumb for good mental housekeeping, and one that reason unfailingly gives to itself. The unity that reason seeks is not a unity of experience. However, this harmless and useful subjective law to seek for every cognition some other or higher condition turns, by an almost imperceptible twist, into a principle: namely, the existence of, 'for understanding's conditioned cognition, the unconditioned whereby the cognition's unity is completed' (A307=B364). *This* principle is indeed synthetic, because it makes a claim about something (the unconditioned or, as we will see in some passages, the totality of conditions) which is not analytically given in its concepts. Kant calls this the supreme principle of reason, and any other principles it gives rise to will be 'transcendent' (A308=B365). 'Transcendent' is meant in a sense related to the use of 'transcendental' in describing the noumenon in the positive sense in the 'Phenomena and Noumena' chapter. However, the transcendental use of the category seemed to be suggested (but only suggested) by the noumenon as an outcome of transcendental reflection upon the conditions of experience: why, it seemed reasonable to ask, should the categories as pure forms of thought and thus as different from sensibility, be nonetheless restricted to sensibility? Here, however, a transcendent principle demands that we 'tear down all those boundary posts [of the limits of experience], and to claim to an entirely new territory that recognises no demarcation at all' (A296=B352). This demand is new: reason is troubled not because it makes slipshod judgements about how to apply categories, which can be easily corrected by careful critical analysis, but because its own principles place upon it the demand that it cease to respect the limits of cognition (see Allison 2004, 328–9). (Kant may not be consistent in the distinction between transcendental and transcendent, however.)

Kant uses the term 'idea' for a concept of reason. The ideas are always of the unconditioned, or the totality of conditions. The idea of the unconditioned is tantamount to the idea of a totality of conditions; the former is the basis of the latter, the latter always entails the former (A322=B379). Kant distinguishes the ideas of reason from the pure concepts of the understanding in the following fashion (A310=B366–7): ideas are inferred from the governing principles and activities of reason, whereas concepts are discovered in reflection upon the conditions of experience. (See also the 'Amphiboly of the Concepts of Reflection', above.) It follows, Kant argues, that by virtue of their origin, the categories have no meaning other than the experiential. Ideas of the unconditioned or the totality of conditions, by contrast, include the whole of experience as a *part* of their purported content. However, they have not the built-in limits that would prevent their extending beyond experience or even, according to reason's principles, demanding that extension. 'By an idea I mean a necessary concept of reason for which no congruent object can be given in the senses' (A327=B383). They are 'necessary' in the sense that they follow inevitably, in the above described manner, from reason's natural and perfectly acceptable function. Reason gives these ideas to itself as part of its necessary functioning. No congruent object can be given in appearance because these ideas are the product of transcendent principles. For these reasons Kant talks about 'illusion' – which as we know is entirely unrelated to 'appearance'. The illusion is that the ideas have been properly arrived at, and the existence and nature of their objects properly inferred. That is, the illusion is that uncritical metaphysics (in the sense Kant attacked in his Prefaces and Introductions) is possible. Kant writes, 'Even the wisest among all human beings cannot detach himself from [the transcendent illusions]; perhaps he can after much effort forestall the error, but he can never fully rid himself of the illusion that incessantly teases and mocks him' (A339=B397). It is the task of the 'Transcendental Dialectic' as a whole to explore these illusions. 'Dialectic' here means a type of reasoning which looks plausible, but which in fact is found to be playing fast and loose with the most basic truths; the term derives from the Aristotelian tradition of understanding the relation between 'science' or philosophy, on the one hand, and rhetoric on the other.

Of what ideas is Kant talking? This is answered in the section 'On Transcendental Ideas'. (Note that despite his own warning, Kant often uses 'transcendental' and 'transcendent' interchangeably.) For each of the three types of syllogisms, there will be a corresponding idea of the unconditioned. For categorical syllogisms, the idea of the unconditioned subject (the 'I', the self); for hypothetical syllogisms, the idea of the unconditioned totality of a series; for disjunctive syllogisms, the idea of unconditioned totality of a system (A323=B379–80). Kant elaborates these further starting at A334=B391. The first is the idea of the self or subject as an absolute unity: the soul. The associated metaphysical illusions are entitled 'transcendental psychology'. The second is the idea of the totality of appearances in space and time: that is, the cosmos, and thus 'transcendental cosmology'. The third is the idea of the condition of the possibility of the existence of all things: God, and thus 'transcendental theology'. To each of these three is dedicated a famous chapter in Book II of the 'Transcendental Dialectic'. The task of each of these three chapters is 1. to examine the origin of each idea in the functions of reason, 2. to identify and subject to critique the illusions to which it gives rise, and 3. not to *cure* us of these illusions, for they are natural and inevitable, but to *neutralise* their effects upon philosophy as far as this is possible. To these three chapters we will now turn.

Roughly, the 'Dialectic' divides into five sections. 1. An introduction of the notion of dialectical illusion and the ideas of reason in general (A293–340=B349–98). We have just finished discussing this. 2–4. A detailed discussion of each of the three general types of illusions, and the problems they get metaphysics into (A341–642=B399–670). 5. In the appendices, a general discussion of the role the ideas have (A642–704=B670–732). The 'role' played by the ideas is, as we shall see, related to the 'subjective law' of reason for managing the multiplicity of knowledge in the understanding. It is important for us to note, right up front, that although the 'Dialectic' is often read as a primarily negative treatment of the illusions of metaphysics, that should be seen as secondary to Kant's main purpose, which is to elaborate a critical theory of the faculty of reason and its principles (Allison makes this point forcefully, see Allison 2004, 308).

Transcendental Dialectic
Book II, Chapter 1 (The Paralogisms)
The 'Paralogisms' are the first (in the order of Kant's presentation) of the three main types of dialectical illusion. (Note that the 'Paralogisms' chapter is one of those that Kant substantially rewrote for the second edition of the *Critique*. We are reading mainly text from

the second edition.) A 'paralogism' is a type of dialectical inference; specifically, a hidden error in the logical form of reasoning. Below, we shall see Kant identifying two basic paralogisms that are in play in this illusion: the error of equivocation, and that of 'begging the question'. The idea in question in this chapter concerns the soul, and through this idea we are purported to have knowledge of the self as if it were a thing in itself – that is, separated from the conditions of sensibility (inner sense) under which alone the self can show itself. Already at B66–9 and again at B157–9, Kant had insisted that we only have an intuited relation to ourselves – as we appear to ourselves under the pure form of time. Separated from this condition of time, the 'I think', or pure self-consciousness, is an empty, formal function that does not contain any information about the underlying self. It is, rather, the vehicle of thoughts (A341=B399), and the 'poorest' of presentations (B408). If, alternatively, I consider a real *instance* of the 'I think' – in the sense of 'I think: my dog is wet' – then the whole thing is empirical, and designates that some judgement has occurred employing concepts and intuitions, subjected to the categories and ultimately to the unity of apperception. The reference of the 'I think' here to the 'I' is under the form of time and occurs through the synthesis of time. We find, then, that we are already familiar from earlier in the book with the basic moves Kant will make in the 'Paralogisms'.

In each paralogism, the first and only premise is the mere 'I think'. Such purported knowledge of the self in itself Kant calls 'rational psychology' (A342=B400). Such a rational psychology makes four types of claims (in accordance with the four-fold division of the table of categories). The most famous of these (and the one that Kant too spends the most time treating) is the claim that the soul is substance (A344=B402). Now, it is normal in commentaries on the 'Paralogisms' to go through each of these four. However, Kant in the second edition spends more time treating them as inter-related. Accordingly, here we will discuss rational psychology as a whole, looking at the various types of errors Kant identifies.

In the end, Kant claims that rational psychology is impossible, although its snares are difficult or even impossible to avoid. Clearly, one of Kant's key philosophical targets here is Descartes, with the latter's famous claims about the self as *res cogitans*: a substance the whole essence of which is to think. Interestingly, Kant's treatment of

Descartes here seems to read the latter's argument as a syllogism arguing from 'I think' to 'I exist'. Descartes himself claims the move is not an inference of this type (second *Objections and Replies*). Nevertheless, this misinterpretation on Kant's part does not necessarily mean that his general accusation of Descartes – that he confuses the function 'I' with the object 'I' – is unsound. The discussion of permanence beginning at B413 should also remind you of the arguments of Plato concerning the immortality of the soul in the *Phaedo*. In fact, Kant has in mind an explicitly Platonic work of the same title by his contemporary, Moses Mendelssohn. The course of the 'Paralogisms' is interrupted by a brief refutation of an argument of Mendelssohn. Because of Kant's focus on the particular claim of the immortality of the soul, commentators such as Ameriks argue that he is forced to overlook more modest versions of rational psychology which do not necessarily fall into the same dialectical traps (Ameriks 1982a, 68).

Kant's arguments against the 'Paralogisms' as a whole take three main forms, which not surprisingly are closely related to each other. The first type of argument is the one we are most familiar with from earlier in the book. This argument he uses four times with respect to each of the paralogisms on B407–9. The paralogisms confuse 1. an analytically true proposition, but one also thereby empty of any determining content, with 2. a synthetic statement about the nature of the soul. The latter is only possible with reference to actual or possible experience – that is, the proposition can only acquire determining content through intuition. The paralogism proceeds, then, either by ignoring Kant's whole account of how cognition can have an object; or by falsely believing that the analytic statement does have determining content. Take for example the fourth paralogism (B409). Here, it is analytically true that my existence is distinguished from other things outside me. That is just what 'other things' means. But the proposition that my existence is also *independent* of things outside me – and thus that I am an immortal soul – is a synthetic proposition.

The second argument is to show that rational psychology confuses the 'I' in the logical sense of an 'absolute subject' of all cognition, on the one hand, with 'I' in the sense of a substantial *object* that exhibits all mental properties, on the other hand (for example, A349–51, or B411–12 and n.). By the former Kant means something that is always in the subject position of a proposition. The former is the notion we talked about in the 'Transcendental Deduction': that the 'I think' should always be possible is a universal demand on or principle of cognition, but is not a *thing* or an *intuition* of a thing. If, empirically speaking, the 'I' has a thing-like character (You can talk about me, I can determine the time and order of my thoughts, etc.), this is because of a transcendental synthetic act that creates the continuity of the 'I'. The 'I' is a necessary and universal synthetic *construction* and not a *basis*. Thus, the 'I' as substantial entity is just a different concept from the former. The argument Kant is criticising has a basic logical error, which is called 'equivocation': the same word is used in two different senses. The type of error in reasoning is similar to: 'All sweet things are edible and contain a lot of sugar. You are a sweetie. Therefore you are edible and contain a lot of sugar.' This second argument reveals a version of what Kant had earlier claimed was the basic dialectical illusion: the move to a totality of conditions or the unconditioned. Here the 'I think' is thought of as *something* unconditioned when it is, rather, a merely *formal* condition. The third argument Kant employs also uncovers this kind of error.

The third type of argument that Kant employs is to show that the move from 'I think' to some claim about what the 'I' is, or how it exists, is to confuse the *condition* of consciousness with an *object* of consciousness (for example, A346=B404). The 'I think' – understood as the principle of apperception – is what makes it possible for there to be any actual (empirical) consciousness. Therefore, any attempt to make the 'I think' an object of consciousness can only do so by first presupposing the 'I think', and thus it begs the question. It is impossible to get 'behind' the 'I think' to ask what it is, in itself, separated from the condition of its presentation (which is, in part, the 'I think' itself). In short, in thinking about the 'I', our thought always arrives 'too late' to capture the 'I' as a pure, unconditioned object (thing in itself).

So the substantiality, permanence, immortality, and so on, of the soul are dialectical propositions that cannot be proved by what Kant generally calls 'theoretical' or 'speculative' reason. (He tends to use the adjective 'speculative' precisely when it is a question of reason positing an unconditioned object; see A634–5=B662–3.) However, it is important to note, such propositions *also cannot be disproved* by this type of reasoning. The existence and nature of the object of the idea is unknowable. Thus, the immortality of the soul, for example, is possible (but not possible in the sense of an object of experience; or, again, not possible as an object for science). This means that speculative reason has two immediate uses with respect to rational psychology: first, as a 'discipline', it serves as a perpetual reminder of the limits of reason (B421; the point is similar to the 'negative' meaning of noumena in the 'Phenomena and Noumena' section). Second, since both sides of a debate in rational psychology are equally untenable, speculative reason provides a battery of weapons against materialists or spiritualists (B424); that is, against dogmatic accounts of the soul that particularly worrying because they have, for example, disturbing *moral* consequences.

However, as we shall see, theoretical reason is not the only, or even the most important, mode of our faculty of reason. Practical reason – Kant's name for the type of reasoning that deals with the basis of, and laws of, morality – is not the same as theoretical reason. Practical reason is concerned with the principles of free action; theoretical reason is concerned with the principles of knowledge. So, there remains the avenue of asking whether the proposition of the soul's immortality might be demonstrable within practical reason, in relation to morality. Kant introduces these new ideas at B424–6. This is indeed what Kant claims later in the *Critique of Pure Reason* (see the 'Canon of Pure Reason'), and in the *Critique of Practical Reason* (the *Second Critique*): moral action contains an implicit faith in the immortality of the soul. We shall see this move from theoretical to practical reason in each of the three chapters.

Book II, Chapter 2 (The Antinomies)
The 'Antinomies' are the second of three 'dialectical' illusions. The 'Antinomies' concern 'cosmological ideas' – about the totality and completeness of the conditions in the synthesis of phenomena. What is distinctive about this set of illusions is that these questions do not give rise to one type of illusory answer, but in each case to *two incompatible answers*. Kant calls this a 'natural antithetic'. Again, there are four of these antinomies. Section II of the 'Antinomies' presents the parallel, contradictory arguments. Sections III and IV of this chapter explain further the relationship between these antinomies and our

ability to reason. Section V says that maybe nothing is wrong with the answers, perhaps it is the *question* that is at fault. Section VI sets up Kant's solution by way of Transcendental Idealism, and in particular that strange consequence of such idealism, the phenomena–noumena distinction. Section VII carries out the solution.

It will be useful here to say a few words about the notion of 'totality' [*Totalität*], especially in distinction to 'whole' [*Ganzes*], because in ordinary language these can be interchangeable. Whole is used in a number of ways, but here are the three most important: first, space and time are said to be wholes; second, individual moments of experience are said to be in relation to the whole of experience; third, a system (of reason, of a science, etc.) is properly a whole. Of course, these are all very different notions; however, in all these cases what is at stake is a structure of the whole being understood to be prior to the parts. In other words, the presentation of the whole is a relation to that which is actually or potentially within it. Wholeness is thus a description of an *inner* structure conceived of as complete and exhaustive. By 'totality of conditions', Kant means the sum of all possible conditions of things, conceived of as given to cognition. Totality is the object of an idea, and is demanded by the principles of reason. It would have to be contrasted with a a limited presentation. The totality of conditions is a description of a (impossible) presentation in terms of its *relation to something outside it* (in this case a lack of relation, since there is no further condition outside it, excepting perhaps the supersensible). Totality is thus a kind of mirror image of a whole. There are many other terms Kant uses that appear to have a related meaning to these two (allness, completeness, sum), but the above discussion will have to suffice.

Here, we will be discussing only the third 'conflict'. In section II, you will read, side by side in parallel columns, two arguments which (Kant claims) are both fully successful in arguing opposite sides of the free will/determinism problem. Kant is claiming that both of these arguments are equally valid, on their own terms. The metaphysical illusion, then, is that one can prove almost anything concerning the unconditioned origin or totality of a series.

At stake for Kant is the ability to understand the following apparent paradox. First, that the world must, here and everywhere, now and always, be subject to the causal laws of phenomena. This we know from the 'Second Analogy of Experience' concerning cause and effect. But, second, *at the same time* certain phenomena must be seen as the effects of human free action (which freedom is defined at minimum as a *freedom from* the laws of phenomena: 'the power to begin a state *on one's own*', A533=B561). This is of course one of the historical problems that, at the beginning of this book, we said were Kant's key philosophical motives. The problem can be understood in two different ways. First, as the problem whether or not *all* events are caused, and *none* are free. Or second, 'whether the disjunctive proposition that "every effect in the world must arise *either* from nature *or* from freedom" is correct, or whether – rather – *both* [sides of this disjunction] can, with one and the same event but in different reference, take place simultaneously' (A536=B564, translation modified). This second version of the problem takes us to the real difficulty, Kant thinks. Kant says, 'What in an object of the sense is not itself appearance I call *intelligible*' (A538=B566). The intelligible object is the object that appears, but not as it appears. Let us hypothesise that this intelligible object might harbour within itself the power (freedom) to be the 'cause' of something without also being part of the phenomenal series of causes and effects. To this extent, this intelligible character of the object is not an 'object' in the ordinary sense, but rather a freely acting 'subject', such as you or I. That is why Kant in this passage uses most consistently the phrase 'intelligible character', rather than 'thing in itself' or 'noumenon' (although these, too, are used). This phrase helps make it clear that he is speaking (at least in the first instance) not of just any object, but of free and thus moral subjects conceived as far as this is possible using the ideas of theoretical reason.

Now, we can consider this intelligible character 'from two sides': on the one hand there are the sensible effects of this causation, but on the other hand its action is merely intelligible. These are not two different things, but the same thing considered under two different aspects: one intelligible, the other phenomenal/empirical. Imagine phenomenal causes and effects laid out across time in a horizontal row: A, B, C, etc. Kant is hypothesising that there might be vertical 'causations' (appearances as the effect of a spontaneity in the noumenon) as well as horizontal ones (the appearance of effect as subject to the law of cause and effect among phenomena). The second type of causation is the only legitimate use of the concept, of course – the use with reference to the noumenon is illegitimate, but is not unintelligible, as a kind of analogy. Kant writes, 'Thus regarding such a subject's power we would frame an empirical as well as an intellectual concept of its causality, these concepts occurring together in one and the same effect' (A538=B566). This is possible precisely because appearances are not things in themselves. What we *mean* in saying that one appearance is the cause of another is that there is a necessity to the rule governing their time-order. Something that exists outside this time-order, then, could have an effect on the time-order without thereby contradicting any determination of this time-order. (Nor of course could it in principle be effected by this time-order.) 'Hence according to its empirical character this subject, as appearance, would be subject to all laws of determination in terms of causal linkage. . . . But according to its intelligible character . . . the same subject would nonetheless have to be pronounced free from any influence of sensibility and determination by appearances' (A540–1=B568–9). Of course, all this demonstrates is that it is *in principle possible* for there to be freedom in the sense of a noumenal 'causality'. Kant has not demonstrated freedom at all – although he goes on to claim that the concept of 'ought' would be unintelligible without the hypothesis of freedom (A547–9=B575–6). Kant will make stronger, but importantly different, claims in the writings on ethics. The mere possibility is enough, however. For it demonstrates that the attempt by reason either to understand the *totality* of the world as entirely determined by causation to the exclusion of freedom, or to exhibit freedom in the world of appearances, must fail. That is, the third 'Antinomy' is a confusion (by reason) of appearance and thing in itself, together with the assumption that the category of causation applies to both indiscriminately. These confusions allow illegitimate antinomic inferences: judgements are made that are, in themselves, illusory because they seem to be experiential in nature, but are only reason whistling in the dark.

A broader version of this solution holds for all four 'Antinomies'. Consider a series of appearances: that is, a series of relations of before and after in time, of enclosure in space, of division or composition of things, or of cause and effect. The major premise of all antinomic inferences is: if some conditioned object within a series is given, then the whole series of conditions must also be given (A497=B525). (This again is the supreme principle of the dialectical use of reason in general, see A308=B365.) For how could any element of the series not be in principle given? To be sure, a moment of time a billion years ago is not, in fact, given to me. But there is nothing *intrinsically* unavailable about it; it is a moment of time like any other. All the elements of a series are of the same type as that which is given. Thus, the major premise appears perfectly true: it seems as though the totality of the world is an appearance just like any particular thing in the world.

However, these series one and all involve time and/or space. These are forms of intuition. They are empirically real (thus the givenness of a conditioned object) but are transcendentally ideal. If it were the case that appearances were things in themselves, then indeed if one element of a series is given, then the whole must be given. But appearances are not things in themselves. As we have seen, appearances in space and time are originally dispersed as relational, or as uncombined manifolds. Thus, the givenness of one element is an *actual* act of cognitive synthesis; the next element in the series is a *possible* act of synthesis. All the elements of the series are not and could never be, as we put it above, 'of the same type' (A499=B527). To be sure, Kant insists, the task of pursuing the regression of conditions is 'assigned' to us by reason (this is a specific application of its 'subjective law') (A498=B526). But the series is given only to the extent that this regression has been pursued (A499=B527). Thus, the whole series is never and could never be given in fact. Speculating about the nature of that whole series has no basis, and thus the quarrel between the two opposing sides equally has no basis. No one wins the debate not because both are right or both are wrong, but because the question itself is nonsensical. Russell makes a famous objection to Kant here, claiming that Kant in conjoining our synthetic apprehension of things and the notion of infinity, is making a basic mistake. Kant's notion of infinity thus is 'infected' with mental attributes and serves as a defective starting point for his arguments (Russell 1914, 160–1). In reply to this, it should be noted that Kant is distinguishing 1. a mathematical or logical notion of infinity from 2. the possibility of the givenness of a totality to a being whose cognition is always synthetic.

This solution works most clearly with respect to the first 'Antinomy', which is about whether space and time are infinite, or finite, in extent. It would make sense to claim that space was *either* infinite or finite only if space were transcendentally real; that is, if it were a thing in itself (A504=B532). Similarly, in the third 'Antinomy', it does not make sense to form an exclusive disjunction and ask whether all *phenomenal* events are caused, or if some *intelligible* events are free, because these are not the same type of thing: phenomena are not things in themselves. Gram argues that the first 'Antinomy' at least can be solved without requiring transcendental idealism as the ground of the solution. He sees it as a linguistic problem, the assumption that the expression 'totality of the world' refers to something; if however 'world' is not referring then the question of its magnitude cannot arise (Gram 1969, 509–12). This does not appear to capture the force of the problem Kant is concerned with, nor the complexity of the notion of world.

Let us think again about the 'subjective' law of reason: reason is not satisfied with a conditioned given, but must strive to pursue the series. This, Kant says, arises entirely properly from the nature of reason's perfectly legitimate activity, but only as a 'regulative' principle of reason (A509=B537). By 'regulative' is meant something about the nature of the relation of the principle to its purported object. This principle assigns a task without anticipating the nature of the object to be found. Kant contrasts this with the dialectical principle (the major premise given above) which is termed 'constitutive' – this principle illegitimately claims in advance the nature of its object (the unconditioned totality) (A509=B537). It claims to 'constitute' the object in advance. The distinction between 'regulative' and 'constitutive' is generalised and elaborated by Kant at the end of the 'Dialectic'.

Book II, Chapter 3 (The Ideal of Pure Reason)

The 'Transcendental Dialectic's third and final major part is called the 'Ideal of Pure Reason'. The first part concerned itself with illegitimate inferences of speculative reason concerning the subject or soul; the second with cosmology. The topic of the third is, essentially, God. Every philosophy student knows that over the centuries many attempts have been made to demonstrate using rational principles the existence of God, where the notion of God is defined as, at least, an all-powerful, necessary, creating Being.

It is often noted that Kant's criticisms of metaphysical arguments tend to focus on traditional metaphysical themes, such as the immortal soul or God. This might be seen as a contingent historical fact, and Kant's attempt to make it architectonically necessary (through the analysis of syllogistic forms, for example) is contrived. Both Bennett (1974, 258) and Strawson (1966, 159–60) complain about this, and thus focus their appreciation on the 'Antinomies', which seem less scholastic. No doubt there is some truth to this claim; Kant is, after all, entering into a debate with his contemporaries. Nevertheless, Allison defends the structure of the 'Dialectic', seeing it as a deeply suggestive account of the rational (rather than merely historical or psychological) grounds of the attempt to think totality (Allison 2004, 321–2).

Traditionally, these arguments are divided into three sorts. First, the ontological argument which, in its most famous expression in St Anselm goes something like this: I have an idea of a being no greater than that which can be conceived; either this being exists or it does not; to exist is greater than to not exist; if the object of my idea did not exist, then it would not be a being no greater than which can be conceived; therefore, this being must exist. The second is the cosmological argument, which occurs in diverse forms (Aquinas alone discussed four, the fifth being a design argument). The most familiar is probably this one: Everything contingent has a cause; if something contingent exists then a whole series of prior causes must exist; either this series runs on infinitely in time, or it has an end; it cannot run on infinitely, otherwise it would not be a whole series; therefore it has an end; the only possible end is a necessary being. The argument continues, Kant believes, in identifying this necessary being as the 'maximally real' being. The third is generally called the argument from design; Kant calls it the 'physicotheological proof' (A620=B648). This argument tries to demonstrate that the order, regularity, beauty and so forth – in short, the designedness – of the universe is impossible to understand without positing a designing creator with both intelligence and power consummate to the infinite cosmos itself. Significantly, there is a fourth argument, introduced in no small part by Kant himself: the moral argument. Here, this fourth gets only oblique mention in the 'Ideal of Pure Reason', because it is an issue within the practical dimension of reason, not the theoretical/speculative. It is treated, instead, first at the very end of the 'Critique of Pure Reason' (see our discussion, below, of the 'Canon of Pure Reason'), then in the *Critique of Practical Reason* and, in still more detail, towards the end of *Critique of Judgement*.

Kant criticises each of these three arguments in turn, and his accounts have been enormously influential. We will be looking at his criticisms, to be sure, although only briefly. We will also spend some time on the 'Ideal' itself; that is, on the rational idea of God. Much of what Kant wants to say about the illegitimacy of the famous proofs is already contained in his account of the ideal.

Kant begins at A567=B595 with a four-way distinction between 'pure concepts', 'conditions of sensibility', 'ideas' and 'ideals'. Most of this is, by now, familiar. Here, Kant is emphasising that the categories reach our experience only by means of the conditions of sensibility (space and time); on their own, they have no real meaning. An idea, however, is still more distanced from 'objective reality' than the categories; it is a notion the object of which could not in principle be presented in space and time at all. Kant is of course referring to the ideas of reason that he discussed in the first two parts of the 'Dialectic'. An 'ideal' is different again: this is an idea, but one whose purported object is an individual, a single thing that would embody the maximum or origin of something. If we have any notion of a God, it will be the object of an *ideal* – an individual being that is a maximum (of power or knowledge, etc.) and an absolute origin (of all creation).

Kant begins section II with a discussion of the meaning of 'determination'. Concepts of all kinds are indeterminate with respect to all properties that are not part of the concept: for example, the concept of a t-shirt in general makes no mention of whether it is blue or not, whether it is size 12, or whatever. But concepts are 'determinable' with respect to their content. This means of every two incompatible sub-concepts, only one can be true: the t-shirt is either made of fabric, or not, and it is the former that is true. (These claims are all part and parcel of what Kant means by discursivity.)

Real things, however, do not have any indeterminate bits. This is part of what we mean when we say 'real thing'. For every possible 'predicate' of the thing, we have to be able to say true or false: this real t-shirt is either blue, or not; it is either a gorilla, or not; it is either cotton or not, and so forth. This raises the possibility of a 'complete concept' (Kant is here using a notion from Leibniz; see also our discussion in the 'Phenomena and Noumena' section). A complete concept is so rich with determinate content for its object that nothing indeterminate is left. Such a concept practically equates to the object. Kant claims this is quite impossible as an ordinary concept. Our ordinary concepts are limited (they are discursive); they determine some content and not others. However, we do have an idea of such a complete concept, the idea of the 'sum of all possibility'. What is this idea like?

Now, if I say that something is 'not an X', then that claim is parasitic upon the notion of X. Negative properties require the possible existence of the positive property. '[N]egations are then nothing but *limits*' (A576=B604) on some prior *total* set of properties. The idea of a 'sum of all possibility' has evolved into the idea of a 'total of reality': 'the entire supply of the material from which all possible predicates of things can be obtained'. In short, an idea of the totality of all possible Xs. Kant then argues that this notion is not, in fact, an idea – but an ideal. That is, the notion of a single and separate individual that is ground of all possible positive properties. If it existed, it has to be a single entity: if there were more than one such, then it would not be the origin of all possible properties. As it is expressed later on: 'the total without limits is absolute unity and carries with it the concept of a being that is single' (A587=B615).

Of course, we are not saying that there actually is something corresponding to this ideal. All we are saying is that, to understand how it is that all real things can be fully determined, we need to think about the sum total of all the properties of real things. Kant writes: 'All manifoldness of things is only a way . . . of limiting the concept of the supreme reality – the concept of which is their common substratum – just as all geometric figures are possible only as various ways of limiting infinite space' (A578=B606). Let us pursue this analogy. Space is not the mere 'aggregate' of all possible geometric figures, a sort of bucket full of geometry. Nor, when we draw a line, are we actually cutting space in half. Rather the form of space is and remains something in itself single and whole, and figures are inscribed by drawing lines or limits. So, Kant argues, the object of the ideal is not just an aggregate of all possible positive real properties, nor are properties parts of the object of the ideal. Rather, the object is their 'basis'. '[T]he manifoldness of . . . things would rest not on the limitation of the original being itself, but on that of its complete consequence.' This ideal, Kant claims, is our notion of God, and he has been giving an account of the origin of that notion. This argument is important, because it directly disproves Descartes's famous 'trademark' argument. Descartes tried to demonstrate that the mere fact that I have an idea of God is explicable in no other way than as a direct result of God's creation of our minds – thus proving the existence of an infinite creator.

But, Kant claims, these last couple of steps although natural to reason also involve an illegitimate use of reason. How has this happened? In the last three paragraphs of the section (starting with 'The answer arises . . .', A581=B609), Kant tries to explain. Every real thing experienced in the world is determined to be the thing that it is by affirmation or negation of *sensible* properties contained elsewhere in the world. This t-shirt is the same colour as that tree; it does not smell like that rose, etc. This is because sensations are already relational properties that are presented in the whole of experience; it makes no sense to say that the colour of the t-shirt *cannot be compared* to some other colour. To *fully* determine a thing's sensible qualities requires, at least potentially, a comparison to every other thing in the world. This is because one cannot a priori determine the extent of sensible relationality. But real things are fully determined. Again, part of what we mean by a real thing is that, for any quality, it must be possible to say it is or is not that; and this in turn means, at its most general, the thing is in a real relation to this or that. 'The matter for the possibility of all objects of the senses must be presupposed as given in one sum' (A582=B610), and this is just what we mean by the world itself. So, 'nothing is an object *for us* unless it presupposes the sum of all empirical reality as condition of its possibility' (A582=B610). Something can be cognised as real only if it is understood to appear within the horizon of the world as a whole. But this principle holds only for empirical things – it does not apply to all things as such. (Nor does it apply to pure objects such as a perfect circle. It doesn't make sense to ask if a perfect circle is the same colour as that tree.) There are two dialectical 'subreptions' (a hidden, illegitimate swap or theft; that is, the error or sleight of hand behind the illusion). *First*, the substitution of what Kant calls a 'distributive' unity (the understanding must conceive of a set of *possible* comparisons that would fully determine the quality) with a 'collective' unity (the whole of experience given all at once). This dialectical move is another version of the supreme principle of dialectical reason (see A308=B365); although, like the cosmological illusion, the 'unconditioned' is in the first instance the totality of conditions. The 'illusion' out of which the transcendental ideal is constructed is then, *second*, the appropriation of this collective unity, which if it has any validity at all would only be for appearances, and its application to things as such (A582–3=B610–1). Accordingly, even the ideal of God, much more any proof of God's existence, turns out to be based upon an error.

Starting with section IV, Kant focuses on the ontological and cosmological arguments in detail. (The 'physicoteleological' argument, or argument from design, is in section VI.) Then, in the second half of section V, subsection 'Exposure and Explanation . . .', Kant shows that both arguments ultimately rest on the same defect. Both the arguments are 'transcendent', meaning they are conducted and concluded outside the limits of experience (outside space and time, in other words). It is worth pointing out, in general, that Kant's objections are commonly encountered, isolated from the rest of the book, in for example the context of the philosophy of religion. There, they are almost inevitably misread, because what will be missing is the whole of the critical philosophy upon which they depend. Section VII concludes with a summary of the inability of speculative reason to make any positive contribution to theology (it is practical reason that has success in this area), but does acknowledge that it may have a negative use. That is, speculative reason can clarify notions that come from elsewhere (from the practical theology Kant will be putting forward later, perhaps, or even from revelation or doctrine) and defend them from contradiction, empirical admixture, or other external influences. Such an employment of theoretical reason within theology can be found at work in Kant's *Religion within the Limits of Reason Alone*.

The ontological argument. This is discussed throughout section IV. At issue is whether, from a concept that includes necessary existence, one can deduce the actual existence of the object of that concept. First of all, he wonders whether it makes any sense to speak of an 'absolutely' or 'unconditionally' necessary being, rather than simply a necessary one. Examples are commonly put forward, such as the proposition that 'every triangle has three angles' being 'absolutely necessary'. But such examples are of judgements, not of things, and 'the unconditioned necessity of a judgement is only a conditioned necessity of the thing' (A593=B621). That is, a thing that is a triangle must, with absolute necessity, have three angles, *only under the condition that the triangle first exists*. In the judgement, to 'annul' the predicate 'has three angles' is a contradiction. But there is no contradiction in saying 'Triangles have three angles but there are no triangles'; that is, 'annulling' both subject and predicate (A594–5=B622–3). Accordingly, there is no contradiction in the proposition 'God (if existent) exists necessarily (but does not exist).'

Kant then asks: is the claim that 'X exists' an analytic or a synthetic proposition? If analytic (like the statement about triangles above), then it is indeed necessarily true, but 'you add nothing to your thought of the thing' (A597=B625). You are either speaking of a thought itself (which would then have necessity, but also be curiously trivial, like Descartes's 'I exist'); or you have begged the question by presupposing existence and then allegedly deducing it. Existential propositions, Kant argues, must be synthetic; but then the predicate 'exists' can be annulled without logical contradiction. However, Kant recognises that talking about synthetic propositions might be misleading in this context. A synthetic judgement was defined (in the Introduction) as one that adds to the subject concept, expanding it. Does the predicate 'exists' expand the concept in this way? Kant argues not: to claim that the object Xc of some concept C exists does not 'add' anything, but rather 'posits' the object and all of the predicates contained in C. 'Being', he famously writes, 'is not a real predicate' (A598=B626). (By 'real predicate' is meant one that would expand the concept, such as 'is wet' expands the concept 'my dog'.) A hundred real thalers (the old Prussian currency) is no more than a concept of a hundred thalers (as much as it matters to your finances); if it were, the one would not be the concept of the other.

So, then, what does it mean to say that existential propositions are synthetic? Kant answers, it means 'the coherence of these objects, according to empirical laws, with some one of my perceptions' (A601=B629). Whereas an ordinary synthetic judgement – such as 'my dog is wet' – expands our knowledge of the subject concept *by way of my experience*, an existential synthetic judgement posits the existence of the concept but again, by way of my experience. No synthetic judgement is possible without the mediation of either the a priori conditions of possible experience (in the case of synthetic a priori judgements), or the mediation of actual experiences (in the case of synthetic a posteriori judgements). Existential judgements are a special case of synthetic judgements which do not, to be sure, add to the concept, but nevertheless are valid or invalid only by reference to what lies outside the concept: experience. But, Kant concludes, 'for objects of pure thought there is no means whatsoever of cognising their existence' (A601=B629).

The cosmological argument. This discussion takes up the first part of section V. Kant breaks his treatment down into two parts. First, the move to a necessary being. Second, the identification of this necessary being as 'maximally real'. The latter of these is discussed at A605–6=B633–4. It is a brief restatement of the account of reason's 'natural' arrival at the notion of a supreme being. We will not here say anything about this discussion, except to note two things. 1. Kant claims it is the ontological argument in disguise. That is, the cosmological argument depends upon a surreptitious employment of the ontological, and is accordingly vulnerable to the same objections. 2. Kant has shown the illegitimacy (although 'natural') of this derivation of the Ideal. Accordingly, the second phase of the argument presents no new difficulties.

This first phase is treated by Kant at A609–10=B637–8. It is essentially identical with the proof of the thesis of the fourth 'Antinomy': 'there belongs to the world something that, either as its part or as its cause, is an absolutely necessary being' (A453–4=B481–2). Accordingly, Kant here in the Ideal says what he says there about the 'Antinomies'. Namely, that the principle that for every contingent thing there must be a cause is a perfectly valid principle, but only for phenomena; here, though, it is used to move 'beyond the world of sense' (A609=B637) and is thus employed outside the limits of its legitimacy; and the principle that an infinite regress of causes is impossible is not a valid principle, even in the world of sense (because a 'total' series could not ever be given; see our discussion at the end of the 'Antinomies' section). Such a principle is thus certainly not valid *beyond* the phenomenal.

The following principle leads us astray, Kant believes: 'If something – whatever it may be – exists, then we must grant also that something or other exists *necessarily*' (A584=B612). A necessary being is a being such that it is not possible for it not to exist. A 'contingent' being, on the other hand, is one such that it is possible for it not to exist; its existence depends upon (is 'contingent upon') something else outside it. Is there any concept of a being that contains 'nothing that conflicts with absolute necessity'? (A585=B613). The concept of the being that is the basis for all other beings certainly agrees with this principle: there is nothing left for it to depend upon. Since only one concept fits the bill, and since the necessary being must exist, the claim is made that the object of this concept must exist. Actually, Kant claims, the argument is already defective for one simple reason: we cannot rule out 'limited beings' – beings that are not the basis of all reality, but rather a part of that reality – also being necessary existences. That is, it hasn't been demonstrated that the object of the Ideal *uniquely* 'fits the bill'.

There seem to be two principles at work here, both of which appear to be important: first, that I cannot think of any natural thing existing without inferring the existence of something that exists necessarily; second, that I cannot *think* the necessity of anything – that is, there is nothing I can name that I cannot perfectly well imagine not existing (A615=B643). The latter principle forms the basis of the naive objection to the classic arguments for the existence of God, to be sure, but it is also in fact a necessary part of the cosmological argument insofar as the series could only be completed by a uniquely necessary being. Above, we saw that Kant had already noticed a flaw: why can there not be limited beings (that is, 'ordinary' experienced beings) that are necessary? The answer is that ordinary beings are thinkable (that's what we mean by something being experiencable), but necessity is not. (This was the significance of Kant's questioning of the 'thinkability' of a necessary being, in connection with the ontological argument.) This second principle then is what shows that the object of the Ideal uniquely fits the bill of a necessary being.

However, these two principles are, in a curious way, in contradiction. The one demands that I try to think something the other says I cannot. I must, in my attempt to think the possibility of things, try to think to their necessary ground; but I can never *get there*, because wherever I arrive in such thinking, will not yet be necessary. This contradiction is a sign, Kant argues, that we are misunderstanding these principles. This principles describe a movement of thought; they do not describe things. We are taking them for objective principles

(principles that apply to things) when they are in fact subjective (applying to and 'regulating' our thought). A regulative principle is a naturally emerging and indeed necessary guide to our thought, one that is very helpful, as Kant explains. Without such a principle we would not search for greater unity in our empirical concepts, and might also rest content with some particular explanation or other. In other words, without these principles, human beings would not *inquire* into the nature of their world. (We will discuss this notion of the 'regulative' more extensively in our treatment, below, of the Appendices to the 'Dialectic'.) As such 'regulative' principles, he claims, the two are compatible principles (A616–7=B644–5), and it is possible for both to be true, provided we posit the absolutely necessary being as *outside* the world (supernatural, outside of space and time). However, that only shows it is *possible* for us to posit such a being, not that we have grounds for so doing. By a 'subreption' we turn a merely regulative principle into a 'constitutive' one – a principle that tells us how real things actually are. (At the end of this subsection, Kant discusses the Greek philosophy of 'matter' as an example of the different conclusions that arise when the principles are taken to be objective or subjective.) And that is the inner move, and the inner flaw, of *all* 'transcendent' arguments that purport to prove the existence of God.

However, importantly, the same flaws would have to occur in any argument that tried to prove the opposite conclusion: that there *cannot* be a God. Thus, as far as theoretical reason is concerned, the existence or non-existence of God is a necessarily open question. The existence of God is possible insofar as that existence (understood to be outside the domain of experience) does not contradict the conditions of experience. This provides the 'space' within which faith can properly operate. Kant thus famously writes, that he had to 'annul knowledge in order to make room for faith' (Bxxx). That is, through critique, he had to expose the limits of the function of pure reason in order to rescue theology from either positive or negative interference from speculative metaphysics.

The physicotheological argument. This is the subject of section VI. The tone of this section is interesting. Kant's attack on the ontological argument is quite scathing, for he can see little value in its concepts. His account of the cosmological argument is more forgiving, precisely because here he recognises the natural movement of reason towards dialectical illusions but also, precisely in this, an employment of the ideal of reason that is at least akin to its properly valuable role (see the discussion of the regulative role of reason below). The account of the physicotheological argument is still more respectful, for the same reason. On the other hand, the physicotheological argument is also the easiest to disprove: for it so obviously employs empirical concepts beyond their sphere of validity.

Kant adduces two simple counter-arguments. First, the argument employs an analogy between God's design and creation of the cosmos, on the one hand, and an artisan's design and manufacture of some object. This analogy is perfectly acceptable, within its limits, for we have no other conceptual resources to understand creation (A626–7=B654–5). However, even ignoring these limits there remains a problem, for God's act is a *creation* of the substance of things, and not just (like the artisan) the *manipulation* of existing substances. Second, the argument requires that the cause of the infinitely complex and also infinitely huge order and harmony be 'proportionate' to it. But this complexity and scale are experienced relationally, with respect to my human powers of conceiving and making; that is, the complexity is more excellent than anything I could imagine, and the scale more vast than anything I could make. Kant writes, 'Now, I trust that no one will presume to have insight into the relation of the world's magnitude observed by him . . . to omnipotence' (A628=B656). Experiences like 'gosh, that's big!' are incapable of giving 'determinate' content to the concept of the deity. Faced with these problems, Kant claims, the argument quickly falls back on the cosmological argument, which in turn relies upon a disguised version of the ontological – and that, as we know, Kant thinks is 'unnatural' and a mere product of scholastic ingenuity (A603=B631). (Incidentally, these passages are filled with references to the 'schools'. Kant means the style, methods and topics of philosophy and theology, as they were carried out within institutions dominated by religious orders, from the Medieval period on. Kant has a sneaking admiration for the rigour of these methods and the precision of the concepts, both of which he is happy to borrow regularly – see for example A344n=B402n; but also a contempt he does not try to hide for its 'dogmatic' 'monopoly' of philosophy – see Bxxxii–xxxvi.) Thus, the respect the physicotheological argument is due has nothing to do with its apparent validity, and certainly not with its hidden recourse to other, less reputable arguments, but rather that reason is here so close as to be almost indistinguishable from its proper role. And that proper role is where we now turn.

Appendices: 'Regulative Use' and 'Final aim'
There are two appendices to the 'Dialectic'. The first lays out in more detail the notion of a positive, though 'regulative', use of the ideas of reason. We have encountered this idea before, in the treatment of the dialectical inferences of speculative reason, but most often as a brief mention at the end of a lengthy, negative discussion. The second continues the discussion with the aim of providing something analogous to a deduction of the ideas.

'What has its basis in the nature of our powers must be purposive', Kant asserts in what here appears to be a curiously dogmatic voice. That is, how could any basic type of thinking not have some positive function? Reason arrives at its ideas through its 'natural propensity' to overstep its critical limits; these ideas bring about illusions that we can only barely resist 'even by means of the most rigorous critique' (A643=B671). This natural propensity, though, belongs to reason at its most fundamental level. It is not the propensity that is at fault, but only poor judgement in the employment of it; namely, the judgement that asserts that reason's activity amounts to a determining concept of an object. Reason's proper domain, though, is not objects (either within or without experience), but rather the concepts of the understanding. '[J]ust as the understanding unites the manifold in the object by means of concepts, so reason in its turn unites the manifold of concepts by means of ideas' (A644=B672). This makes it clear that the difference between the understanding and reason is not one just of a quantitatively higher generality (as in Bennett 1974). Concepts of the understanding can be as general as you like, but remain concerned with the cognition of appearances. The ideas of reason are not *wider*, but of an essentially different function: reason's 'objects' are concepts.

Accordingly, Kant distinguishes between a regulative and a constitutive use of the ideas. The latter is the dialectical illusion unrestrained by critical judgement whereby the ideas are taken to be determinative of objects; here, by 'determinative' is meant that the ideas would provide, directly and of themselves, knowledge of these

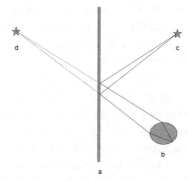

Figure 2. Simple diagram of a *focus imaginarius*. The mirror (a) reflects two rays of light from object (c) to the eye (b) where they come together (are focused) on the retina. The eye sees object (c) at position (d) which is imaginary or virtual.

objects. The regulative use is also termed 'hypothetical', and this 'aims at the systematic unity of the cognitions of understanding' (A647=B675). The various and diverse concepts employed by the understanding are not thereby unified in a higher concept, but rather set the task of such a unification. Kant employs an elaborate optical analogy to explain this. The idea is a *focus imaginarius*: when facing a mirror, what lies behind us appears in front of us but behind the mirror, just as if the rays of light had proceeded in uninterrupted straight lines (see Figure 2). The *illusion* of the virtual image is what makes it possible for us to 'direct our understanding' towards *knowledge* of things 'behind our back' (A644–5=B672–3). In other words, the illusion of the idea of reason, despite and perhaps even because it is illusion, enters employment in order to further the expansion of knowledge towards that which is not yet known. On this, see the discussions in Grier (2001, 37–8) and Allison (2004, 425ff); the latter sees what is at stake in the 'behind our back' as the problem of induction.

Kant's various examples of such guidance by ideas (all of them outdated, but generally pretty clear despite this) include the unification of various particular chemicals under classes, the unification of botanical or zoological species under genus and family, and the unification in empirical psychology of various specific mental functions under 'basic powers'. These examples might suggest that the regulative employment of the ideas of reason has a significance that is confined to Kant's understanding of specifically natural science (see for example Buchdahl 1992 or Kitcher 1994). There is this significance, to be sure, but Allison argues that we must not thereby overlook the importance of the notion of regulation to Kant's account of reason as a whole and its relation to transcendental illusion (Allison 2004, 424–5). The task of such unification of concepts, Kant says, is a 'logical principle' (A648=B676), and we should identify this with the 'subjective law' (A306=B362) that we discussed in our treatment of the Introduction to the 'Dialectic'.

However, at A650=B678, there is an important shift in the discussion. Kant says three surprising things: concerning the necessary presupposition of the objectivity of transcendental principles; concerning the necessity of the function of reason for empirical cognition; and concerning the apparently contradictory diversity of the principles of reason.

First, it is insufficient, Kant claims, to understand the positive role of the ideas of reason merely through this notion of a 'logical principle'. He writes, 'It is, indeed impossible to see how there could be a *logical* principle concerning the rational unity of rules [i.e. concepts of nature], if we did not presuppose a *transcendental* principle whereby such systematic unity, construed as attaching to the objects themselves, is assumed a priori as necessary' (A650–1=B678–9). The merely logical principle would have, even on its own terms, no legitimacy whatsoever unless it included also a 'presupposition' that the unity which it (subjectively) demands is there to be found in the cognition of the object (that is, in nature). On the face of it, however, this sounds just like the 'poor judgement' that asserts the objective determinacy of ideas. There are two important differences, however. First, and most obviously, the object here is the unity of the concepts of sensible nature; although this unity is unattainable (it is, Kant says, approached 'asymptotically' A663=B691) it nevertheless must be conceived of as immanent to nature, otherwise it could not be 'approached' at all. On the other hand, the quite illegitimate and dialectical object of a idea is a unity of *super-sensible* nature. Second, the important point is the notion of 'presuppose', which ties in with the earlier notion of 'hypothetical'. Understanding and reason do and must function *as if* the unity demanded by the ideas of reason were a real unity of nature, without that idea being constitutive of precisely what concepts or laws would make up that real unity. This 'as if' principle is a new class of principles, neither objective nor subjective in the ways we have been defining these up to now, and leading to a new class of judgements. It is not reducible to either a merely logical (or subjective) principle, nor to a constitutive principle.

Kant explicates the notion of an 'as if' principle (Kant also calls it a maxim at A666=B694) by way of the notion of a schema (A664–6=B692–4). The understanding has as its purpose the unification of manifolds in the presentation of objects, but is indeterminate without a schema of sensibility. The schema, that is, is a description of the conditions under which a concept of the understanding obtains determinate meaning. Reason has as its purpose the unification of the manifold of concepts of the understanding; this too remains a merely formal requirement without something analogous to a schema. 'The idea of reason is an analogue of a schema of sensibility' (A665=B693). The object determined through this schema, however, is not *directly* an object of sense. Rather, the direct object is a procedure for the systematic unity of, and bringing into harmony with itself of, the understanding, and is thus has at best an *indirect* object of sense. In this analogue of a schema, reason's otherwise merely logically formal idea of a maximum comes to have a determinate meaning in terms of the procedures of the understanding. The 'as if' principle is more than a merely logical or formal 'begging' insofar as it is determinative of objective procedures of the understanding whereby the hypothetical maximum of unity could be discovered; it is not a constitutive principle, though, insofar as it is by no means directly determinative of objects of sense. These maxims have 'objective but indeterminate validity and serve as rules of possible experience' (A663=B691).

We must think this material in connection with the so-called second Copernican revolution that Kant discusses in the B-Preface. There it is a question of understanding what is meant by a science. Kant writes, 'all we cognise a priori about things is what we ourselves put into them' (Bxviii). In discussing the 'Transcendental Analytic', it seemed obvious that what Kant meant that 'we put in' were the forms of intuition, the categories, and the principles that govern their legitimate employment in the cognition of nature. It is now clear that Kant all along meant *also* the determination by ideas of reason of procedures of investigation by the understanding, through which higher, more complete and above all more systematic concepts of nature become possible. A science is only possible when it presupposes a priori that its object so constituted as to be understood systematically. In the Preface, Kant wrote that reason must approach nature 'in the capacity of an appointed judge who compels the witnesses to answer the question that he puts to them' (Bxiii). While here in the 'Regulative Use', Kant writes in direct parallel, 'reason here is not begging but commanding' (A653=B681).

The second surprising new idea is found in passages like this one: 'without this law [of reason] we would have no reason at all, but without reason would have no coherent use of the understanding, and in the absence of such use would have no sufficient mark of empirical truth' (A651=B679). The demands of reason that are embodied in reason's ideas are, therefore, not merely 'useful' as Kant has (apparently) hitherto been claiming. Rather, they are necessary for there to be something even as concrete and everyday as a criterion of empirical truth. What is meant in saying that an empirical proposition is true? It means that the content of the proposition is in accord with the whole of experience. If the dog *looks* wet but *feels* dry, then one or the other of these cannot be true. However, the requirement that, and the procedures for determining if, experience is in accord with itself are not a function of the understanding, but rather of reason. Indeed, Kant goes so far as to argue that no empirical concept would be possible at all without the transcendental presupposition of the underlying homogeneity in the unity of manifolds of concepts (A654=B682). The maxims of reason are thus *indirect* 'rules of possible experience' (A663=B691). Now, because they have no direct objective employment, the ideas of reason cannot be subjected to a deduction (A663–4=B691–2); however, this argument concerning the possibility of empirical experiences is a kind of deduction. Kant uses this analysis of reason being the condition of the possibility of empirical concepts and criteria of truth in their use as a further demonstration that the 'as if' principle is not merely logical, but transcendental insofar as it must be presumed (that is, in the mode of the 'as if') to have objective validity. (The treatment of the possibility of empirical truth should be compared with the account Kant gives in the 'Analogies'. These two accounts are different, but not incompatible if we understand them as both parts of a richer picture of truth.)

The third surprising thing Kant claims in this appendix is that we misunderstand the demand of reason for unity in concepts if we think of this merely as a search for ever *higher* concepts. On the contrary, the unity of concepts is of no value without also a maximum in the specificity of, or richness in the content of, concepts (A654ff=B682ff). So, it is a requirement of reason that the understanding also presuppose for each of its concepts of a species, also a manifold of subspecies. (In turn, there is a third principle of the continuity across this increasing or decreasing specification (A657–8=B685–6).) The interest of reason in expanding the range of concepts (through ever higher concepts), and the interest of reason in expanding the content of concepts (through ever more specific and thus richer concepts), appear to be contradictory. Certainly, Kant says, they are the source of many conflicts among scientists who as individuals may have a disposition to one or the other. These principles would indeed be contradictory if these principles were directly objective (the situation would be akin to the antinomies); but as maxims that only regulate or determine only procedures for the understanding, they are compatible. More than this, they are together necessary for conceiving what would be meant by a maximally complete *system* of the cognition of nature; that is, a maximum of both range and content and continuity of specification between. This notion of a system, as a defining aim of any science as such, has been quietly important throughout the first *Critique*, since the Prefaces.

The second appendix to the 'Transcendental Dialectic' is entitled 'On the Final Aim of the Natural Dialectic of Human Reason'. As mentioned above, this section appears to be a continuation of the previous on regulative ideas, and we will pick out from it just four points for discussion: the deduction of ideas; relative as opposed to absolute presupposition; purposiveness; and the answerability of the questions of reason. But why is it entitled the 'Final Aim'? Kant states that 'the proper vocation of this highest cognitive power [reason]' is to employ all its tools to trace nature 'to its innermost core' along all possible dimensions of systematic unity (A702=B730). In short, providing the deduction legitimates Kant's claim earlier that 'whatever has its basis in the nature of our powers must be purposive' (A642=B670).

Kant reiterates that a deduction strictly speaking of ideas is impossible, for essential reasons. Nevertheless, if they are to have some 'indeterminate' objective validity, then something like a deduction must be attempted. So, we can expect Kant to ask: how does our experience becomes possible through the regulative use of the ideas? Kant puts it this way: 'if one can show that . . . under the presupposition of such an *object in one's* idea [the as if object], all rules of reason's empirical use lead to systematic unity and always expand experiential cognition' then this will be akin to a deduction of the ideas. For this *expansion* of cognition towards system is indeed experienceable, and would not be possible for cognition on its own (without the guidance of reason). For each of the three ideas, Kant provides this sort of deduction at A681–8=B710–6. However, Kant in the previous section made still greater claims for the role of the regulative ideas (for example, that there could not be a criterion of empirical truth as such without the regulative function of reason), so what he writes here seems anticlimactic.

Kant here finds yet another new way of thinking the 'as if' object of an idea, and this is in terms of a distinction between a relative and an absolute presupposition. We know from the 'Regulative Use' section that Kant argues that a merely logical principle of reason is insufficient to understand the role of the ideas; instead, we need to presuppose the objects of reason in the mode of the 'as if'. Here Kant describes this by saying the objects of ideas are posited not absolutely in themselves, but rather 'I merely think the relation that a being, in itself quite unknown to me, has to the greatest systematic unity of the world whole', and I think this relation employing categories analogously. (See the discussion of analogy at A626–7=B654–5.) In other words, the 'as if' judgement of the object of an idea concerns not the object as such but rather the function that object would have with respect to reason's interest of a maximum in the systematicity of cognition.

Above, we did not discuss the fourth 'Antinomy', which concerns the question of whether the phenomenal series of contingent beings requires a necessary being. Expressed in that way, the fourth 'Antinomy' looks like a version of the cosmological argument. But Kant insists that the 'Antinomies' are issues of the totality of series, whereas the Ideal concerned the totality of interconnections. Here in the 'Final Aim' he gives us a way of understanding this distinction with the notion of the 'purposive'. By 'purposive' (*Zweckmäßig*; sometimes translated as 'final') is meant a cause and effect that should be understood as an intention of a rational agent. So, my walking to the front door can be understood either as a series of mechanical acts, or as a series of acts organised by my intention of answering the doorbell. In certain contexts (for example, the study of the body's physiology and thus *how* I am walking) we employ the first way of understanding; for others (asking *why* I am walking) we use the other. Kant's point here is that it can sometimes be useful to think of nature (that is, non-human nature) as purposive – opening new ways of conceiving the systematicity of nature – and doing so requires that one treat nature 'as if' it were the product of a rational creator. For example, in evolutionary biology – which is of course precisely the science that did most to discredit any purposive view of nature – it remains a very useful and generally harmless mental short-hand to talk about 'why' a certain new genetic feature developed. Kant says more than this, however: this manner of conceiving of the systematicity of nature according to purposes is the most important (A702=B730), partly because purposive unity does not exclude other unities (and is thus most comprehensive), partly because its schema of nature conceives of nature as a domain within which the interests of reason (theoretical and practical) itself can be unified. We will return to this latter point in discussing the 'Canon of Pure Reason' later.

The 'Final Aim' ends with a striking *tour de force* wherein Kant demonstrates that, because reason's concern is always with itself (A680=B708), all the questions of reason can be answered (A695–701=B723–9). The trick is, as always, not to confuse subjective and objective bases (and thus take an object presupposed in the mode of the as if and functioning regulatively for an object posited directly and determinately) and, accordingly, to understand the limits of the implications of one's answers.

Transcendental Doctrine of Method

The 'Transcendental Doctrine of Method' forms the second 'volume' (for lack of a better word, since Kant provides no label) of the *Critique of Pure Reason*. The first volume, the 'Transcendental Doctrine of Elements', includes the 'Aesthetic', 'Analytic' and 'Dialectic' and is roughly five times the number of pages. Kant uses a building metaphor to compare the roles of these two volumes. The first assesses the 'elements' of the building, the materials and tools available, and evaluates what type of building they might be suited to. The second concerns itself with the method of building and, in particular, with the plan. Here Kant provides 'the determination of the formal conditions of a complete system of pure reason' (A707–8=B735–6). This second volume is much less frequently read and referred to, but in terms of the structure of the book Kant evidently regarded it of equal importance. Moreover, there is plenty of evidence to suggest that the content of the 'Canon' chapter in particular is quite literally the end towards which the rest of the book has been striving. This volume is divided into four chapters, the last of which is on the history of philosophy and, although influential on subsequent (and still current) standard accounts of history, is very brief indeed and forms a most unsatisfying anticlimax to the titanic whole. We shall here briefly sketch out the key ideas from each of the first three chapters.

The 'Discipline' of pure reason concerns itself with the 'negative' function of the critical enterprise insofar as this makes a contribution to the method. Based upon what we now know concerning the critical limits of (theoretical or speculative) pure reason, Kant is asking: what should be the shape of philosophical debate? This chapter is divided in four topics: 'Dogmatic Use', 'Polemic Use', 'Hypotheses', 'Proofs'. The section on the 'Dogmatic Use' of pure reason is especially notable for the detailed account of mathematics it provides, in contrast to a characterisation of transcendental philosophy. Mathematics is an example of a science, according to Kant's much more brief account in the Prefaces and Introduction; and we know also that Kant wants to show that a certain limited philosophical metaphysics can also be a science. Both comprise synthetic a priori judgements. However, while mathematical knowledge advances 'without the aid of experience', this would only be true of a 'dogmatic' philosophy. The discipline of reason requires us to avoid falling into the trap of believing the example of mathematics can be successfully followed in this respect.

Mathematics (Kant is thinking of geometry) is cognition through the construction of concepts (A713=B741). By this is meant that I allow the geometric properties of space to reveal themselves, as a priori and universal, in and through the rule-governed activity of drawing spatial figures. In constructing individual figures, because space is an a priori form of intuition, it is possible to 'contemplate the universal in the particular' (A714=B742). Philosophy, on the other hand is cognition simply through concepts, and the particular is contemplated only in the universal (A714=B742). Now, the principle of causation, for example, is a synthetic a priori principle. But it is not determinate cognition of some real thing in empirical space and time. That is, the principle does not constitute an object as given, though it does provide a condition of the possibility of our experiencing objects. Nor is it determinate cognition of some pure thing in pure space and time (there are no pure causes). Rather, causation is 'a principle of the synthesis of possible empirical intuitions' (A722=B750 and n.). To the extent that it can be determinate at all, it becomes so only under conditions of the givenness of some real, empirical thing or event that we can judge to be a cause or effect. (This should be compared with Kant's warnings, in the 'Deduction', for example, at B165 about particular concepts and laws.)

The polemic use of pure reason concerns the manner in which reason can resolve, or should intervene in, debates of speculative reason. That is, when *others* are employing reason in illegitimate ways. In other words, this section concerns the public face of philosophical debate and thus part of what it means to be a good 'citizen' of reason. The basic principle is stated up front in the strongest possible terms: 'The very existence of reason depends upon' the freedom of its critique. This is a barely disguised, and very modern-looking, *political* claim. Kant elaborates: 'to expect enlightenment from reason and yet to prescribe to it beforehand on which side it must necessarily sally forth is quite absurd' (A747=B775). This is true even in the training of philosophers in universities (A754–5=B782–3). Now, there is no 'antithetic' of reason at all (A743=B771); all disputes involving reason are the result of failures to respect the critical limits of reason. Such disputes will continue, and *should* continue. For if both sides are arguing well, he says, reason can only gain (it is 'cultivated' and 'corrected') even if resolution is impossible (A744=B772). Critique being the 'tribunal' of reason, the critical philosopher has a certain tranquillity in the face of such debate (A751=B779), and also a reserve confidence that the practical domain of reason will not offer so little grounds for conviction. The section on 'Polemic' ends with a brief section on skepticism, which is largely about Hume. Scepticism, Kant argues, is always directed towards dogmatism, and thus is highly useful in preparing the ground for a proper critique of pure reason. However, scepticism is not yet critique, for although it is successful in laying waste to dogmatism, it has no basis for evaluating any future endeavours of reason. Its account of the limits of reason is empirical (up to now, no rational argument for X has been successful), not transcendental.

A 'hypothesis' of pure reason would be the invention of an object for an idea under the acknowledgement that knowledge of this object is impossible. Although he does not make it clear here, Kant is concerned to ward off misunderstandings of the notions of the regulative and 'as if' presuppositional use of the ideas of reason. In the sciences, it is often seen to be a vitally useful procedure to hypothesise an explanation for some phenomenon far in advance of any empirical evidence for it. Exploring the hypothesis might speed up, focus and clarify the search for the evidence. However, in the empirical sciences, the hypothesis has more than logical possibility, it has 'real' possibility (see our discussion of the types of possibility at the beginning of our account of the 'Deductions'). But the real possibility of an idea can be established no more than its actuality. Moreover, the object of a scientific hypothesis, if borne out by evidence, will have a direct and determining relation to objects of experience. Even in the hypothetical mode, this is claiming too much for the object of an idea. Therefore, what from within pure reason might be called 'hypothesis' could at best be the 'raving' of imagination (A769–70=B797–8). A transcendental hypothesis would be 'no explanation at all' (A772=B800). Such a hypothesis of reason might have use in reason's polemical use, as a strategem for showing just how shaky is the ground upon which a dogmatic opponent stands (Kant gives an example of such use at A778–9=B806–7). Kant also notes, in passing, that the first and best opponent is within oneself – since reason is naturally and inherently dialectical (A777=B805). This quick move takes the political notion of the freedom of reason that was developed in the previous section, and extends it into philosophical self-consciousness. Reason must be allowed to be free *within oneself* as a condition for its continued existence.

The brief section 'The Discipline of Pure Reason in Regard to its Proofs' is quite a useful discussion of the notion of a transcendental argument, and a comparison with the types of arguments adduced by reason in its speculative use. Kant's discussion proceeds through three 'rules'. First, and most familiarly, transcendental proofs do not proceed directly from some concept to either an object or another concept, but can only do so by a detour, so to speak, through a deduction of the validity of the concept with respect to possible experience. This was of course the strategy of the 'Transcendental Deduction', but it is likewise true of the arguments in the 'Principles'. In the 'Principles', in each case, the principle is arrived at synthetically by way of a demonstration that experience would not be possible without that synthetic connection. In the arguments of pure reason such a deduction should be sought, but of course always in vain. The first rule of the proofs of pure reason is the requirement of a deduction of principles employed in them (A786–7=B814–5). The second rule (or 'peculiarity') of transcendental proofs is that, in each case, there is only one possible argument. A transcendental proposition always begins with a single concept, and the proof can only proceed by treating the concept as the synthetic condition of the object. Thus, Kant writes, 'as soon as we see the dogmatist come forward with ten proofs, we may safely believe that he has none at all' (A788=B816). As we have seen in, for example, our discussion of the principle of substance, Kant seems to have more than one argument. Here, Kant is insisting that we understand these as attempts to restate, ever more clearly, one underlying proof. The 'one argument' rule is true also of the speculative arguments of pure reason; it now becomes clear why Kant insisted that the three proofs for the existence of God all depend upon the ontological.

The third rule is that transcendental proofs should be 'ostensive' rather than 'apagogic'. Kant means they must be of the form where the antecedent is affirmed (If p, then q. p, therefore q) rather than by denial of the consequent (If p, then q. Not q, therefore not p). The reason is that in transcendental proofs there is the unique danger of confusing a subjective and an objective basis. So, for example, in the 'Paralogisms' we saw the arguments of rational psychology over and over again confusing the subjective requirement of 'I think' with an objective claim about substance. Because of this possible confusion in the meaning of q, one can never be sure that 1. q and not-q are actually mutually exclusive, and thus that 2. an argument by denial of the consequent is sound. Kant thus claims, 'the apagogic kind of proof can be permitted only in those sciences where there is no possibility of *substituting* the subjective [element] of our presentation for the objective' (A791=B819). Now, this is a nice way of summarising the structural anomalies in the dialectical inferences of pure reason. However, many of Kant's proofs in the 'Analytic' seemed to be 'indirect' in a closely related sense (for example, *reductio ad absurdum*). For example, in the proof of the 'First Analogy of Experience', an argument might proceed roughly as follows: suppose things (and not just the determinations of things) could arise absolutely; that leads to an absurdity; therefore things cannot arise absolutely, that is to say, they are permanent substances. In this case, we would *also* have to prove that 'things can arise absolutely' and 'things are permanent substances' are indeed exclusive alternatives. That is, we need to show that 'substance' has as one of its objective meanings 'things *cannot* arise absolutely'. Now, in transcendental arguments in the 'Analytic' the whole point of the argument is to show the objective validity for possible experience of the concept; that was the first rule, above. This deduction is what Kant here means by a 'direct' or 'ostensive' proof: one that not only shows the truth of something, but also the basis of that truth (in the conditions of possible experience). So, apparently apagogic argument forms in the 'Analytic', Kant insists, should be understood as explanatory fragments of a larger, unique and complete direct argument. This may be one reason why Kant, for the second edition, adds new first paragraphs to the 'Analogies of Experience' which seem to contain just such direct proofs.

Canon of Pure Reason

Kant defines 'Canon' as 'the sum of a priori principles governing the correct use' of a faculty (A796=B824). The 'Analytic', then, was a canon of the understanding. However, the synthetic principles of theoretical reason are illusory, so there can be no canon. And yet, if reason also has a *practical* dimension, then there one might find a canon of governing principles. This practical reason is opened up for us first of all by the incapacity of theoretical/speculative reason to understand (from its point of view) its own overwhelming interest in that which lies outside experience (A796=B824, A798–9=B826–7). '*Practical* is everything that is possible through freedom' (A800=B828), and in particular moral actions (indeed, other 'actions' are not actions, strictly speaking, insofar as they originate in nature, A798=B826). Kant defines moral laws quite conventionally as telling us 'what ought to occur' while natural laws tell us only what in fact occurs (A802=B830). Kant claims (here with little argument) that such a priori moral laws exist (A807=B835). Moreover, the fact of practical freedom is clear from experience (we do make decisions according to rules of conduct). Even were it the case that in such decision making we are determined by remote *natural* causes (an important question for theoretical reason), that is of no concern within the practical. Thus, moral laws (as principles of practical reason) have objective validity, in the way no speculative principles ever could (A807=B835).

The 'Canon of Pure Reason', then, is going to be Kant's first major sketch of his specifically critical moral theory, and of some of the important consequences of that theory. This moral theory receives considerable elaboration in subsequent books (such as the *Second Critique*), so we will not dwell long on it here. However, the study of practical reason will indeed reveal the 'ultimate purpose' of pure reason if two conditions can be met. These are: that theoretical and practical reason are harmonised, and do not contradict one another; and that practical reason can provide insight into why reason as a whole is obsessed by the attempt to determine transcendent objects (freedom, immortality, God); which obsession leads both to dialectical illusions and also to the regulative governance of the systematicity of the understanding.

The three problems of speculative reason from the three chapters of the dialectic become two problems of practical reason (freedom, as we have just seen, is a fact for practical reason) (A800=B828). In the 'Canon' Kant wants to establish that, within the domain of practical reason, the existence of God and of a future life must be asserted; asserted not, however, as objects of knowledge, nor merely 'as if' objects that are presupposed in order that a regulative function might be conceived of as having sense, but rather as objects of 'moral faith'. The argument commences in section II of the 'Canon'; section III then determines the relationship between knowledge and faith. The former begins with Kant's famous three questions: What can I know? What ought I to do? What may I hope? (A804–5=B832–3) (Importantly, at the beginning of his lectures on logic (IX, 25), Kant adds a fourth: What is the human being? This can be interpreted as the last and widest question, including the other three insofar as the answers to these all lie in transcendental subjectivity as a characterisation of the human as a finite being.) The first question is answered by theoretical reason; the second by practical reason in its moral laws; and the third also through practical reason as an immediate entailment of the possibility of morality.

Kant defines 'happiness' as the satisfaction of our inclinations; that is, it concerns us as natural, worldly beings. Obedience to moral law then amounts to 'worthiness to be happy' (A806=B834). The world as it would be if in accordance with these laws he calls a 'moral world' (A808=B836). The question of 'hope' then becomes: if we are worthy, can we hope happiness will follow? The only way of answering this from within pure reason would be to answer a slightly different question: is it the case that worthiness to be happy and happiness are necessarily connected within reason's principles? The answer to this second question is 'yes', Kant asserts (A809=B837). For this reason, reason must assert whatever conditions would be necessary for the first question to also have 'yes' for an answer. Now, if everyone always followed moral laws, then the moral world would be real, and happiness would follow; but this is, at best, unlikely (A809–10=B837–8). Therefore, the hope of happiness 'cannot be cognised through reason if mere nature is laid at the basis' (A809–10=B837–8). Kant continues: 'Rather, this connection may be hoped for only if a *supreme reason* that commands according to moral laws is also laid at the basis of nature, as nature's cause' (A809–10=B837–8). This supreme reason is a notion of God as not only creator but morally wise designer of nature. Only in such a morally purposive nature could there be a necessary connection of worthiness for happiness and happiness itself. Kant swiftly adds that this moral world can also only be conceived of as a future world. Thus 'God and a future life are two presuppositions that, according to principles of pure reason, are inseparable from the obligation imposed on us by that same reason' (A811=B839). If we acknowledge the command of moral law *at all*, then we *must also* presuppose the existence of God and a future life. Indeed, if we hold a moral 'maxim' as in fact a law of our action, the we already (implicitly) assert these objects, however sceptical or atheistic we may believe ourselves to be. (This point is picked up most famously by Nietzsche, who outlines the various ways in which a belief in morality is tied to other metaphysical and theological beliefs.) This seems a remarkably strong, and unexpected, conclusion. Kant's concern in the next section is to understand its limits.

Section III consists of a rapid series of distinctions. Two are key. First, Kant makes a distinction between 'holding something to be true' (Pluhar renders this as 'assent') upon a subjective basis, and upon an objective basis. Something that is held true on an objective basis is called 'knowledge' (A822=B850). Only in the latter case can I communicate this basis to others (A820–1=B848–9). That is, only for an objective basis must it be the case that all others will have and agree the cognitive principles needed to understand and evaluate this basis, and thus likewise share the world within which knowledge is empirically verified or at least employed. This emphasis on communicability as a key indicator of objectivity is clearly here very important (and was again very important in twentieth-century philosophy) but was something Kant did not earlier stress. Moreover, the distinctively *public* quality of objective inquiry here relates nicely to the political points concerning the freedom of reason and the expression of reason that Kant was making in the 'Discipline of Pure Reason'.

The second key distinction is between doctrinal and moral faith (A825–8=B853–6). The German word *Glaube* means 'faith' or 'belief'. Within the sphere of theoretical reason, Kant argues, there is no holding-true on a subjective basis (A823=B851). As before, the practical sphere is defined in terms of human free actions; that is, in relation to *purposes*. However, there is a curious 'analogue' of practical judgements within the theoretical, and that is when theoretical reason takes as *its* purpose pursing the systematicity of *nature's* purposes (A825=B853). Kant is trying to employ his distinctions here between knowledge and faith to understand the 'as if' objects presupposed by reason in its regulative use. The 'as if' objects are objects of a holding-true that Kant calls 'doctrinal faith'. (This relation to the practical could explain why, in the 'Discipline of Pure Reason', Kant rejected the model of hypothesis for such as if judgements.) However, Kant's other examples here (of a doctor making a diagnosis, or of life on other planets) seem entirely inappropriate *from a theoretical point of view*. There is nothing intrinsically impossible about the doctor's diagnosis being shown, objectively, true or false; likewise with life on other planets. But in the case of the 'as if' objects of regulative reason, there is such an impossibility. Kant's point, perhaps, is not that the *theoretical* contents of these judgements are similar, but rather that they have a similar *practical* structure.

The type of holding-true that pertains when purposes are necessarily given to reason, however, Kant calls 'moral faith'. This remains only a subjective basis, and thus 'I must not even say, *It is* morally certain that there is a God, etc., but must say, *I am* morally certain, etc.' (A829=B857). Kant is here explicating the distinctive features of the type of assent that his 'moral argument' leads to, and specifically differentiating it both from mere opinion, on the one hand, and knowledge (or even possible knowledge) on the other. All of the topics in the 'Canon' – the 'moral argument' itself, the proper manner of understanding it, and the manner in which it brings into harmony the theoretical and the practical and thus unifies the whole of transcendental thought – return in the *Second* and *Third Critiques*. Clear now, for the first time, is Kant's famous statement in the B-Preface that he had to 'annul knowledge in order to make room for faith' (Bxxx).

Architectonic of Pure Reason

A science is only a science properly called if it exhibits a comprehensive and rational systematicity. A science, therefore, is organised according to an idea of reason (A832=B860). To be sure, in the history of a science this rational organisation may in fact emerge very late, and perhaps in an unexpected way, but it will always have been aimed at (A834=B862). This idea of rational organisation, under the conditions of the particular a priori domain of objects of a science (that is, its 'manifold' of parts and problems), is an architectonic schema. Kant's aim here is to sketch out the architectonic schema of philosophy.

Along the way, Kant makes a couple of interesting asides, such as that concerning the difference between learning philosophy and learning to philosophise (A835–8=B863–6). The former, Kant writes in a striking phrase, is like wearing 'the plaster cast of a living human being'. Kant's conclusion was hugely influential on the development of modern systems of education (and not just university philosophy departments): 'We can learn only to philosophise, i.e. to practice reason's talent of complying with its own universal principles upon certain already available attempts at philosophy – but always while reserving reason's right to investigate these principles themselves in their sources and to confirm or reject them' (A838=B866). There is also an important discussion of the distinction between the 'school concept' of philosophy and its 'world concept' (A838–9=B866–7). The former has as its purpose the systematic completeness of philosophy in and of itself. Kant's two-sided attitude towards scholasticism shows itself here. This systematic completeness must be part of what is meant by a science, on the one hand, but on the other its distinctive tendency to be closed in on itself is both mistaken and dangerous. The world concept sees this purpose of completeness as called forth by and always in the service of the essential purposes of human reason in general. These essential purposes are either identical to, or subsidiary to, morality. In other words, the meaning that philosophy ought to give to itself, and the underlying reason for any pursuit of a merely philosophical end, is a moral one.

Returning to the concept of 'architectonic', this section is thus providing the backdrop to earlier discussions of the necessary structure of Kant's work, such as that at the end of the Introduction (A10ff=B24ff), or the following passage from the B-Preface. We obtain the same systematic results in critical philosophy, Kant writes there, 'whether we proceed from the minutest elements all the way to the whole of pure reason, or proceed backward to each part when starting from the whole (for this whole also is given by itself, through reason's final aim in the practical sphere)' (Bxxxviii). As it happens, then, Kant's *Critique of Pure Reason* was written 'synthetically' so to speak, building up to the whole from its elements. However, Kant could have written it backwards, 'analytically' from the whole to the parts. That is, we can imagine a *Critique of Pure Reason* that begins with reason's final aim in the practical sphere, explicates the regulative employment of theoretical reason as a necessary component of this, then finds it necessary to contrast that to an illegitimate and deceptive constitutive or 'transcendent' employment, and finally turns to the synthetic cognition of appearances as the demonstration of the only proper 'immanent' use of theoretical cognition. Any volunteers?

3. Study Aids

Glossary

aesthetic
Having to do with sense. In the *Critique of Pure Reason*, Kant's treatment of space and time is as a priori forms of intuition, and thus the condition of sense perception.

analysis
The resolution of complex concepts or judgements into constituent parts.

analytic
A judgement is analytic if the subject concept already contains the predicate. 'Analytic' is also used by Kant as a stage of critique, in which the basic principles and operations of a faculty are laid out.

antinomy
One of the types of dialectical illusion, in which two contradictory theses both appear rationally demonstrable.

a posteriori
Refers to any presentation or judgement that comes from experience, either directly or indirectly. *See* a priori.

appearance [*Erscheinung*]
That which is given/presented in an empirical intuition. Appearance is thus empirically real, and not to be confused with the notion of 'illusion' in any sense. The term 'appearances' is often used by Kant to designate the sensible world in general. Appearances are or can come to be experienced, and thus also known.

	'Appearance' is contrasted with the thing in itself.
apperception	Self-consciousness. In the 'Transcendental Deduction', Kant distinguishes empirical self-consciousness from the 'transcendental unity of apperception'. The latter is the requirement for all acts of judgement that the self-sameness of the 'I think' be discoverable across all syntheses of the manifold of experience.
a priori	That which is completely prior to, or independent of, anything which depends upon experience. Most, perhaps all, presentations have to be understood to be complex in their origin: thus Kant also speaks of pure or impure a priori presentations. A priori judgements are universal and necessary. *See* a posteriori.
architectonic	The systematic coherence, given in an idea of reason, of any set of cognitions that can be called a science.
autonomy	The property of a faculty which is free in that it gives the law of its operation to itself.
category	A pure concept of the understanding which forms the intelligible component of the transcendental conditions of experience. There are twelve categories, arranged in four groups: quality, quantity, relation, modality.
cognition [*Erkenntnis*, or 'knowledge' in some translations]	Normally in Kant, thought which is directed towards knowledge of possible or actual objects, either a priori or through experience. *See also* judgement.
concept [*Begriff*]	A discursive presentation of a *type* of thing, or of a set of individuals that have properties in common; Kant thinks of concepts as rules for judgements that bring synthetic unity to a manifold.

condition [*Bedingung*]	That which makes something else possible or actual. Often, in phenomenal terms, this means a material cause. Metaphysically speaking, then, the unconditioned would be that which requires nothing outside itself (except perhaps God) in order to be possible. In transcendental terms, a condition is the operation, according to its immanent principles, of a cognitive faculty, such that thereby cognition and its objects are made possible. Thus, the 'conditions of possible experience' are the set of presentations (including the forms of intuition and the categories) and operations (the synthetic operation of the imagination in the formation of judgements according to the principle of the transcendental unity of apperception) of the cognitive faculties.
constitutive [*konstitutiv*]	Of the relation between a principle and an object wherein the former gives a determinate law of the latter's possibility.
contingency [*Zufälligkeit*]	Of that which could have been otherwise or is dependent. *See* necessity.
critical/critique	One name for Kant's overall philosophical project: 'critique' meaning determining through transcendental analysis the limits of the validity of a faculty or power.
deduction	A transcendental argument to show the validity of a priori concepts with respect to experience, normally by showing that the principle is a necessary or constituting condition of the possibility of that experience. Kant expresses this with a legal metaphor: *by what right* are these concepts employed in experience?
determinate [*bestimmend*]	Something is 'determined' if it has (or through a particular presentation is known

to have) a definite set of properties and not others; in a passive sense, something 'is determined' if its definite set of properties are conditioned.

dialectic

What happens (illusion or paradox) when the function of a faculty is assumed to be transcendent with respect to its critically determined limits. 'Dialectic' also refers to the study of this phenomenon as a phase of critique. *See* analytic.

discipline

The critique of reason can be a 'discipline' – allowing for vigilance against the effects of rational illusion – even where it cannot be 'doctrine' – that is, where knowledge is not possible.

discursive

Of the manner of presentation typical of concepts: not singular, and requiring the mediation of intuitions for cognition of the real.

empirical

Of that which comes from experience.

experience [*Erfahrung*]

Our encountering of the real world through the receptivity of our sensibility. The 'transcendental conditions of experience' are those a priori forms and principles of their application through which any synthetic a posteriori judgement can be formed. 'Possible experience' refers to: either these conditions insofar as they make experience possible and thus limit it; or a presentation of the set of objects or events that are transcendentally possible but not given.

faculty [*Vermögen, Facultät*, sometimes *Kraft*; also translated 'power']

An ability of the mind to produce some presentation or to act in a certain way. For instance, the ability to form concepts, to perform a synthetic act, to receive sensible intuitions, or to reason about concepts and propositions. Kant is interested in showing *that there must be* such faculties universally, and *the principles and consequences of their actions.* He is not interested in speculating on the empirical, material conditions of them (for example, the brain). *See also, especially*, principle.

faith/belief [*Glaube*]
The holding-true of a judgement on compelling or necessary subjective grounds but an acknowledged insufficiency of objective grounds.

form
The structure of a presentation, as opposed to its 'content' or 'matter'. Space and time are pure forms of intuition; the categories, considered merely with respect to the understanding, are called 'forms of thought' or 'forms of judgement'.

freedom [*Freiheit*]
The ability of the rational human will to act autonomously; that is, to act in a way conditioned only by the laws that it gives itself.

ground/foundation/ basis [*Grund*]
Figuratively, that which underlies something. So, a set of reasons (for a rational argument) or motivations (for the will); a cause; or the thing in itself as that which is the ground of appearance.

idea
A concept formed by pure reason which seems to demand the cognition of 'objects' beyond the limits of possible experience, and which thus gives rise to dialectical illusion. The ideas are of the soul, the cosmos, and of God.

ideal
An idea with the special additional feature of having as its 'object' *an individual entity* (God).

illusion [*Schein*]
Distinct from 'appearance'. 'Illusion' refers to the misunderstanding of the 'objects' or results of a dialectical inference.

imagination [*Einbildung(-skraft)*]	The faculty of presenting that which is not present. Kant thus usually claims that the imagination must be that which actually performs acts of synthesis. Kant distinguishes between reproductive and productive imagination – the latter has an important transcendental role in the Deduction and the Schematism.
immanent	A principle is immanent insofar as it is employed within its critically determined limits of validity.
intelligible	Of an *object* considered separate from the conditions of *sensible* appearance. Kant uses this notion particularly in his account of unconditioned freedom in its relation to the series of appearances.
intuition [*Anschauung*]	An immediate presentation of a object in space and time. Pure, a priori intuition is the presentation of the form of space or time itself.
judgement [*Urteil*]	Any act of subsumption of a particular under a universal, or a decision concerning whether a particular is, or is not, something. That, at least, is the *logical* definition; but Kant claims that judgement needs to be re-understood. Especially in the Deduction passages, judgement is the name given to the act of synthesis by means of which the unity of consciousness across a manifold is realised and, in the same act, coherent and meaningful experience of objects is achieved.
knowledge [*Wissen*]	A cognition/judgement that is held to be true by the faculty of cognition, and either given a priori or in principle verifiable in experience. Knowledge is the purpose of theoretical cognition, considered on its own.

legislative	A faculty (or the principles of a faculty) considered as producing laws that are necessarily valid for its objects.
logic	The rules governing the validity of relationships among pure concepts or propositions. While ordinary, general logic abstracts from any sense that concepts might have or be about objects, what Kant calls 'transcendental logic' deals with concepts insofar as they are taken to refer a priori to objects in general.
manifold [*Mannigfaltige*]	The field of as-yet-unsynthesised presentations. Thus, the 'manifold of intuition' is a notion that looks a little like the idea of 'sense data'. Also, Kant sometimes speaks of a manifold of concepts or thoughts.
matter/material	The content, as opposed to form, of a given intuition; thus equivalent to 'sensation'. Such 'matter' of intuition is what, in our subjective presentation, corresponds to the empirically real.
metaphysics	We need to distinguish between 1. traditional metaphysics (that practised by Plato, Aristotle, Descartes, and so on) which Kant considers an a priori deductive system, without reference to intuition, that makes claims about reality; and 2. metaphysics as a genuine science, which is also metaphysics in a restricted sense, which is the system of synthetic a priori principles. Only the second is possible; the first just results in nonsense.
nature [*Natur*]	The realm of all objects of which experience is possible and which are determined as a whole by the laws of the understanding such as cause and effect. ('World' is similar, but looser: it is simply

everything which appears, without further specification.) 'Nature' is sometimes used by Kant in other senses, for instance, 'the nature of something', if he is referring to human beings, this nature may include that which is not natural in the first sense.

necessity [*Notwendigkeit*] Of something that could not have been otherwise. *See* contingency.

noumenon A thing understood as an object of non sensible intuition. In the 'negative' sense, this means simply the recognition of the limits of sensible cognition; in the positive sense, the noumenon becomes a purported object of knowledge. *See* thing in itself.

object [*Objekt, Gegenstand*] Generally, an object is what is presented through judgement. In certain contexts, 'object' is used in a way that abstracts from our conditions of sensible presentation (for example, when Kant talks about the 'transcendental object', or the supposed object of a rational idea). In other contexts, it refers to ordinary, particular objects (or events) within experience.

objective [*objectiv*] Something is 'objective' if it relates to the possibility of experience; that is, objectivity is determined by the universal conditions of possible experience. *See* subject/subjective.

paralogism One of the types of dialectical illusion involving unavoidable but illegitimate inferences. The paralogisms in particular concern what Kant calls 'rational psychology'.

phenomenon Roughly, 'phenomenon' is equivalent to 'appearance'.

possibility [*Möglichkeit*] Something is possible if it conforms to the laws governing such a thing. The set of things logically possible is larger than the set of things transcendentally or 'really' possible, which in turn is larger than the set of things empirically possible. Correspondingly, Kant also speaks of thoughts being possible or impossible: this involves the question of whether the concepts and intuitions the thought involves are possible. For example, it is possible for us to *think* the supersensible, but not for us to have *cognition* thereof.

power
: *See* faculty.

practical philosophy
: That philosophy that deals with human purposive action in general, and with human free (and thus potentially moral) action specifically. For Kant, it is opposed to 'theoretical' or 'speculative' philosophy.

practical reason
: *See* reason.

presentation [*Vorstellung*, or 'representation']
: The manner in which the mind apprehends something (for example, my concept of a 'horse' is a presentation of the general quality of being a horse; my intuition of Desert Orchid is my immediate presentation of that particular horse). There are some contexts, however, in which Kant evidently restricts the meaning of 'presentation' to *sensible* presentations.

principle [*Prinzipien*, *Grundsätze*]
: Broadly, any fundamental law. More specifically, a proposition stating the fundamental legislative or regulative contribution of a faculty. Thus, the basic principle of sensibility is that all appearances must be subject to the form of space or time. (Kant also speaks of space and time as themselves principles of sensibility.) And the 'Analytic of Principles' (A130=5B169) is a treatment of the

various principles of our faculty of the judgement of appearances in accordance with the categories; the principle that governs all the others in this treatment is the 'highest principle of all synthetic judgements' (A154=B193).

pure [*rein*]   Not mixed as to origin.

reason [*Vernunft*]   Broadly speaking, Kant uses reason to stand for 'higher thought' of all kinds. More specifically, reason is one of the cognitive faculties, with at least three 'employments': first, merely logical, as that which forms or identifies logical connections between cognitive propositions – that is to say, forms proofs; second, reason in its theoretical/speculative employment, which seeks to pursue these logical connections in order to arrive at a 'maximum' in the completeness or systematicity in its accounts of things (thus its meaning of 'higher thought' in general); reason will pursue such connections even beyond the proper grounds of cognition, and thus forms 'ideas'; third, as practical, supplying the principle of the moral law for the free will.

receptivity   *See* spontaneity.

regulative   Of a principle (or concept or idea) that does not constitute the possibility of its object, but nevertheless 'guides' the activity of the faculty.

representation   *See* presentation.

sensation [*Empfindung*]   The hotness, redness, sourness, etc. of an intuitive presentation. Kant also calls sensation the 'matter' (as opposed to the form) of our experiences. Notice above all that 'sensation' is not the same as 'sensibility' (they are not even related words in German).

sense [*Sinn*], inner	Sensibility as empirical self-consciousness; time is the form of inner sense.
sense [*Sinn*], outer	Sensibility as a relation to things in space; space is the form of outer sense.
sensibility [*Sinnlichkeit*]	The faculty by means of which, or the manner in which, I am in a direct 'receptive' or 'passive' relation to particular objects; thus, the faculty by means of which immediate, singular presentations of all kinds are given. This includes all presentations from mere sensations to pure intuitions, and including imaginings. (Thus 'sensible' is *not* the same as 'empirical'.) As the 'manner' in which we relate to objects, sensibility can be studied a priori. For Kant, it is a fundamentally important characterisation of human cognition that our intuition is *sensible* intuition, and that the relation of cognition to objects is always in the manner of receptivity; or, expressed another way, that the faculty of intuitions is different from the faculty of concepts.
speculative reason	A sub-class of theoretical reason in general wherein reason is employed in the impossible task of knowing objects that lie beyond the limits of experience.
spontaneity	The self-initiated and self-governed activity characteristic of the understanding, for example. In this, Kant contrasts it with the 'receptivity' or 'passivity' of the sensibility that must first be affected by its objects.
subject/subjective	The 'subject' is the human being considered as *that which has* intuitions, concepts, experiences, memories, etc., or as *that which acts*, mentally or physically. (This remains true whether we think of the

subject as a thing – for example, a sub-stance – or as a mere function or construc-tion.) 'Subjective' thus means pertaining to the nature of the subject. But this is ambiguous: 'subjective' could mean 'indi-vidual' or 'personal'; for example, my indi-vidual likes or dislikes (because such things are *in principle* personal, they lack univer-sality and necessity characteristic of objec-tive experience). Or, it could refer to a universal characteristic of the subject. The latter is the more important to Kant; but the reader has to judge which meaning is in play according to the context. Finally, in the context of the 'Transcendental Dialectic', Kant speaks of 'subjective necessity' (A297=B353), meaning a way of reasoning which is 'natural' and neces-sary in human beings, but which can never be objective because it does not agree with the conditions of possible experience.

supersensible
[*Übersinnliche*]

That realm of 'objects' considered separ-ate from the conditions of possible expe-rience, and especially when purported to be the ground of all objects of experi-ence. *Similar:* thing in itself; noumenon; intelligible.

synthetic/synthesis

A 'synthetic' judgement is one in which the concept of the object does not already contain the predicate; that is, the concept and predicate are initially unrelated. 'Synthesis', more generally, is any act of combining or relating together presenta-tions.

theoretical philosophy

That branch of philosophy that deals with objects of possible experience, and deals with them as objects of possible knowledge. *See* practical philosophy.

thing in itself	The thing or object considered without reference to the conditions under which it can be experienced. Often used as roughly equivalent to noumenon, or intelligible.
thought/thinking [*Denken*]	Kant's most general term for any mental activity whatsoever involving a concept or idea, with the emphasis (not exclusive) on the non-intuitive nature of the activity.
transcendent	Distinct from 'transcendent*al*'. Of a principle that *demands* application beyond the limits of experience. A transcendent object is thus the object of an idea of reason that has been posited according to such a principle. Opposite: immanent.
transcendental	Concerning that which forms the a priori conditions of the possibility of something (in particular, of either knowledge or experience). Transcendental knowledge, then, is knowledge of such conditions and how those conditions function. Transcendental knowledge is therefore strictly speaking different both from ordinary knowledge about things, and even from metaphysical knowledge (although Kant sometimes uses 'transcendental' in a broader sense).
understanding [*Verstand*]	The faculty of cognition which legislates for the cognition of nature by supplying a priori concepts (categories), and which in general forms and employs concepts of all kinds.
universality [*Allgemeinheit*]	That which applies, or is the same, everywhere and always.
will/choice [*Wille, Willkür*]	The determination to act, including the ability to choose an action from several possibilities, including non-action. As part of the lower faculty of desire, choice [*Willkür*] is always partly determined by

inclination. As part of the higher faculty of desire, will is autonomous, determining itself rationally according to the principle of the moral law.

Types of Question You will Encounter

Our research, sourced from universities all over the English-speaking world, suggests that there are a number of types of assignment you are likely to encounter. These are:

1. *Exposition*: A typical assignment would be to take a short passage from the *Critique* and explicate it. This means: to lay out in detail the structure, meaning of key terms and overall sense of the passage; to put it into context with respect to what Kant is doing in surrounding passages; possibly also to contextualise it with respect to Kant's work as a whole, and with other philosophers (for example, Hume or Descartes); possibly also to bring to bear on the passage the varying interpretations, and reasons behind these interpretations, of commentators on Kant; you may also be asked to assess the validity of Kant's views here.

2. *Issues in Kant Interpretation*: In the book above, we sometimes referred to key places where different interpretations diverge as 'pivot points'. The Copernican revolution is one such, and there are quite a few others. This type of assignment typically focuses on such key points. The aim of this type of assignment is for you to adjudicate between what Kant says on the subject in all relevant passages, and how a variety of commentors have interpreted him. You should try to give a balanced and fair representation of all these, but also to provide a reasoned verdict. Again, you may be asked also to assess not only the correctness of your interpretation but also the validity of it as a philosophical view. An example of such a question would be: 'Critically assess what Kant means in saying that space is transcendentally ideal but empirically real. Can Kant's views be upheld?'

3. *Modern Philosophy Problems*: Here the focus is on a debate characteristic of Kant's historical period (usually conceived of as seventeenth- to eighteenth-century thought). An obvious example would be 'Assess

to what extent Kant refutes Hume's treatment of causation.' Again, you will probably be expected to bring to bear and assess the interpretations of commentators.

4. *Philosophical Problems*: The task is to use a Kantian analysis to try to illuminate a philosophical problem that is of contemporary significance. An example is 'Does natural science require a sense of system? Discuss with reference to Kant's regulative ideas.'

Common Assessment Criteria

Your work will be inspected for some or all of the following virtues:

1. The ability to precisely and accurately explain the meaning of a piece of terminology, a passage, an argument or an idea.

2. The ability to philosophically enrich and clarify a particular notion with respect to Kant's work as a whole, and other philosophers (for example, Hume or Descartes).

3. The ability to use secondary commentators. This means showing the ability to: find them (through intelligent use of all the resources available to you); digest them (to not get caught out by changes in style or language, and to not get lost in details or irrelevant side-issues); summarise them correctly; and employ them usefully (to be critical with respect to both primary and secondary writers, rather than assuming they have a point; and allowing their work to inform your own thought rather than be a substitute for it).

4. The ability not merely to report on the meaning of a bit of philosophy, but to intelligently and fairly assess its merits or truth.

Tips for Writing about Kant

1. Reference passages in the *Critique of Pure Reason* using the style used in this book, that is, by the original pagination of the first (A) and second (B) editions. References to other works by Kant is by the volume and page number of the standard Akademie edition, and looks like this: (*Critique of Judgement*, Ak. V: 197). There may be times when the translation you are using does not give the Akademie numbers, in which case you would have to reference by the physical page number of the book you are using.

2. Cross-referencing terms that you find in your reading against the original German words is essential. Different translators render these terms differently, and you do not want to be making a point in your essay based upon a difference in translation. So, for example, *Vorstellung* might be translated as either 'presentation' or 'representation'; *Glaube* as either 'faith' or 'belief' and so forth. Most English translations provide many helpful footnotes about the translations of terms, as well as bilingual glossaries or indexes. Your library will most likely have the original German text of the *Kritik der reinen Vernunft*. If not you can find it online. The Project Gutenberg ebook website has nicely laid-out etexts of both editions.

3. Kant uses a very specific technical vocabulary. Admittedly he is sometimes inconsistent, or the meaning of terms is allowed to stray; but this is no excuse for *our* being sloppy. When you mean one of Kant's terms, use it in the first instance; try to not employ some other word in English that strikes you, at the time, as equivalent.

4. However, the opposite extreme is also to be avoided: writing *like* Kant. Your writing will be more clear and effective if you use Kant's technical terms and phrases in the first instance, and *then* try to explain them using your own words, examples or analogies.

5. Do not quote Kant and then move on, as if the quotation were self-explanatory. If it were, you wouldn't need to write an essay! Instead, write a sentence like 'What Kant means is this. . .', or even 'There are two ways of interpreting what Kant means here. . .'.

6. It is particularly important with Kant to be clear about the difference between an example and an analogy. Both are useful only to illustrate or clarify. However, in Kant an example is also often an opportunity to analyse a certain cognitive act; in other words, the example is an argument in disguise.

7. Pay particular attention to what the essay or examination question is asking. Is it asking you to explain what Kant meant by X? Is it asking you to evaluate the validity of X? Or is it asking you to try and solve a philosophical problem that is related to or analogous to X? See above the common types of assessment.

Bibliography

Works by Kant

Kant, I. (1987) *Critique of Judgement*, trans. Werner S. Pluhar (Hackett: Indianapolis, IN/Cambridge).

Kant, I. (1996) *Critique of Pure Reason*, trans. Werner S. Pluhar (Hackett: Indianapolis, IN/Cambridge).

Other Sources

Allison, H. E. (1973) 'Kant's Critique of Berkeley', *Journal of the History of Philosophy* ii: 43–63.

Allison, H. E. (1990) *Kant's Theory of Freedom* (Cambridge: Cambridge University Press).

Allison, H. E. (2004) *Kant's Transcendental Idealism: An Interpretation and Defence* (New Haven, CT: Yale University Press).

Ameriks, K. (1978) 'Kant's Transcendental Deduction as a Regressive Argument', *Kant-Studien* 69: 273–87.

Ameriks, K. (1982a) *Kant's Theory of Mind: An Analysis of the Paralogisms of Pure Reason* (Oxford: Oxford University Press).

Ameriks, K. (1982b) 'Recent Work on Kant's Theoretical Philosophy', *American Philosophical Quarterly* 19: 1–24.

Ameriks, K. (1992) 'Kantian Idealism Today', *History of Philosophy Quarterly* 9: 329–42.

Aquila, R. (1979) 'Personal Identity and Kant's "Refutation of Idealism"', *Kant Studien* 70: 259–78.

Aquila, R. (1983) *Representational Mind: A Study of Kant's Theory of Knowledge* (Bloomington: Indiana University Press).

Azm, S. al- (1972) *The Origins of Kant's Arguments in the Antinomies* (Oxford: Oxford University Press).

Baum, M. (1986) 'The B-Deduction and the Refutation of Idealism', *Southern Journal of Philosophy* 25 (Supplement), 92–9.

Baumer, W. (1969) 'Kant on Cosmological Arguments', in L. W. Beck (ed.) (1969b).

Beck, L. W. (1963) 'Can Kant's Synthetic Judgements Be Made Analytic?', in R. P. Wolff (ed.) (1967b).

Beck, L. W. (1969a) 'Kant's Strategy', in Penelhum and MacIntosh (eds) (1969).

Beck, L. W. (ed.) (1969b) *Kant Studies Today* (La Salle, IL: Open Court).

Beck, L. W. (ed.) (1974) *Kant's Theory of Knowledge* (Dordrecht: Kluwer).

Beck, L. W. (1978) *Essays on Kant and Hume* (New Haven, CT: Yale University Press).

Beck, L. W. (1979) *Early German Philosophy* (Bristol: Thoemmes Press, 1996).

Beiser, F. (1992) 'Kant's Intellectual Development: 1746–1781', in Guyer (ed.) (1992b).

Bell, D. (1987) 'The Art of Judgement', *Mind* 96: 221–44.

Bencivenga, E. (1992) 'Knowledge as a Relation and Knowledge as an Experience in the *Critique of Pure Reason*', in Chadwick (ed.) (1992) [vol. 2].

Bennett, J. (1966) *Kant's Analytic* (Cambridge: Cambridge University Press).

Bennett, J. (1974) *Kant's Dialectic* (Cambridge: Cambridge University Press).

Bieri, P., R.-P. Horstmann and L. Krüger (eds) (1979) *Transcendental Arguments and Science: Essays in Epistemology* (Dordrecht: Kluwer).

Bird, G. (1962) *Kant's Theory of Knowledge: An Outline of One Central Argument in the 'Critique of Pure Reason'* (London: Routledge & Kegan Paul).

Brueckner, A. (1983) 'Transcendental Arguments I', *Nous* 17: 551–75.

Brueckner, A. (1984) 'Transcendental Arguments II', *Nous* 18: 197–225.

Buchdahl, G. (1992) *Kant and the Dynamics of Reason: Essays on the Structure of Kant's Philosophy* (Oxford: Blackwell).

Burnham, H. D. (2004) *Kant's Philosophies of Judgement* (Edinburgh: Edinburgh University Press).

Buroker, J. V. (2006) *Kant's Critique of Pure Reason: An Introduction* (Cambridge: Cambridge University Press).

Cassam, Q. (1987) 'Transcendental Arguments, Transcendental Synthesis and Transcendental Idealism', *Philosophical Quarterly* 37: 355–78.

Cassirer, E. (1981) *Kant's Life and Thought*, J. Haden (trans.) (New Haven, CT: Yale University Press).

Caygill, H. (1995) *A Kant Dictionary* (Oxford: Blackwell).

Chadwick, R. (ed.) (1992) *Immanuel Kant: Critical Assessments*, 2 vols (London: Routledge).

Dancy, J. (1984) *An Introduction to Contemporary Epistemology* (Oxford: Blackwell).

Deleuze, G. (1984) *Kant's Critical Philosophy*, H. Tomlinson and B. Habberjam (trans.) (London: Athlone).

Engel, S. M. (1967) 'Kant's "Refutation" of the Ontological Argument', in Wolff (ed.) (1967b).

Ewing, A. C. (1938) *A Short Commentary on Kant's 'Critique of Pure Reason'* (Chicago, IL: University of Chicago Press).

Falkenstein, L. (1995) *Kant's Intuitionism* (Toronto: University of Toronto Press).

Förster, E. (ed.) (1989) *Kant's Transcendental Deductions: The Three 'Critiques' and the 'Opus Postumum'* (Stanford, CA: Stanford University Press).

Foucault, M. (2001) *The Order of Things* (London: Routledge).

Friedman, M. (1991) 'Regulative and Constitutive', *Southern Journal of Philosophy*, 30, suppl., 73–102.

Friedman, M. (1992) *Kant and the Exact Sciences* (Cambridge, MA: Harvard University Press).

Gadamer, H. G. (2005) *Truth and Method*, J. Weinsheimer and D. G. Marshall (trans.) (London: Continuum International).

Gardner, S. (1998) 'Kant', in Grayling (ed.) (1998).

Gardner, S. (1999) *Kant and the Critique of Pure Reason* (Routledge: London and New York).

Genova, A. C. (1992) 'Kant's Notion of Transcendental Presupposition in the First *Critique*', in R. Chadwick (ed.) (1992).

Gram, M. (1969) 'Kant's First Antinomy', in Beck (ed.) (1969b).

Gram, M. (1976) 'How to Dispense with Things in Themselves (I), (ii)', *Ratio* 18: 1–16, 107–23.

Gram, M. (1982) 'What Kant Really Did to Idealism', in Mohanty and Shahan (eds) (1982).

Grayling, A. C. (ed.) (1998) *Philosophy 2: Further Through the Subject* (Oxford: Oxford University Press).

Greenwood, T. (1989) 'Kant on the Modalities of Space', in Schaper and Vossenkuhl (eds) (1989).

Grier, M. (2001) *Kant's Doctrine of Transcendental Illusion* (Cambridge: Cambridge University Press).

Guyer, P. (1987) *Kant and the Claims of Knowledge* (Cambridge: Cambridge University Press).

Guyer, P. (1992a) 'The Transcendental Deduction of the Categories', in Guyer (ed.) (1992b).

Guyer, P. (ed.) (1992b) *The Cambridge Companion to Kant* (Cambridge: Cambridge University Press).

Guyer, P. (2006) *Kant* (Routledge: London and New York).

Harper, W., and R. Meerbote (eds) (1984) *Kant on Causality, Freedom, and Objectivity* (Minneapolis: University of Minnesota Press).

Harrison, R. (1982) 'Transcendental Arguments and Idealism', in Vesey (ed.) (1982).

Hegel, G. W. F. (1977) *Phenomenology of Spirit*, A. V. Miller (trans.) (Oxford: Clarendon Press).

Heidegger, M. (1990) *Kant and the Problem of Metaphysics*, 4th edn, R. Taft (trans.) (Bloomington: Indiana University Press).

Heidegger, M. (1996) *Being and Time*, J. Stambaugh (trans.) (Albany, NY: SUNY).

Henrich, D. (1982) 'The Proof-Structure of Kant's Transcendental Deduction', in Walker (ed.) (1982).

Henrich, D. (1989a) 'The Identity of the Subject in the Transcendental Deduction', in Schaper and Vossenkuhl (eds) (1989).

Henrich, D. (1989b) 'Kant's Notion of a Deduction and the Methodological Background of the First Critique', in Förster (ed.) (1989).

Henrich, D. (1994) *The Unity of Reason: Essays on Kant's Philosophy* (Cambridge, MA: Harvard University Press).

Hintikka, J. (1972) 'Transcendental Arguments: Genuine and Spurious', *Nous* 6: 274–81.

Hopkins, J. (1982) 'Kant's Visual Geometry', in Walker (ed.) (1982).

Horstmann, R. (1976) 'Space as Intuition and Geometry', *Ratio* 18, 17–30.

Hughes, F. (2007) *Kant's Aesthetic Epistemology* (Edinburgh: Edinburgh University Press).

Hume, D. (1975) *Enquiries Concerning Human Understanding* (Oxford: Oxford University Press).

Kemp-Smith, N. (1930) *A Commentary to Kant's 'Critique of Pure Reason'*, 2nd edn (London: Macmillan).

Kitcher, P. (1994) *Kant's Transcendental Psychology* (Oxford: Oxford University Press).

Kitcher, P. (ed.) (1998) *Kant's 'Critique of Pure Reason': Critical Essays* (Oxford: Rowman and Littlefield).

Körner, S. (1967) 'Kant's Conception of Freedom', *Proceedings of the British Academy* 53, 193–217.

Körner, S. (1969) 'The Impossibility of Transcendental Deductions', in Beck (ed.) (1969b).

Leibniz, G. W. (1989) *Philosophical Essays*, R. Ariew and D. Garber (trans. and eds) (Indianapolis, IN: Hackett).

Longuenesse, B. (1998) *Kant and the Capacity to Judge: Sensibility and Discursivity in the Transcendental Analytic of the 'Critique of Pure Reason'*, C. T. Wolfe (trans.) (Princeton, NJ, and Oxford: Princeton University Press).

Matthews, H. E. (1982) 'Strawson on Transcendental Idealism', in Walker (ed.) (1982).

Meerbote, R. (1984) 'Kant on the Nondeterminate Character of Human Actions', in Harper and Meerbote (eds) (1984).

Melnick, A. (1973) *Kant's Analogies of Experience* (Chicago, IL: University of Chicago Press).

Miller, A. (1998) *Philosophy of Language* (London: University College London Press/Routledge).

Mohanty, J. N., and R. Shahan (eds) (1982) *Essays on Kant's 'Critique of Pure Reason'* (Norman: University of Oklahoma Press).

Neiman, S. (1994) *The Unity of Reason: Rereading Kant* (Oxford: Oxford University Press).

Nietzsche, F. (1998) *The Genealogy of Morality*, M. Clark and A. J. Swenson (trans.) (Indianapolis, IN: Hackett).

Parsons, C. (1992) 'The Transcendental Aesthetic', in Guyer (ed.) (1992b).

Paton, H. J. (1936) *Kant's Metaphysics of Experience: A Commentary on the First Half of the 'Kritik der reinen Vernunft'*, 2 vols (London: Allen & Unwin).

Penelhum, T., and J. J. MacIntosh (eds) (1969) *The First Critique: Reflections on Kant's 'Critique of Pure Reason'* (Belmont, CA: Wadsworth).

Pippin, R. (1982) *Kant's Theory of Form: An Essay on the 'Critique of Pure Reason'* (New Haven, CT: Yale University Press).

Plantinga, A. (1966) 'Kant's Objection to the Ontological Argument', *Journal of Philosophy* 63: 537–46.

Powell, C. T. (1990) *Kant's Theory of Self-Consciousness* (Oxford: Oxford University Press).

Prichard, H. A. (1909) *Kant's Theory of Knowledge* (Oxford: Clarendon Press).

Quine, W. (1961) *From a Logical Point of View* (New York: Harper and Row).

Remnant, P. (1969) 'Kant and the Cosmological Argument', in Penelhum and MacIntosh (eds) (1969).

Robinson, R. (1969) 'Necessary Propositions', in Penelhum and MacIntosh (eds) (1969).

Rosen, M. (1989) 'Kant's Anti-Determinism', *Proceedings of the Aristotelian Society* 89: 125–41.

Russell, B. (1914) *Our Knowledge of the External World* (London: George Allen Unwin).

Schaffer, J. (1969) 'Existence, Predication, and the Ontological Argument', in Penelhum and MacIntosh (eds) (1969).

Schaper, E., and W. Vossenkuhl (eds) (1989) *Reading Kant: New Perspectives on Transcendental Arguments and Critical Philosophy* (Oxford: Blackwell).

Schopenhauer, A. (1966) *The World as Will and Representation*, 2 vols, E. F. J. Payne (trans.) (New York: Dover).

Schrader, G. (1967) 'The Thing in Itself in Kantian Philosophy', in Wolff (ed.) (1967b).

Schwyzer, H. (1990) *The Unity of the Understanding: A Study in Kantian Problems* (Oxford: Oxford University Press).

Strawson, P. F. (1966) *The Bounds of Sense: An Essay on Kant's 'Critique of Pure Reason'* (London: Methuen).

Stroud, B. (1982) 'Transcendental Arguments', in Walker (ed.) (1982).

Stroud, B. (1984) *The Significance of Philosophical Scepticism* (Oxford: Clarendon Press).

Vesey, G. (ed.) (1982) *Idealism Past and Present* (Cambridge: Cambridge University Press).

Walker, R. (1978) *Kant* (London: Routledge & Kegan Paul).

Walker, R. (ed.) (1982) *Kant on Pure Reason* (Oxford: Oxford University Press).

Walker, R. (1988) *Real in the Ideal: Berkeley's Relation to Kant* (New York: Taylor & Francis).

Walsh, W. H. (1969) 'Kant on the Perception of Time', in Beck (ed.) (1969b) and Penelhum and MacIntosh (eds) (1969).

Walsh, W. H. (1975) *Kant's Criticism of Metaphysics* (Edinburgh: Edinburgh University Press).

Walsh, W. H. (1982) 'Self Knowledge', in Walker (ed.) (1982).

Wartenburg, T. (1992) 'Reason and the Practice of Science', in Guyer (ed.) (1992b).

Wittgenstein, L. (1958) *Philosophical Investigations*, trans. G. E. M. Anscombe (Oxford: Blackwell).

Wolff, R. P. (1963) *Kant's Theory of Mental Activity: A Commentary on the Transcendental Analytic of the 'Critique of Pure Reason'* (Cambridge, MA: Harvard University Press).

Wolff, R. P. (1967a) 'A Reconstruction of the Argument of the Subjective Deduction', in Wolff (ed.) (1967b).

Wolff, R. P. (ed.) (1967b) *Kant: A Collection of Critical Essays* (London: Doubleday).

Wood, A. (1978) *Kant's Rational Theology* (Ithaca, NY: Cornell University Press).

Wood, A. (1984a) 'Kant's compatibilism', in A. Wood (ed.) (1984b).

Wood, A. (ed.) (1984b) *Self and Nature in Kant's Philosophy* (Ithaca, NY: Cornell University Press).

Index